THE NOTORIOUS CAPTAIN HAYES

Also by Joan Druett

NON FICTION

Lady Castaways

Eleanor's Odyssey, Journal of the Captain's Wife on the East Indiaman
Friendship, 1799-1801

The Elephant Voyage

Tupaia, The Remarkable Story of Captain Cook's Polynesian Navigator

Island of the Lost

In the Wake of Madness

Rough Medicine

She Captains

Hen Frigates

The Sailing Circle (with Mary Anne Wallace)

Captain's Daughter, Coasterman's Wife

She Was a Sister Sailor, Mary Brewster's Whaling Journals, 1845-1851

Petticoat Whalers

Fulbright in New Zealand

Exotic Intruders

FICTION

Abigail

A Promise of Gold

Murder at the Brian Boru

A Watery Grave

Shark Island

Run Afoul

Deadly Shoals

The Beckoning Ice

THE NOTORIOUS CAPTAIN HAYES

THE REMARKABLE TRUE STORY OF
WILLIAM 'BULLY' HAYES, PIRATE OF THE PACIFIC

JOAN DRUETT

HarperCollins*Publishers*
New Zealand

HarperCollins*Publishers*
First published in 2016
by HarperCollins*Publishers* (New Zealand) Limited
Unit D1, 63 Apollo Drive, Rosedale, Auckland 0632, New Zealand
harpercollins.co.nz

HarperCollins*Publishers*
Unit D1, 63 Apollo Drive, Rosedale, Auckland 0632, New Zealand
Level 13, 201 Elizabeth Street, Sydney NSW 2000
A 53, Sector 57, Noida, UP, India
1 London Bridge Street, London, SE1 9GF, United Kingdom
2 Bloor Street East, 20th floor, Toronto, Ontario M4W 1A8, Canada
195 Broadway, New York NY 10007, USA

A catalogue record for this book is available from the National Library of New Zealand

ISBN 978 1 7755 4097 7 (pbk)
ISBN 978 1 7754 9135 4 (ebook)

Cover design by Darren Holt, HarperCollins Design Studio
Cover image by shutterstock.com
Map from Rolf Boldrewood, *A Modern Buccaneer*, London, 1894
Typeset in Bembo Std by Kirby Jones
Printed and bound in Australia by Griffin Press
The papers used by HarperCollins in the manufacture of this book are a natural, recyclable product
made from wood grown in sustainable plantation forests. The fibre source and manufacturing
processes meet recognised international environmental standards, and carry certification.

CONTENTS

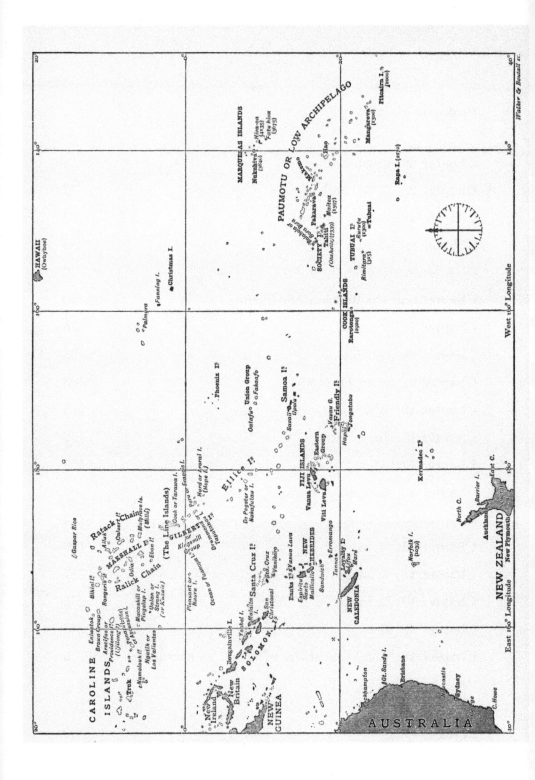

PROLOGUE

Talk in the South Seas is all upon one pattern; it is
a wide ocean, indeed, but a narrow world: you shall never
talk long and not hear the name of Bully Hayes.
— Robert Louis Stevenson, *The Wrecker*

Romance has coloured stories of the Pacific ever since the day in 1769 when the first European seamen came home from Tahiti, firing the public imagination with tales of beautiful bare-breasted girls beckoning seductively from groves of swaying palms. From that pivotal moment an enduring passion for stories about tropical islands was born, as amazing yarns drifted back from those who were exploring this great new ocean. The trouble was, the Pacific did not have a legendary pirate — America had Captain Kidd, the Caribbean had Captain Morgan, the Mediterranean had Barbarossa, and the Atlantic had Blackbeard, but the Pacific had just whalers and explorers. Though hardy and adventurous folk, they were not the stuff of sensational newspaper stories.

But then, in the mid-nineteenth century, Captain William Henry Hayes arrived.

Wherever he went, a tsunami of headlines seethed in his wake, starting with the storm he raised in the Eastern ports of Hong Kong and Singapore. 'THE HISTORY OF A CONSUMMATE SCOUNDREL' blared a Honolulu paper in September 1859, just months after he had arrived in Hawaii, while Australian papers ran their own exposés the following year, under the heading 'THE NOTORIOUS CAPTAIN HAYES', describing with relish 'one of the most systematic and unmitigated scoundrels' who had ever dropped anchor in the colony.

This was addictive reading. Subscribers were fascinated, and news stands were besieged by eager buyers who wanted to know the latest grisly details. The name of the 'remarkable scoundrel' became so well known that the simple heading 'CAPTAIN W.H. HAYES AGAIN' was all that was needed to advertise the latest exciting escapade of 'the notorious maritime swindler'. Everyone wanted to know more — *much* more — about him, creating such a ready market that newspaper editors hastily reprinted the articles they found in rival papers, no matter how tenuous or suspect the content might be.

Recapping what already had been told was yet another option. 'For years he followed a course of plunder, stealing entire cargoes and sometimes even running away with ships,' revealed the *Straits Times* of Singapore in 1872, in a long summary of his nefarious career that was copied all over the Pacific. Hundreds of papers not only reprinted stories like this, but filled columns with editorial comment. 'He has hitherto successfully eluded every attempt to bring him to justice,' thundered the editor of the *Herald* of Fremantle, Western Australia, 'but thief, pirate, plunderer, kidnapper as he is, there can be but one termination in the eternal fitness of things to such a career as this!'

Hayes' gory demise five years later, in 1877, did not bring the respite the editors had expected, however — the rogue might be dead, but the public still demanded stories about him, no matter how wildly rehashed. Though the newspapermen had never realised what was happening, their headlines and columns had turned Captain William Henry 'Bully' Hayes into an iconic figure — he had become 'the last of the buccaneers' and 'the pirate of the Pacific'. Nor did the passing of time alleviate their problem of what to write to feed the public appetite, as the myth they had built about Bully Hayes refused to fade. 'Romance is weaving itself around this picturesque character, and it becomes more and more attractive as the years roll on,' mused the editor of the *Sydney Mail* in 1928, and generations of other editors found that the writer was right.

No one is even sure what this notorious American looked like, and yet his impressive physical appearance is part of the Bully Hayes legend. Most of the people who met him agree that he was six feet tall, and hefty in physique, that he had a bluff and hearty manner and a soft, persuasive voice, but otherwise descriptions vary. Some reckoned he had blue eyes, others that they were brown. Sometimes he is described as bald, while in other yarns he has long, curling hair. Everyone agrees that he had a beard, but whether it was cut to a point (like Captain Morgan) or flowing down to his belt varies according to the narrator, and whether it was brown, black or grey is equally vague. What everyone is sure about is that he loved women. Captain Bully Hayes had several wives on shore and kept a constant stream of beautiful brown girls on board. And they also say that he had a magnetic personality. Today they would call it charisma.

'Of all the buccaneers and pirates of my acquaintance Captain Hayes had the most winning ways,' wrote the famous solo-sailor

Captain Joshua Slocum to a friend. Another of those who met him thought that his charm owed much to the fact that he was an actor of exceptional ability. 'He bought and stole ships, cargo and women,' this fellow added, 'and yet so persuasive was he in his ways that even some of his victims laughed at the ingenious methods he employed to gain his ends.' One copra trader who was tricked by Hayes had no reason to respect the American adventurer, yet described him as 'a fine upstanding man, was well dressed and had a most charming personality', while another who had been cheated admitted that 'he was a fine sailor and generous and kind-hearted — *except for those whom he robbed!!'*

'For half a century, waterfront gatherings throughout the Pacific have been enlivened with tales of Captain "Bully" Hayes and his famous pirate crew,' wrote J.B. Musser, in an article for the magazine of the United States Naval Institute, *Proceedings*, which was published in September 1927. 'From San Francisco to Sydney his exploits are recounted' — for the simple reason that he was 'as charming a rascal as ever broached a keg of stolen port'. Even pious missionaries enjoyed his boisterous company, while suspicious shipmasters, naval commanders, angry shopkeepers and pompous Customs officials were unwillingly captivated by his charm. As one of his passengers (who had not been cheated) declared, a voyage with Hayes was highly recommended — he was certain that he would make any of his paying guests 'as welcome as he did me; for I am sure I could not have been better cared for had the vessel been my own'. Not only did Captain Hayes look after his guests, but he entertained them with yarns. A generous host who plied the bottle freely but drank very little himself, he enjoyed himself immensely by spinning outrageous stories of how he had cheated merchants and governments, and tricked men out of their ships — tall tales that were never questioned, but instead retold all about the ocean, adding to his swashbuckling image.

Not only did Hayes brag like a buccaneer, but according to a neighbour in Samoa, he dressed like a storybook pirate too. As he strode along the Apia waterfront, the skirts of his long alpaca coat swished back from his black broadcloth trousers and black boots, revealing that his broad chest was covered with a white frilled shirt with a white flowing necktie, and that instead of a waistcoat he wore a brightly coloured sash about his waist. A wide-brimmed black slouch hat was propped aslant his head, and his white teeth shone through his moustache and beard when he grinned. He even smelled good, a man who knew him well testifying that he 'oiled and scented himself before going on shore'.

Yet, despite this exotic appearance, his wild tales of his own misdeeds and his reputation for stealing ships, cargoes and women, Hayes cannot be called a 'real' pirate. The pirates of history are known by their actions, and there is no record at all of Captain William Henry Hayes sinking a ship with a broadside of cannon, or storming on board with a knife between his teeth. As a crook, in fact, he was nothing out of the ordinary. On 9 January 1917, a Honolulu paper ran an interview with Captain Callaghan, 'one of the few men alive who sailed with Bully Hayes, having been with him six months before the mast'. The vessel was the *Leonora*, and 'Hayes was not as bad as nearly everyone says he was', the old shipmaster reckoned. And another neighbour in Samoa, Charles Netzler, declared that Hayes 'was no better or worse than other people in the South Seas then were; he had only one fault, which a lot of people still have today: he always forgot to pay his bills!'

*

The ocean was replete with colourful characters at the time. All over the tropical Pacific, men in wide-brimmed planters' hats turned atolls into their private kingdoms — men like 'His Majesty' David Dean O'Keefe, the king of the island of Yap — and yet their names are almost forgotten. Many other flamboyant men feature in the Bully Hayes story — men like George Buckingham, actor, buffoon, and pioneer in colonial theatre; Eli Boggs, who slaughtered his victims with his own hand and forced the survivors to walk overboard; Ebenezer 'Aloe' Pitman, who drank his way out of many a command, then used the proceeds from selling a stolen ship to spend a virtuous retirement in Marblehead, Massachusetts; and Ben Pease of Edgartown, Martha's Vineyard, who kidnapped a Chinese gang and stranded them on the island of Pohnpei, and may have buried his ill-gotten gold there. But their names are lost to history, too, while the name of Captain Bully Hayes is as evocative as ever.

No one ever boasted about meeting Ben Pease or His Majesty O'Keefe, but Bully Hayes was so famous that right up until the middle of the twentieth century, obituaries noted that the deceased had met Hayes, once in the same sentence recording that the late lamented had seen the Charge of the Light Brigade too. 'He assisted in the pursuit of Bully Hayes', noted the obituary of an old seaman, Mr Edward Laing. The memorial to Mr G.F. Smith, who died in Hamilton, New Zealand, in September 1922, thought it worth recording that he 'agreed to ship with Bully Hayes, but fortunately he got an inkling about his true character in time'.

Visiting missionaries giving presentations about their good works in the South Seas were badgered with questions about the notorious so-called pirate. The 'distinguished' Methodist missionary, Dr George Brown, D.D., was quizzed about 'some of the characters he had come in contact with during his long experience in the Pacific' by the reporter from the Christchurch *Press* in February 1915, 'and mention was made especially of that notorious buccaneer Bully Hayes'. And yes, Dr Brown had met him, 'but that was all history now', he protested, and hastily changed the subject to his meeting with Robert Louis Stevenson, leaving the interviewer (and his readers) frustrated. 'No, no', he had not met 'anyone who could be termed as bad as Bully Hayes', protested the Reverend W.E. Clarke, in the 'splendid lecture' he gave in Apia, in April 1914, but, as he added rather weakly, he had met Robert Louis Stevenson, who walked in bare feet. Eccentric as he might have been, though, the great writer of *Treasure Island* was not as newsworthy as Captain Bully Hayes.

*

'From one end of the Pacific to the other the name of Bully Hayes may still be heard,' wrote a traveller a dozen years after his death, and over a century and a quarter later the same still applies. Travel guides to islands like Pohnpei, Guam and Hawaii relate romantic yarns of Bully Hayes to make their destinations more attractive. In Rarotonga, a real estate agency uses his name to promote the properties on their books. Local histories of towns and cities in Australia, California, Hawaii and New Zealand never fail to say what Captain Hayes got away with there. He is featured in museums, the Western Australian Museum proudly displaying a necklace that the notorious Captain Hayes gave to one of the many women he jilted. No academic study of the history of the Pacific, Australia and New Zealand is complete without a mention. Some part of the Bully Hayes saga is quoted in every learned discussion of topics ranging from the coconut oil and copra trade to European colonisation of the atolls, political manoeuvring in Samoa, the markets in Tahiti, the shipping trade in New Zealand and Australia, gold rushes in California, New South Wales and Otago, and the establishment of law and order.

There are other weird and wonderful ramifications. An American racehorse was named 'Bully Hayes', galloping on to make his owners a lot of money, and in Australia the 'Bully Hayes Stakes' draws eager punters. In 1983, a film was made by Paramount, called either *Nate and Hayes* or *Savage Islands*, depending on where it was released. Starring Tommy Lee Jones as the hero, Hayes, and Australian actor Max Phipps as the villain, Pease, it still has a loyal following. In 1986, the Federated State of Micronesia issued a five-stamp souvenir block of postage stamps commemorating 'Bully Hayes, Buccaneer', and on Kosrae the international airport is nicknamed 'Bully Hayes Airport'. On the same island, 'Bully Hayes' sunken pirate ship' is a popular scuba-diving site. The ancient flagstaff on Signal Hill, Port Chalmers, in New Zealand, is still advertised as being a mast from 'the pirate ship *Cincinnati*' and until the old ship collapsed completely, timbers of the rotting hulk were fashioned into curios that were sold as relics of 'the last pirate of the Pacific'. In Pearl City, on the Hawaiian island of Oahu, there is a Bully Hayes club, where the patrons quaff rum cocktails out of bamboo mugs. In Fiji, they brew a Bully Hayes hard cola, while in Cleveland, Ohio, a 'Portside Bully Hayes Rye I.P.A.' is brewed.

And then there is the loot that Hayes is supposed to have buried on Suwarrow, Niue and Kosrae, ranging from three big chests of bullion to bags of pieces-of-eight. It is treasure that is hunted to this very day, encouraged by whispers of crabs coming out of their holes with nuggets of gold in their claws. In 1989, the Singapore *Straits Times* held a 'Bully Hayes treasure chest' hunt, where the lucky finder collected a case of Ballantine's Scotch whisky. And Bully Hayes has been listed on the Hong Kong city website as one of Hong Kong's 'top 10 pirates' — 'Not completely evil, he was also known for his brave commitment to saving lives during times of shipwreck,' runs the text. He has his own Facebook page, courtesy of the Bully Hayes Restaurant and Bar in Akaroa, New Zealand. And a 'Bully Hayes' shirt — 'a pirate shirt with attitude' — is advertised by an online store.

Somehow, this dishonest charmer has become the dashing corsair demanded by the popular history of that most romantic of oceans, the Pacific — the kind of person who is pictured on the labels of bottles. But what was the real man like? And what did he really do? In 1957 the best-selling author James A. Michener declared that so many tall tales had been told about Bully Hayes that it had become almost impossible to separate truth from fiction — 'upon a slim thread of proved incident has been hung all the romantic canvas of a great ocean'. But, as he also said, the subject can be grasped 'before the sifting of legend becomes completely hopeless', and, by following the headlines, announcements, shipping lists, advertisements, reports from police court proceedings, and the solemn warnings that were published during this flamboyant man's life, it is indeed possible to sift the reality from the myth and tell the true story of the notorious Captain Hayes.

AUTHOR'S NOTE

The common currency of the Pacific in Captain Hayes' time was the silver dollar. Five of these dollars were the equivalent of one pound sterling. As an indication of the scale of the thefts described in the book, the usual seaman's pay was £2 10s (two pounds, ten shillings, or $12.50) a month.

CHAPTER 1

Otranto

The date was 14 August 1849, and the place was the port of New Bedford, on the eastern seaboard of the United States. Thirty-one men were gathered on the quay ready to board their ship, and there was an unusual buzz of excitement in the air. It was the start of a great new adventure.

Though New Bedford was the premier whaling port in the world, they were not on the brink of yet another interminable whaling voyage — instead, they hefted gold-washing pans and shovels, and were wearing brightly checked shirts, broad-brimmed hats, dungarees and knee-high boots. All of them were experienced whalemen, with famous whaling family names like Hussey, Ricketson, Leonard, Brownell, Manchester, Luther and Luce. None of them was named William Henry Hayes. At this part of the story it is the ship that takes centre stage.

The ship, like the men, was in the whaling business. Her name was *Otranto*, and she had been built in Guildford, Connecticut, in 1832, and brought into the New Bedford whaling trade ten years later. Since then, though just 150 tons and seventy-five feet long, she had cruised all over creation, from the fevered coast of Africa (where some of her men had died of tropical disease) to the Bay of Bengal and the southern Indian Ocean. On 30 April 1849, she had arrived back in New Bedford from her last voyage, a 22-month cruise to Madagascar, the East Indies and Western Australia, and since then she had been bought by the men who were filing on board her.

As the *New Bedford Whalemen's Shipping List* reported in the 21 August issue, they had made the purchase in the name of the Bristol County Mining Association. The mining they had in mind was nothing to do with coal or tin. Instead, they were heading off to dig for gold. Reports were flooding in from the Pacific coast — that San Francisco was full of ships that had been abandoned by their crews, that Panama was crammed with Americans crazy to get to Eldorado. Such huge amounts were being paid in New York, Boston and New Bedford for passage to the land of promised riches that it made economic sense for seamen to club together, form a company, buy a local ship, and sail it themselves to the Golden Gate.

Once California was reached, however, it was common for the ship to be forgotten, and this is what happened with the Bristol County Mining Association. After arriving at San Francisco in March 1850 (to report the salvage of a drifting boat), and working the ship up the San Joaquin River to the mining town of Stockton, every single member of the company walked away from the *Otranto* to dig on his own account, leaving the decks echoing emptily. After that, she sat neglected in the mud.

*

The next episode in the *Otranto* story begins on 11 December 1851, when a New Bedford whaling master, John P. Davenport, dropped anchor at Tahiti. Davenport's vessel was a small schooner by the name of *Alfred*, and for the past six years he had been cruising about Australia and New Zealand, trying with little success to fill his ship with oil. Hearing talk in Papeete of the huge prices that fresh fruit and vegetables were fetching in San Francisco, he invested in a cargo of oranges, set sail, and steered for the Golden Gate. It was a felicitous decision. Not only was he greatly impressed by the potential of California as a market for oranges, but he had spied great schools of whales on the way into port. Hastening about Cape Horn, he arrived in New Bedford in April 1852, and no sooner had he handed over the schooner to the owners than he set himself in motion, collecting whaling gear, marrying a local girl, and buying passages for San Francisco.

That was when Davenport's luck ran out. Their transport sank off Nicaragua, forcing his party to cross the swampy, fever-ridden Isthmus of Panama on foot, and then the ship they boarded in Panama foundered off the coast of San Simeon. Rescued from this second wreck, Davenport bought passage on a steamer, which ran so short of fuel that bulwarks, bunks and furnishings had to be burned to get them to their destination. But, though worn down by the long journey, he summoned the energy to locate the *Otranto* and fit her out for chasing whales. And so, on 3 October 1852, the *Daily Alta California* duly reported John P. Davenport taking the bark *Otranto* on a whaling voyage.

Sadly, nothing improved. Not only did the whales prove elusive, but other ships got in his way. When Davenport was beating back into port on 18 November 1852, with just a few barrels of oil from one whale on board, he had the misfortune to run into a small sloop. The *Otranto* sustained little damage, but the sloop went down like a rock. Luckily, her crew of two was saved from drowning, but it was a definite embarrassment. Nonetheless, Davenport reprovisioned the ship, hired a new crew, and went out again.

Persistence did not meet its due reward. The basic problem was that while there were plenty of good whalemen in California, they were all digging for their fortunes in the hills, and so John Davenport was reduced to the sad cases who had run out of money and had drifted to the wharves in the hope of a job. Within months he gave up the idea of deep-sea whaling and instead became the pioneer of shore whaling on the Californian coast. Stripping the *Otranto* of her whaling boats and gear, he established a station on the beach, and then sent out the ship on trading voyages, employing a captain by the name of Kendrick.

Kendrick was as dogged as his employer, sailing the wide Pacific in search of profitable cargoes. He was also quite an adventurer. In July 1853, a notice in the *Alta California* revealed that Captain D. Kendrick, 'of the American barque *Otranto*' had been presented with a purse for $1000, raised by grateful Irish gold-diggers in recognition of his rescue of the famous Irish patriot O'Donohue from the penal colony of Van Diemen's Land, now known as Tasmania. The arrival and departure of the *Otranto* were not noted by the Australian papers, so it was a stealthy and daring operation.

This unexpected wealth led to Kendrick's retirement as master of the bark — though not before the little whaleship was involved in another collision. On 26 October, she was run into by the ship

Oscar, and this time came off very much the worse. Not only did the *Otranto* lose her foremast, along with all its rigging, but her bottom was badly damaged, forcing Kendrick to run her up onto an Oregon beach, to fix her for the passage home. Once he arrived, it was easy for Davenport to decide to put the battered and leaky old vessel on the block. On 16 May 1854, the *Otranto* was listed for sale, 'well found with sails and rigging for a voyage'.

And the man who took her over was named William Henry Hayes.

*

Like much about Hayes, his early past is murky. Most people say he was born in Cleveland, Ohio, about 1828 or 1829, and that his father was a hotel proprietor. After learning his seamanship on the Great Lakes, he may have joined the United States Navy. At least, that is the story that was told by Captain Cocks, the harbourmaster at Levuka, Fiji. He was posted to the China Station, and seems to have done well, reaching the rank of master-commander. In 1846, this career came to an abrupt end when Hayes was court-martialled for the crime of hanging twenty-five Chinese pirates without bothering with the formality of a trial. After quitting in disgrace, he joined the Imperial Chinese Navy and took command of a gunboat. His orders — or so the harbourmaster's story went — were to hunt down pirates, but at the same time he levied protection money from the merchants of the coast.

The fact that Hayes was not quite twenty years old at the time casts some doubt on this. However, Henry Wolcott, an American adventurer who was the head of Russell & Co., in Shanghai, and served informally as the United States Consul there from about 1845, confirmed the gist of it, adding that Hayes' confederate in the protection racket was another American, Benjamin Pease of Martha's Vineyard, who had joined the Chinese Navy after deserting from a whaler in the Caroline Islands. If the story is indeed the truth, then it was after leaving this partnership that William Henry Hayes sailed for San Francisco, where he bought the whaler *Otranto*.

Whether the purchase was fraudulent or not is hard to tell, but the fact that he made no attempt to rush out of the territory infers it was reasonably legitimate. Additionally, John P. Davenport, the man who had sold the ship to Hayes (and may still have been backing him), gave him a contract. Two months after the purchase, the *Daily Alta California* noted in the 1 July 1854 issue that the *Otranto*, Captain Hayes, had come into port with a freight of timber for Davenport & Co., which he had loaded in Monterey.

Hayes did have the Orient in mind, though, as the records reveal that he arrived at the Chinese port of Amoy in November. And there he approached a company of merchant adventurers who were most unlikely to be fooled — Jardine, Matheson & Co., the firm that pioneered and dominated the tea-for-opium trade between London, Calcutta and Hong Kong. Opium-trading, while illegal in both China and Britain, had a certain glamour, mostly because of the elite captains of beautiful ships who unloaded the pernicious stuff onto smuggling craft at little offshore islands, then dashed home with the fabulous cargoes of tea and China goods they had bought with the booty. No such romance for Captain Hayes, though. Instead, he entered into an agreement to freight indentured labourers from Swatow to Singapore.

This was the infamous 'coolie trade', where hapless Chinese men, made desperate by drought, flood or rapacious landlords, were herded into holding pens in the port of Swatow, to sell themselves to captains who would carry them to some far-flung plantation or railroad construction site. Years later, Hayes was to adapt the skills he learned in this miserable business to blackbirding, where natives from the Gilbert Islands (now Kiribati) and the New Hebrides (modern Vanuatu) were captured and carried to market, but right now he was a novice.

To get established, Hayes needed financial backing, which he received from none less than the famous Captain Robert McMurdo of Amoy, master of the crack opium clipper *Red Rover*. The bond, dated 30 November 1854, and now held in the Jardine, Matheson archives at Cambridge University, describes Hayes as 'master and part-owner of American barque *Otranto*'. In return for $1259.50, he pledged to repay McMurdo from the earnings of the first voyage from Swatow to Singapore, 'with the appropriation of passage money and hypothecation of freight serving as security'. And this he did, arriving in Singapore with his first cargo on 6 January 1855.

It is a testament to Hayes' engaging personality that as he called from port to port on the Chinese coast over the next few months, he made many influential friends, though this was helped by the fact that he was a Mason. A fellow lodge-member was the United States Consul in Amoy, Charles William Bradley, and another was Bradley's son, C.W. Bradley Junior, who acted as the Spanish consular agent in Swatow and managed the Bradley business there. Hayes played billiards with George W. Heard, the Hong Kong representative of Augustine, Heard & Co., and was often seen in the Victoria Hotel, Hong Kong, drinking with dashing opium-clipper captains like 'Long John' Saunders of the *Chin Chin* and

'King Tom' Donovan of the *Spray*. Another friend was Captain Edward Vansittart, commander of the British gun-brig *Bittern*. And it was through this last contact that Bully Hayes snared the deposit to buy a much better ship than the leaky old *Otranto*.

This was a neat little American-built clipper bark that was often seen in Oriental ports, a vessel for a man to be very proud of indeed. When she had first arrived in Singapore, on 11 July 1854, she had been named *Canton*, and her commander was Captain Elisha Gibbs, who had orders to sell her for the best price he could get. Within days she had been bought by John Harvey, the Singapore representative of a Scottish firm, who handled the affairs of Rajah Brooke of Borneo and needed a craft to sail between Singapore and Sarawak. He renamed her *Santubong*, after the beautiful mountain that rose from the jungle behind the Rajah's palace, and gave the command to an experienced South China Sea shipmaster by the name of Dufretay.

And so it was that the clipper bark was sailing under the name of *Santubong* when Captain Hayes of the *Otranto* arrived in Singapore on 6 January 1855, and it seems that he eyed her enviously for several months. Then, in March 1856, he had his chance to acquire her, as John Harvey had been appointed 'Manager East' of the newly constituted Borneo Trading Company, meaning he had to return to Britain. Accordingly, his ship's agent, Tek Tye, had orders to sell, and Hayes was an eager customer. All he needed was the deposit.

And he raised the money in the most melodramatic way possible — by catching the notorious American pirate Eli Boggs.

*

Information about Boggs is so scanty that very little has been written about him. According to people who saw him at his trial (on 4 July 1857), or when he was in prison awaiting trial and sentencing, he was a most unlikely pirate. Only in his twenties, Eli was a dandy with striking looks — as a correspondent to the London *Times* wrote, his face was one 'of feminine beauty', while his abundant hair was black, his complexion was 'delicately white', and his eyes were described as 'lustrous'. He was also, it seems, well educated and eloquent, as he spoke for two hours in his own defence. His cruelty, however, was legendary — it was said that after he captured some Chinese merchants he chopped up one and sent the pieces on shore in a bucket, to speed up the payment of the ransom. At his trial it was charged that he had boarded a junk and personally killed fifteen men, then drove the survivors overboard. He may even have been the man who invented walking the plank, a cruelty that the buccaneers of the Caribbean never practised, despite the popular myth.

What was important to Hayes, however, was that the Hong Kong authorities had put a bounty of $1000 on the renegade seaman's head — and at the perfect moment his chance to earn that bounty arrived. According to a lively account in Captain A.G. Course's *Pirates of the Eastern Seas*, one evening in September 1855 Hayes walked into the billiard room of the Victoria Hotel in Hong Kong, accompanied by George W. Heard. While playing, they were joined by two opium clipper captains, who revealed that they had raised a pirate fleet in the Gulf of Liaoheng. And both were positive that Eli Boggs had been at the helm of the leading lorcha — a vessel with junk sails on a European hull.

Hayes went on board the gun-brig *Bittern* to report this to his Royal Navy friend, Captain Vansittart, and after a short consultation both the *Otranto* and the *Bittern* set out on the chase. The pirate fleet was raised in Fuchow Bay in the Liaotung Peninsula. At once the junks formed up into two columns and commenced a spirited attack. Vansittart gave the order to pretend to flee, craftily drawing the junks into shoal water, where some of them grounded. The dirty weather was against him, however, and though eight stranded pirate junks were seized, the rest escaped. Prisoners reported that Boggs had indeed been at the helm of one of the two leading lorchas, going on to relate stories of his horrifying treatment of his latest captives, which served to fire up the hunting spirit even further. Joined by the steamer *Paoushun*, Vansittart and Hayes searched the creeks of the peninsula, capturing eleven more junks as they went.

The following morning a lorcha was sighted, so close to the shore that the gun-brig could not approach her. Two armed cutters were lowered and manned, Hayes taking charge of one. In a demonstration of reckless courage, he led the way shoreward through a murderous hail of cannon balls and flaming stinkpots, though the cutters seemed doomed. Then, all at once, the lorcha blew up, its magazine hit by a lucky shot. Peering through the fire and smoke, Hayes saw Boggs jump overboard and swim for shore. He promptly dived into the water himself. And after a frantic struggle where the unarmed Hayes had to fend off the pirate's short sword, Boggs was captured.

The authorities were thrilled with the success of the exercise. Grace Estelle Fox, in her account of British admirals and Chinese pirates, relates that Ningpo bankers, along with Shanghai traders, raised $22,000 to be presented to Captain Vansittart. This was for him to distribute among the crews of H.M.S. *Bittern* and the steamer *Paoushun* for the gallant part they played 'in the destruction of the piratical fleet in Sheipoo Bay, 18 September 1855', specifying that a generous part be paid to the mother of the sailing master of the *Bittern*, who lost his life in the battle, and smaller sums given to those who had lost limbs.

Hayes got the purse of $1000. Stories add that he appropriated a portion of the pirate treasure too. At once he sailed to Singapore, to pay the deposit on the *Santubong*, ex-*Canton*, and raise a mortgage for the rest.

*

According to gossip, Hayes mortgaged the bark to Dare & Webster, chandlers, for the sum of $3000. The problem with this is that the firm of Dare & Webster did not exist. However, there was a firm called G.J. Dare & Co., who acted as Captain Hayes' agents. The business was owned by George Julius Dare, a sailing master in the Royal Navy who had settled in the port in February 1848, setting up as one of the four chandlers in town, but in 1855 Dare had returned to his home in Dorset, England, where he died in September 1856. The firm was left in the hands of his head clerk, Josiah Webster, who, according to *An Anecdotal History of Old Times in Singapore*, was 'a very plausible man, with a particularly pleasant manner' who 'turned out to be most untrustworthy, and ruined the business, as well as his employer'. So, if Hayes cheated G.J. Dare & Co., it must have been through Josiah Webster, which means it was either a case of one rogue outwitting another or of two rogues working in concert.

Whatever the means, by 18 March 1856, the *Santubong*, ex-*Canton*, was his. After renaming her *C.W. Bradley junior* in honour of his friend, Hayes moved on board and off he sailed, leaving the *Otranto* abandoned at her moorings, with orders to the agents to sell the leaky old craft, if they could.

CHAPTER 2

C.W. Bradley junior

The *Straits Times* for 8 April 1856 records that Hayes left Singapore for Shanghai on 2 April, after a spectacular spending spree. 'During his stay amongst us, he was a daily visitor at the chief stores of the town, and an excellent customer on credit for all kinds of goods,' the same paper reminisced in the issue for 20 August 1859. 'From Singapore he proceeded to Amoy in China. From Amoy his vessel was bound to Hong Kong, but instead of proceeding thither, he made his way back to Singapore!'

He dropped anchor there in November 1856. 'His reappearance renewed confidence among our tradesmen as to his honesty, and the admirable *nonchalance* with which he comported himself, enabled him again to make extensive additions to the large sums which he already owed. He named a day in which he intended to leave the harbour, and requested that his creditors should send on board for the repayment of their respective accounts at a certain hour of the day in question. Long however, before the hour fixed, the *C.W. Bradley junior* had disappeared.' And this despite the fact that the bark was not Captain Hayes' property, 'as she was mortgaged to Singapore creditors, and the mortgage was duly registered at the American consulate'.

But, as the newspaper mused, what cared Hayes for that? 'The next time we hear of our hero — he is at the Swan River,' the writer continued. The bark had called at Java on the way, where the master 'probably pitched into the purse of some of the Dutchmen of the place'. He left in a hurry, it seems, perhaps because 'tidings of legal process' came to his ears — or so the writer speculated.

*

Much of what happened on the voyage is described by one of the crew of the *C.W. Bradley junior*, an Englishman by the name of Hines, whose reminiscences were published many years later (24 July 1900) in the New Zealand *Akaroa Mail*.

Having been discharged from his ship in Hong Kong, Hines 'signed articles as an ordinary seaman on the barque *William Bradley*, Captain W.H. Hayes, with a cargo of tea for Fremantle, West Australia'. At first it looked like an easy berth — 'She was a smart little vessel of about 350 tons, and was kept in apple pie order.' And the captain was a fine-looking man too — 'standing 6 feet 4in in height, and built proportionately. He had an aquiline nose, and light blue eyes that seemed to penetrate one when he looked at you, and long black hair'. But it did not take long for the seaman to find out just how and why the bark was kept in apple pie order. 'Every man aboard was afraid of him, and his discipline was almost as strict as a man-o'-warsman.'

Once, during the run to Australia, Hayes came on deck to find that the helmsman was steering half a point off course — 'he took hold of him by the back of the neck and the strap round his waist, and lifted him up as high as he could reach and flung him down on the deck with such force that he broke his arm and two ribs, and a nasty smash on the face — "There, now, I guess I'll teach you to steer the course I give you next time," said he, as the poor fellow crawled away forward'. Fighting among the crew was not tolerated either — Hayes would wade in and knock the combatants into submission. 'D—n you,' he once shouted at a pugilistic pair; 'you want to fight do you, and catching each of them by the back of the collar he battered their heads and faces together until he was tired.'

No doubt to everyone's relief, the Western Australian port of Fremantle was fetched on 30 January 1857. Adopting his jovial shore-side manner, Hayes quickly became the most popular young man around town, 'speculating in timber on a large scale, and making love to the daughter of a resident there', according to the *Straits Times*. This last must have been a challenge, as according to Hines, Captain Hayes had a Chinese mistress on board, along with a fourteen-year-old boy.

The local *Inquirer* newspaper had nothing but compliments to make, largely because Hayes brought so much interesting news, such as the progress of the war in China — Canton, he said, was in flames on 23 November 1856, 'the day of the *Bradley*'s departure', after being bombarded by the English and Americans. 'The English vessels engaged are, the *Winchester, Barracouta, Hornet, Nankin*, and five others, and the American ships *Levant, Portsmouth*, and one other. The Chinese were offering 50 dollars for the head of each white person killed. Captain Hayes also informs us that when at

Angier [Anjer-Lor, Java], on his voyage hither, he learnt that Mr Sleddon and our Postmaster-General, Mr Helmich, had left that place some days previously in a vessel named the *Swallow*, chartered by the former gentleman for this colony.'

And, though Hayes did not know it, the British schooner *Swallow* also bore his nemesis — the gossipy wife of the commander, Captain Allen.

*

Mrs Allen, who had been christened Sarah Ann Galway in October 1829, soon after her birth in Ireland, had first come to Australia at the tender age of seven, and had married a master mariner, Thomas Allen, in 1850. She was the original source of much that is told about Hayes' career in the Orient and Australia, because in her old age she related a great deal of hearsay, rumour and observation to her nephew, Alfred Thomas Saunders, who was just an accountant at the time, but was so enlivened by her yarns that he became an amateur historian.

According to what Aunt Sarah Ann Allen told him, Captain Hayes had first arrived in Singapore in command of 'an American brig which was seized for debt and sold by the Vice-Admiralty court', after which a Singapore merchant named Webster bought 'a barque of 187 tons' named *C.W. Bradley junior*, and put Hayes in command. 'This,' she said, 'was in December 1856.' The *Swallow* was also in the harbour, loading for Fremantle, so Mrs Allen was able to meet the captain of the *Bradley*, finding him 'a charming young man of good appearance and manners, had a good voice, sang nicely and was generally liked, especially by women'.

While Mrs Allen's gossip about the 'American brig' *Otranto* is obviously wrong (the old whaleship was still languishing unsold at her moorings), her memory was sharp, as her timing was out by only one month. According to the shipping intelligence in the *Straits Times*, the *Swallow* was in the harbour in November 1856, and departed for Fremantle on the 19th. The *C.W. Bradley* departed one day later, the *Straits Times* reporting 'destination unknown', though, according to Mrs Allen, it was generally 'understood that she was to go to Rangoon for rice'. Hayes and the Allens renewed their acquaintance just one day later, as the *Swallow* had to take in sail and lie-to during the night, the wind being foul. The next morning, the *Bradley* sailed up to them, and Captain Allen shouted, 'I thought you were going to Rangoon.' 'Aha,' said Hayes. 'We don't tell our business to everybody. I am going to drift about China.' And so the vessels parted.

The *Swallow* made a very slow passage, so did not arrive at Fremantle until 18 March 1857 — when Mrs Allen found to her astonishment that Hayes had been lionised in port for the past six weeks, and that, in fact, she had only just missed him, as he had sailed for Adelaide just eight days before. Not only had he 'astonished the natives generally', but he had entertained the Chief Justice and other notables on board the bark, and, what's more, he had 'engaged himself to marry Miss Scott, the daughter of the harbourmaster, and had taken her brother with him to Adelaide'.

This is confirmed by seaman Hines, who remembered that Captain Hayes had gone 'into the passenger trade between the Swan River and Adelaide, and carried as many as 250 passengers, at £10 per head', though according to the advertisements placed in the Fremantle paper, it cost £15 to travel in the privileged after quarters.

Two of those on the passenger list were indeed men by the name of Scott, while two others had come all the way from Singapore — B.T. Baker, and Captain Edward Willett. What the Scotts made of the Chinese woman was left to the imagination.

The *C.W. Bradley junior* arrived in the Port of Adelaide on 24 March, 'from Singapore, via Swan River'. Hayes found an interesting ship in the harbour — the American-built, Portuguese-registry *Estrella do Norte*, with Manuel Goularte in command, and a man by the name of Cambridge acting as sailing master (navigator) and supercargo (trading master). There had been nothing but trouble since the *Estrella* had arrived. The same day that the *Bradley* dropped anchor, there was a stirring item in the *South Australian Register* describing the antics of two 'drunk and riotous' seamen on board the *Estrella do Norte*. Cambridge, who had been in charge of the ship, had gone forward to quell some scuffling and had been attacked by the pair, 'one of whom tore his shirt off his back, and the other savagely bit him in the thumb'. Worse, if possible, according to the policemen who carried out the arrest, they had called Cambridge a 'curly-headed son of a Yankee b—h'. Cambridge, retaliating, had grabbed a belaying pin and hit the speaker 'over the nut', which caused him 'to sheer off and run away like a sheep'. The two culprits were fined £5 and £3 respectively, but this would have had to come out of what the ship owed them in the way of pay. This was not forthcoming, the ship's accounts being in the red, so they were both sent to jail.

The *Estrella* had come from the Chinese port of Macao, where Cambridge and Goularte had entered into a contract with a Hong Kong merchant, Lum Sing, to carry 242 Chinese men to Adelaide. The arrangement specified that once the ship had dropped anchor in the South Australian port, the passengers were to be transferred to a steamer that would take them to the little port of Robe, in Guichen Bay. From there, they would walk to the gold-mining towns of Ballarat and Bendigo. It was a 300-kilometre trudge, but by landing in South Australia the Chinese immigrants avoided the £10 poll tax that would have been charged by the government of Victoria, the state where Ballarat and Bendigo are sited. After all, they had already paid Lum Sing the immense sum of $80 (£16) each — as the whole of Adelaide was soon to learn.

The business became a public scandal when Cambridge refused to organise the Chinese fortune-hunters' passage from Adelaide to Robe. Instead, he and Goularte had every intention of stranding them on shore. The Chinese, however, were a spirited lot, as the *Register* reported on 27 March. When Cambridge tried to herd them to the gangplank, they barricaded themselves in the steerage, where some of them 'seized logs of firewood and hurled them at the chief officers and sailors', while others struck out with bamboo staves. As the reporter commented with some awe, the 'uproar was deafening; everyone was talking or shouting with astonishing volubility and singular intonation'. Altogether, considering the 'strange appearance' of the Chinese men, with their half-shaven heads, long pigtails and baggy clothing, it 'afforded an exceedingly novel and striking spectacle'.

The officers and seamen beat a diplomatic retreat, leaving it to the police to get the angry Chinese on shore, but that was certainly not the end of the affair. Through their surgeon, Yung Hing, the passengers took Captains Cambridge and Goularte to court, in an action that was reported on 9 April. In this, they sued for the sum of £3 each, which they reckoned was the cost of the passage to Guichen Bay. The Magistrate, though bemused by the strange situation, found for the 242 plaintiffs, so Goularte advertised for a loan, offering 'bottomry' (mortgage on the hull of the ship) for the sum of £1000.

At this stage, Hayes took an interest, aided and abetted by his own trading master, Robert Parkinson. The arrangement the two rogues proposed was that Hayes should lend the owner of the ship — a merchant by the name of Antonio des Santos, who was far away in Macao and completely unaware of what was going on — not just £1000, but £3000. And the guarantor, or 'garnishee' — the person who would collect on the debt when Hayes called it in — was none other than his supercargo, Robert Parkinson.

Then, with this disingenuous document drawn up and signed, Hayes offered to carry the Chinese to Robe on the *Bradley*. The prospective gold-miners flatly refused. They were 'afraid to go to sea' with him, according to the *South Australian Register* — presumably because of Hayes' reputation in China as a coolie captain. A few were either persuaded or coerced to change their minds, as on 9 April 1857, the *Bradley* sailed from Adelaide 'for Fremantle, via Robe Town, Passengers, 83 Chinese'. However, the captain was not Hayes, but Parkinson, who blithely disregarded the arrangement to drop anchor in Guichen Bay. Instead, he steered for Albany, where he dumped the Chinese, despite their vociferous protests. There, they were worse off than they would have been in Port Adelaide, having over 3000 kilometres further to walk.

Two witnesses to this hard-hearted action were passengers for Fremantle, who came on board at that port — none other than Captain Scott and Mrs Scott. But if they found it odd that their prospective son-in-law was not on board his ship, no public comment was made.

*

It was not until 5 June 1857 that Hayes was mentioned again in the Fremantle paper, when the arrival of 'the *Estrella do Norte*, 389 tons, Goularte, master, from Adelaide', was reported, with 'passenger Captain Hayes' in the cabin. He was acting as sailing master, as Captain Cambridge, Goularte's supercargo, had left Adelaide on the brig *Alarm*, headed for Newcastle, New South Wales.

Once the anchor was dropped, it was a chance for the three conspirators to meet up again, as the *Bradley*, Parkinson, master, was still in port, advertised as sailing for South Australia on 11 June. The *Swallow* was not in Fremantle, since Captain Thomas Allen had sailed for South Australia on 30 April, carrying thirty-five passengers and his wife, meaning that a potentially embarrassing encounter had been narrowly avoided. While Mrs Allen undoubtedly gossiped in the parlours of Fremantle, Hayes' luck was holding — in the meantime.

It was Hayes, and not Parkinson, who took the *Bradley* out on the next voyage to Adelaide, after the departure had been delayed until 27 June. The passage was swift, the *South Australian Register* remarking that the *C.W. Bradley* had arrived on 3 July, 'in the unprecedentedly short time of six days and a few hours'. Both cabin and steerage had been full of paying passengers, so Hayes had money in his pocket. 'Captain W.H. Hayes, of the *C.W. Bradley*, entertained on Saturday evening, on board his vessel, a party of gentlemen in commemoration of the glorious 4th of July,' the same paper reported. The party included Englishmen as well as Americans, but there was 'much cordiality and uninterrupted unanimity of sentiment. Loyal toasts were given and responded to on both sides, and compliments of international esteem warmly reciprocated'.

There was more than one reason for Hayes to enjoy the moment. Before he had left Fremantle, he, with his co-conspirators Goularte and Parkinson, had commenced legal action for the £3000 that was 'owed' to him by the absent owner of the *Estrella do Norte*, via the garnishee, Robert Parkinson. The attorney they retained, George Fred Stone, filed the action on 3 July — 'Between William Henry Hayes, Plaintiff and Antonio des Santos, Defendant' to recover 'the sum of £3000 due for money lent and advanced in the year 1857, at Adelaide'. As the hapless des Santos did not reside in the Colony of Australia, 'a writ of Foreign attachment has been issued returnable the 11th August next', the statement continued, 'wherein Robert Parkinson, Master Mariner, is Garnishee'.

Though nothing better than barefaced robbery, the action was successful. On 15 August 1857, an advertisement was placed in the *Inquirer* by the Sheriff, F.D. Wittenoom, stating, 'NOTICE is hereby given, that, at noon on Monday, the 24th instant, the Sheriff will cause to be put up for sale by Public Auction, at the Custom House, Fremantle (unless the above execution is previously satisfied): — THE ship called the *Estrella do Norte*, now lying at the Vasse.' It did not sell. Instead, by dint of legal legerdemain, the owner of the ship became Captain William Henry Hayes, while the commander was Captain Robert Parkinson and the trading master was Captain Manuel Goularte.

*

On 24 October, when the *Estrella* arrived in Adelaide and Parkinson and Goularte rejoined Hayes, they found that a great deal had happened. On Saturday, 18 July, there had been a 'preliminary notice' posted in the *South Australian Register*, informing all and sundry that 'the American Barque *C.W. Bradley*' was for 'absolute sale, and will be sold to the highest bidder, unless previously disposed of'. This had been followed by an even more peremptory notice in the paper for 20 July, stating the sale would take place 'Tomorrow (Tuesday), July 21, at 12 o'clock sharp'.

According to the usual version of the story, the instigators of the sale were Dare & Webster of Singapore, who had sent authority for collection on the mortgage. However, George Julius Dare being dead and buried in England, any action would have been instigated by Josiah Webster. The rest of the advertisement tends to cast doubt on the legend, too, as it reads, 'For Inventory and further particulars, apply to Capt. Hayes, on board'. So, despite the gossip that Hayes had been put out of the ship, he was still living in the captain's cabin.

Whatever the true circumstances, the *Bradley* was indeed sold — to a Mr John Newman for the sum of £1250, the equivalent of $6250 in American currency, a good price that indicates that Hayes certainly kept her in apple pie order. Did he pocket the money or was it sent to Singapore? In the absence of documentation, it is impossible to tell.

CHAPTER 3

Estrella do Norte

The other big surprise for Manuel Goularte and Robert Parkinson was that on 25 August 1857, at St Mark's Church, Penwortham, Captain W.H. Hayes of New York had wed a widow, Mrs Amelia Littleton of Port Adelaide.

The Chinese woman had left the scene, according to seaman Hines. During the second trip to Adelaide, she and the boy had 'mysteriously disappeared, and it was hinted amongst the crew that they had been dropped overboard'. On the *Bradley*'s 'next trip to Adelaide Hayes persuaded a young lady to go on board with him. She was a barmaid at the railway refreshment rooms'. But she was gone, too, as 'after two trips she also disappeared'. But then there was the engagement to Miss Scott, the Fremantle harbourmaster's daughter, not to mention the one or two wives Hayes was supposed to have abandoned in America. Presumably, Amelia had no idea of any of this when she consented to say, 'I do.'

Though versions of Hayes' earlier history mention a wife or two, this marriage appears to have been legal. According to the marriage certificate, Hayes declared his age as twenty-eight, while his bride admitted to being twenty-four. The man who officiated, an Anglican parson by the name of William Wood, was paid £10 and a roll of lawn cloth to make a surplice — or so Mrs Allen, the gossipy aunt of A.T. Saunders, confided to her nephew. While Sarah Ann Allen would not admit to having much to do with Hayes or his new bride, she had certainly conversed with the Reverend Wood and his wife, so had that titbit firsthand.

Little is known about Captain Hayes' new wife, though it seems that she lied about her age. A family search reveals that Amelia was born in April 1827 in Westminster, England, the daughter of John Moffatt. Her family emigrated to South Australia, where she met William Weston Littleton, originally of Leamington Priors, Warwickshire. He was about two years her senior, having been baptised on 16 August 1825. They married on 5 July 1854, but the union was short-lived, as he died on 12 April 1856, at the age of thirty. Then, as we have seen, after sixteen months of widowhood, Amelia married the handsome and jovial Captain Hayes.

Where William and Amelia lived for the next eight weeks is unrecorded. According to what Aunt Allen told her nephew, after the *Estrella do Norte* arrived, the couple moved on board, taking over the best cabins. How she knew this is impossible to tell, as the *Swallow* cleared out of South Australia for Gallé, Ceylon (now Sri Lanka) on 24 October 1857, so the ship must have passed the *Estrella* as she was coming into port. What is on record is that Hayes distinguished himself during a conflagration that devastated shops, warehouses, houses, taverns and a theatre on the waterfront of Port Adelaide on

7 November — he was one of those who 'peculiarly distinguished themselves in assisting to quell the fire, and in removing goods from the burning houses', and that despite the fact that at least one of the warehouses was stocked with barrels of gunpowder.

And then there was the Port Adelaide regatta, held on New Year's Day.

*

This was a hugely anticipated event, possibly the first formal regatta in Australian history. It was preceded by meetings at Coleman's Exchange Hotel where excitable people argued over such earthshaking matters as the precise definition of a 'gentleman', only 'gentlemen' being allowed to compete for the Ladies' Purse. This, the prime prize, 'will probably excite the ambition and take the attention of numerous amateurs', observed the editor of the *South Australian Advertiser*. Then, once this argument about the qualities of a true gentleman was resolved, 'The only assistance to be now invoked is that of wind and weather.'

The writer's prayer was answered. As the *Register* gloated on 2 January 1858, 'The New Year was ushered in by one of the most lovely days an Australian climate can boast.' The sun shone brightly, the sky was unclouded, and there was a nice breeze to cool the temperature and fill the sails. Hundreds turned up to watch, coincidentally 1858 of them by rail, the railroad company having put on special trains. The glistening water was literally covered with small craft, while all the ships in port were flying colours — 'and it was a general remark that the river looked more like the Thames on a holiday than a watering-place for South Australia'.

The day's racing began at nine-thirty, the starting gun being fired from the flagship, *Gazelle*, which was moored in front of the Government steps. It did not go particularly well, the yachtsmen being inexperienced. To the dismay of all, the wind dropped, and there was a farcical moment when the boat that was coming in second ran into a little dinghy, and the boy who was the sole occupant of the craft jumped up onto the sailboat's bowsprit and clung on like a monkey. Captain Hayes' entry in the fifth race, for 'ships' gigs pulling four oars', was disappointing for him, in that his boat only came second (though the prize, £10, was the same as the prize for the front runner), but he snared the ultimate award. With a hastily assembled crew of local businessmen, he won the Ladies' Purse — which is ironic, since the many tradesmen to whom he owed a lot of money would be unlikely to consider him a gentleman.

This indebtedness was confirmed on 9 February 1858, when Hayes filed for bankruptcy. 'INSOLVENCY NOTICES', ran the advertisement in the *Register*; 'William H. Hayes, Port Adelaide, Master Mariner'. This was followed by the forced sale of the *Estrella do Norte*, which was put on the block by the Government Auctioneer, 'and was bought in at the reserved price of £700' — or $3500 in American money. The buyers were Billy Wells and Joe Coleman, the latter being the proprietor of the Exchange Hotel in Commercial Road. They sent the *Estrella* to the Swan River to collect Jarrah timber, just as Hayes and Goularte had done. Then, in October, they sent her to Melbourne, 'where it is intended she shall be laid on for the Port Curtis gold diggings' and carry fortune-hunters from Melbourne to Port Curtis (now known as Port Gladstone) in the state of Queensland.

Hayes did not hang around to learn the fate of his illicitly obtained ship. 'A FUGITIVE DEBTOR', posted the *South Australian Register* on 17 March 1858:

'It having been known early on Tuesday morning that a certain well-known master of a vessel now in harbour had left in the *Fayaway* for Newcastle, New South Wales, several tradesmen, who were peculiarly interested in the fugitive, obtained warrants from the Magistrates for their respective accounts, and having hired the *Young Australian*, steamed away in search of him, though, from his having had several hours' start, it was problematical as to whether he would be overtaken. The party was accompanied by Sergeant Dyke, who was entrusted with the execution of the warrants.'

The news that Hayes was fleeing on the brig *Fayaway* had come from Goularte, who put on a good show of being distressed and angry. Hayes had gone without paying him £10 owed for wages — or so he declared. The creditors rushed on board the *Young Australian*, the steamer was fired up, and steered downstream in hot chase. 'At the North Arm there lay an insignificant schooner, bound for Portland, but she was only noticed *en passant* as the paddles increased in revolutions, and by the time the outer bar was reached the gallant little steamer was making good headway,' recorded the *Adelaide Observer* in a reminiscent story, published on 6 May 1871. There was no sign of the *Fayaway*, but the steamer chugged on, while the weather became dirty and the creditors became seasick. Worse still, they began to run out of fuel, and, as the *Observer* dryly commented, 'Heaven sends wind, but it takes money to make steam.' Miserably, they were forced to give up and chug slowly home. The same little schooner was passed on the way, and the miserable creditors took just as little notice. They should have paid more attention. The little schooner was the *Perseverance*, and Captain Hayes was on board, bound for Portland, an important gateway to the state of Victoria.

Manuel Goularte braved it out in Port Adelaide, so was still in town on 19 March when the first sitting of the case of W.H. Hayes, master mariner, was called in the Insolvency Court. The insolvent did not appear, 'having left the colony', as the *Register* noted. One of the creditors did take the stand, he being an unfortunate 'who had supplied insolvent with a lot of drapery goods'. As he went on to describe, he and 'other creditors followed the brig in which the insolvent went away; but although they came up with her off Cape Willoughby, they were unable to get on board'.

So, at even that late date, the creditors did not realise the trick that had been played on them, which is a good reason why Manuel Goularte was not called to testify. His immunity was not going to last long, however. In July, he made his own escape, sneaking on board the *Havilah* on a Sunday, so that he could take advantage of a strange embargo that permitted debtors to leave on the Sabbath without arrest.

CHAPTER 4

Orestes

The little schooner *Perseverance* dropped anchor in Portland at 7 p.m. on 1 April 1858, and William Henry Hayes disembarked, headed for further adventure. Melbourne beckoned, and to get there it was possible to travel overland, via the interesting gold-rush town of Ballarat.

Once in Ballarat, it was very tempting to settle for a while. In the surrounding diggings more gold was being mined than anywhere else in the world, and the town that had sprung up in the midst of tents was bustling and prosperous. The likelihood that Hayes took up residence there for a month or so is borne out by a notice in the Ballarat *Star*, dated 6 May, which advertised a summons on W.H. Hayes for town rates. The fields about Ballarat, however, were also famous for being unusually peaceful and law-abiding, so it was inevitable that he would move on to Melbourne — quite apart from the fact that he would have been dodging yet another significant debt.

Melbourne, the hub of the state of Victoria, was a tremendously exciting city. Hundreds of hopeful miners poured in every day, to join the thousands who had already arrived. On the southern outskirts of the town, they set up tent cities, where their wives struggled with endless mud and awful pestilence while the men surveyed the possibilities and raised a grub stake, so that they could get to the diggings. In the business part of town, those who had succeeded beyond their wildest expectations were spending their gold like crazy men, getting rid of their wealth before heading back to the fields to try their luck again.

About the time that Hayes arrived, the notice of an interesting sale was posted daily in the Melbourne newspaper, *The Argus*. On Tuesday, 11 May, at precisely twelve noon, an ex-Peninsular and Oriental bark by the name of *Orestes* was to be sold at the Hall of Commerce in Collins Street. At 600 tons register, and 1000 tons burthen, built of English oak and sheathed with metal, she was a tempting acquisition for 'Merchants, Ship Owners, Ship Masters, and those interested in the Whaling Trades, or Exportation of Horses to India'. Indeed, as the auctioneer, H.A. Coffey, mused, it would be 'almost superfluous' to go into details of 'the many profitable trades that this vessel might be employed in'.

The passenger trade was definitely one of them. Not only did the *Orestes* have a capacious between-decks area for steerage passengers, who would have the luxury of unusually good headroom, the deck head being eight feet high, but her poop cabin contained two large after cabins, six side rooms and a large cuddy — or dining room — 'all fitted up in the newest style, and adapted by every modern improvement to meet the requirements of tropical climates'. Unsurprisingly, in view of all this, the sale went smoothly, the *Orestes* going for the good sum of £1500 ($7500 in current American money), to the senior partner in the American merchant firm of Osborne, Cushing & Co., Daniel Asaro Osborne.

Osborne opted for the passenger trade (though he also revealed that he intended her to carry timber on the way back), and by the end of July passage for the 'Vancouver's Island gold-fields' was being advertised. Not only were the accommodations splendid, as the notice enthused, but the ship would carry a surgeon. On 19 August, departure was imminent, and Osborne advertised in *The Argus* that a boat would be waiting at Ingles' Pier to carry all passengers on board.

But there was a hitch — many of those passengers had failed to pay the balance of their fare. Departure was put off until the 28th, when she would 'positively' sail, leaving behind those passengers who had failed to pay up, their deposits forfeited. Yet again, however, sailing was delayed, so that the first officer, David Keys, could be brought before the court on the charge of beating up one of the seamen, Charles Johnson, 'in the most brutal manner'. It was not until 1 September 1858 that at long last the *Orestes* cleared out of port.

And the man in command was William Henry Hayes.

It is difficult to tell why Daniel Asaro Osborne hired Hayes for the job. Though just twenty-seven, Osborne was a successful entrepreneur, a founding partner in a prosperous firm that had operated in Melbourne since 1855. Typical of the scores of American speculators attracted to Australia by the gold rushes, the partners in Osborne, Cushing & Co. owned several ships, manufactured brooms, acted as agents for an American drilling company, and imported equipment for shipmasters and miners, specialising in

American iron stoves. That their ships were often under-insured or even uninsured indicates that they were risk-takers.

Osborne should have been more careful. There had been a notice in *The Argus* on 17 March that William Henry Hayes, mariner, had been declared bankrupt in Adelaide, but if Osborne or his partners had seen this, it had been forgotten. Like many others, he was taken in by his fellow American's bluff charm, and Hayes' knowledge of sailing the northwest coast of America would have been a definite asset. Hayes also carried the reassuring demeanour of a family man, as Amelia had joined him, probably coming on the steamer *Admella*, which arrived in Melbourne on 21 July 1858, with a 'Mrs. Hayes' in the passenger list.

No sooner was the *Orestes* topgallant-down on the horizon than Daniel Osborne was disillusioned — and the source of his disillusionment could well have been none other than Aunt Allen, as the brig *Deva* arrived from Singapore on 13 September, with 'Captain and Mrs. Allen and family' on board. Shortly after that, Osborne sent to London for the registry papers for the *Orestes*, being anxious to claim ownership in a hurry. Once he had these in hand, he had to apply to the Custom House at the Port of Melbourne for an affidavit of the new registry, 'in favour of the above D.A. Osborne'. Time was fleeting fast, but on 4 February 1859, he was at long last able to write a letter to the British Consul at Rangoon.

Why Rangoon, when the *Orestes* was bound for Canada? The inescapable conclusion is that he had received information from Mrs Allen, including the detail that it was commonly said in Singapore that Rangoon was Captain Hayes' destination, back when he had sailed off on the *Bradley*.

*

'SIR', Osborne commenced, and then introduced himself as 'the sole owner of the Barque *Orestes*, I having purchased the same of the Peninsular and Oriental Steam Navigation Company, and dispatched her to Vancouver's Island with passengers, September 1, 1858, Captain W.H. Hayes as Master, with instructions to return to this port with a cargo of timber'. To his horror, as he went on to describe, he had received 'good and reliable reasons to believe that the said W.H. Hayes is not a trustworthy person to have charge of said vessel', and so he begged for every assistance possible, such as putting 'some trustworthy person on board as supercargo, or in such capacity as shall seem advisable to see her safely back to this Port of Melbourne'.

Once Osborne's letter had been received and read, it was given to the *Rangoon Times* for publication, and reprinted in the *Straits Times* on 20 August 1859, far too late to do any good. Almost a year earlier, the *Orestes* had arrived in the port of Honolulu, dropping anchor on 15 November 1858, en route for Victoria, Vancouver's Island, with seventy passengers who were ultimately headed for the gold diggings at the Fraser River.

Captain Hayes, as usual, had made himself affable, calling at the office of the *Pacific Commercial Advertiser* with a bundle of Australian newspapers under his arm. Over the first part of the voyage he had experienced very rough weather, he said — 'one month from port carried away foretopsail yard in a squall. Crossed the Line in 124° 10', since which have had light winds and fine weather'. Unfortunately, the ship had struck a leak in her topsides, and he would be forced to stop in port for 'two or three weeks to caulk and step a new foremast. All hands have enjoyed good health during the passage', he went on, indicating that everything on board was fine — which was very misleading indeed.

Within days, on the 20th, a notice was posted in the *Polynesian*:

'THE UNDERSIGNED WILL NOT be responsible for any debts contracted on account of bark Orestes, from Melbourne, unless approved by him

'— JOHN CLEMENT, Supercargo and Agent for the Owners.'

Whether Clement had been on board the *Orestes* during the 75-day voyage from Melbourne is unknown, but in view of Osborne's plea for 'some trustworthy person' to be put on board as supercargo, it seems unlikely. Additionally, Clement was acting for J.C. Spalding, a well-established Honolulu firm of ship chandlers and commercial merchants. In the same issue (and the same column) of the *Polynesian*, he called for tenders for repairs to the British bark *Orestes*, going on to say that 'specifications may be seen on application to the office of J.C. Spalding, Esq.'. It was also impossible for him to have received Osborne's letter, since it was not published until late the following year. The inescapable conclusion is that his suspicions had been aroused by Hayes' behaviour in Honolulu. Whatever his standing, he was remarkably efficient. By 10 December, Captain William Henry Hayes had been fired, and by the end of the following week Clement had found a replacement, Captain Thomas Mason. And when the *Orestes* sailed, on 27 December, Clement made sure he was on board as supercargo.

The *Orestes* arrived at her destination in good time, in January 1859, which seemed hopeful, but she then had to make her way to Puget Sound, to be laid up and stripped down before she could be loaded with timber. She finally sailed from Puget Sound in June, but though the ship was supposed to sail directly for Melbourne, on 14 July she was back in Honolulu, with a leak that needed fixing fast. Urgency was not attainable, however. The shipwrights had trouble finding the leak. Captain Mason tried an experiment, solemnly reported by the *Pacific Commercial Advertiser* on 4 August — a barrel was bunged up tightly and a gimlet hole bored in its head, and then it was placed over the likely bits of the floor of the hold, on the theory that any incoming water would make it ring like a bell.

Whether it worked or not, the crew did not find it reassuring, for they all signed a protest saying they refused to go back to sea until the ship was made seaworthy, 'it being entirely rotten, and the water continually pouring in, and in not only one place, but from stem to stern'. William Green, the British Consul, duly ordered a survey, and three gentlemen, including the harbourmaster, made an inspection. They passed the ship as seaworthy, but it could have been in a spirit of sympathy for a fellow shipmaster, as Captain Mason and the supercargo, John Clement, had both confided that they did not have the funds for a thorough repair. A native caulker had gone all over the bottom, they argued, and even though the *Orestes* might still be leaking, Captain Mason had a mechanical pump on board.

This made not just the crew unhappy, but the newspaper as well. 'An unjustifiable risk,' the editor of the *Advertiser* thundered. What if the pump broke down? And one of the seamen was a family man with five children back home! 'Old bachelors should take warning,' quipped the *Advertiser*'s rival, the *Polynesian*, and provide themselves 'with these aids to popular sympathy'. Captain Thomas Mason wrote an angry letter to the paper saying that he was the best judge of the condition of his ship, and so the crew wrote one of their own, declaring that the ship was leaking '*ten* inches an hour, which any gentleman can see by coming on board'. Then, to make matters even more exciting, Captain Mason was accused of killing one of the crew.

As the *Advertiser* headlined on 25 August, 'There was quite an excitement about the town', as Captain Mason had been charged with the murder of Joseph Watson, seaman. According to the testimony of the second mate, Thomas Fitzgerald, he, the captain, and other members of the crew had been in one of the ship's boats at the time, testing it for seaworthiness. Captain Mason had demanded to know if Watson was going to sail or not, and when Watson said no, an altercation had commenced. Vowing that he would force him to buckle under and obey, the captain had grabbed the tiller handle and hammered him about the shoulders, at which Watson, with a defiant yell, had jumped overboard. Whether he intended suicide or not, the leap was fatal. His body sank beneath the waves, never to be seen again.

'Mr. Clement, representative of the owners of the *Orestes*', rose to Captain Mason's defence, saying that he had heard a slightly different story, and, anyway, Watson was 'an unhappy and melancholy man'. This feeble argument did not wash with the judge, who committed Captain Mason for trial. Forthwith, he was thrown into jail — at which Clement hastily posted a notice in the paper that neither he nor the captain could be held responsible for any debts the crew of the *Orestes* might incur. Then, in the captain's name, he advertised a bottomry bond, to raise $2500 to pay expenses, and ordered that the ship should be unloaded so that proper repairs could be made. 'Had this been done a month ago,' wrote the editor of the *Polynesian* with an almost audible sniff, 'there would have been no trouble with the crew, and perhaps no loss of human life.'

It is little wonder that in the midst of all this excitement, the firing of the previous captain — William Hayes — was forgotten. It was finally aired on 1 September, the editor of the *Advertiser* musing, 'It is not often that a vessel visits our port, that is in every respect as unfortunate as this one. She first visited us last fall, and lay in our harbor six weeks repairing. After discharging her captain and taking another, and quietening in a measure the dissatisfaction of her passengers, she went on to her port of destination. There, she hardly had time to land her passengers and freight, before we hear of her as threatened with various suits for ill treatment by her passengers, to escape which she hastily sailed to an American port and procured a cargo of lumber.'

Captain Mason was tried on 19 September, before the jury of twelve good men that the British Consul had demanded, according to British law. Objections were made that the trial was being conducted in a blaze of publicity. Things had obviously never gone well on board, which affected the matter to some unknown degree — and how did the jury know that murder had actually been committed? Even if Watson had jumped overboard in a fit of rebellion, how did they know he was dead? A corpse had never been found.

By the end of the day, the jury had still not made up their collective minds, so they were sequestered for the night to think it over. The next day, they emerged with a request to inspect the scene of the crime. 'The jury in the case of Capt. Mason, of the bark *Orestes*, visited that vessel on Wednesday morning, in charge of the Marshal, examined the boat in which the trouble with Watson occurred,' reported the *Advertiser* on 24 September, 'and after their return to Court, united eleven to one in a verdict of not guilty.' After carefully measuring the distance between the place where Captain Mason had allegedly been standing and the thwart where the dead seaman had been sitting, they had decided that the gap was too great for the attack to have been brutal.

Captain Mason did not pause to celebrate his release. Instead, he hastily returned to his ship and prepared for a swift departure. It was not the end of the drama, however. The two men who had given evidence against the captain applied for permission to leave the vessel, knowing perfectly well that life on board was going to be very unpleasant. The Court of Arbitration decided against them, saying there was no good reason for their discharge, and so they broodingly returned to their berths. But then, as the *Advertiser* reported on 28 September, the captain was arrested for debt! 'A compromise was subsequently effected, and yesterday morning the Captain returned to his ship, which was lying off and on, and the unlucky craft was finally squared away before the wind with some prospect of eventually reaching her port in Australia.'

But was he rightfully acquitted? That was the question. Some of the public reckoned Captain Mason had been the victim of a conspiracy, while others thought differently. 'However, where there are doubts, the accused should have the benefit of them, and we trust that the *Orestes* will safely reach Melbourne without further mishap,' decided the editor, adding on a sardonic note, 'but don't believe it possible.'

CHAPTER 5

Ellenita

The trial of Captain Mason had provided most welcome fodder for the newspapermen at a slow time of year, but interest in the *Orestes* did not end with his acquittal and the departure of the ship. The very same page of the *Pacific Commercial Advertiser* that printed the verdict of the jury (24 September 1859) also carried an intriguing story from their San Francisco correspondent.

'The brig *Ellenita*, Captain W.H. Hayes, which has been advertised for Australia for some time past, has disappeared very mysteriously from our harbor,' the writer began, and then launched himself into the background. 'Capt. Hayes purchased the brig — an old tub — some weeks since, at a Marshal's sale, for $800 — only $500 of which he paid down; and had her thoroughly repaired on the ways of Tichenor & Co., *on credit*. Having laid in an abundance of stores of all kinds with the utmost profusion (all on credit), Captain Hayes quietly dropped out to sea on the night of the 28th, forgetting to clear at the Customs House, or to pay his bills! Even his lawyers are among the cheated ones! The next day, when her departure was discovered, Mr. Solomon, the U.S. Marshal, sent the steam tug *Martin White* to search for her, but to no purpose. The tug returned without seeing the runaway.'

Charles G. Hopkins, the editor of the rival Honolulu newspaper, the *Polynesian*, had received a letter from his own Californian correspondent. 'Our readers will remember perhaps a Captain Hayes, late master of the same British bark *Orestes* which has caused so much talk in this community of late,' he mused that same day, 24 September. 'Capt. Hayes brought the *Orestes* here from Melbourne last fall, but owing to transactions, which we need not repeat, became rather notorious, and was deprived of his command. Having remained here some time after the *Orestes* left for Victoria, V.I., Capt. Hayes obtained passage for San Francisco, where we had lost sight of him until we saw in the journals that he had purchased the brig *Ellenita*. Since then the report from San Francisco, as circulated here, is that the Captain, having paid for the brig "with the foretopsail," and forgotten to pay his respects to the Marshal of the City, under whom the vessel was held in a libel suit for water put on board, left between two days "for parts unknown."'

*

The *Pacific Commercial Advertiser*, a much racier paper than the *Polynesian*, had a great deal more to say, in words that were to ring around the world, and be echoed for over 150 years. Most was in a leading article that was headed 'THE HISTORY OF A CONSUMMATE SCOUNDREL' —

'The story of the life of a notorious rascal,' it began, 'is sometimes both interesting and profitable, as affording to the reader an example to be shunned, and giving to all mankind a knowledge of the practices of rogues, and an opportunity to avoid them.' Then, having given this virtuous reason for indulging in common gossip, the editor went on to repeat a lot of hearsay — that Hayes was about thirty-two years of age; that he had been born in Cleveland, Ohio, where his father was a grogshop owner; that, 'if we are correctly informed', he had been married in that place; that he had learned his seafaring skills there; that about the year 1852 he misappropriated another man's horses, sold them and pocketed the money, but got away with the crime because of a flaw in the law; that he married a second woman and fled with her to California; that on the way he talked his way into another man's confidence, leading to the purchase of the *Otranto* and her fitting out 'in the most costly style for a China voyage'.

In China, Hayes raised a lot of money with a series of bottomries, the story ran on, 'until at length the bark was seized to settle her liabilities', at which point Hayes bought the *C.W. Bradley junior*, 'and after pursuing as long as prudent the same course of borrowing and raising moneys on bottomries, he suddenly *left*'. His last port was Shanghai, where 'he employed a tailor to furnish him with $500 worth of clothing for himself and $40 for each of his crew. The clothing was made and delivered, and on the morning of his departure, the poor knight of the shears came off to get his money. Hayes received him very politely, requesting him to wait a while until he was more at leisure. At length the vessel approached the mouth of the river, and the tailor, beginning to "smell a mice," urged him again for the immediate payment. "Sir," said Capt. Hayes, "it is very inconvenient for me to pay you now; I shall return in two weeks, and then we shall square our accounts. At the present moment I am going to sea, and if you don't get into your boat you shall go with me." The tailor went ashore without his money'.

Instead of Shanghai, the next port was 'Port Adelaide in Western Australia', where Hayes 'conspired with the captain of a ship to defraud the owners of that vessel out of $20,000', by raising a bottomry bond of £4000. This did not work out well, according to what the editor of the *Advertiser* had been told, meaning that Hayes was forced to sell the *Bradley*, but nonetheless he proceeded to Melbourne, where he sold a gang of miners a ship that he did not own — none other than the infamous *Orestes*.

They set out for Vancouver's Island, but had to call at Honolulu, where he made himself notorious — and it is here that the editor of the *Advertiser* at last betrayed some personal knowledge. According to him, 'The voyage thus far had been one continued scene of trouble and bickering between the Captain and his passengers. From one of his passengers he had, while in Australia, procured the sum of $2,000, all the money he had, for the purpose of investing it in liquor and selling it on their joint account, to the steerage passengers during the voyage.' Somehow, however, Hayes forgot to invest the money, and so the passenger was out of pocket.

In Honolulu, Amelia, described by the writer as a 'lady of interesting demeanor and irreproachable character', applied for separation 'by act of law, on account of his brutal treatment towards her; and during the stay of the ship here, Mr. Clement, supercargo of the vessel and agent of the owners, having discovered, besides several dishonest acts on the part of Hayes, a conspiracy with others of the crew and officers to run away with the vessel and cargo, took the responsibility of removing him from the command of the ship. Hayes subsequently left for San Francisco in the *Adelaide*, leaving worthless drafts, debts, &c., behind him, in Honolulu, to the amount of near two thousand dollars'.

Amelia Hayes travelled on the same vessel, but not with her husband. Instead, she intended to join some friends in California. But, once landed, as the writer sighed, the foolish woman relented, and 'returned to the arms of him who had foresworn his vows to love and cherish her'. Then there was the embarrassment of a reunion with the merchant who had financed the purchase of the old *Otranto*. With a hasty reassurance that he had thousands of dollars ready and waiting in China, Hayes managed to persuade that gentleman not to go to the law. Worse still, his second wife made an appearance while Hayes was out walking with Amelia on his arm, but Hayes placated her, too, with the promise of some cash.

Or so the story claimed.

*

This was remarkably detailed, considering the distances involved. While events in Honolulu were part of the writer's own experience, he could not have known about Hayes' background in Cleveland, or his record in China, Fremantle, Port Adelaide and Melbourne. So how and where did the editor of the *Pacific Commercial Advertiser* get all these so-called facts? And how accurate was his information likely to be?

The 35-year-old editor and owner of the paper, Henry Martyn Whitney, had been born on the island of Kauai. Though the son of pious missionaries, in spirit he was a true entrepreneurial American. His aim was to be always the first to break the news, which in his case meant going out in a boat to meet every incoming ship, then boarding by means of a tossed rope, often before that ship had lost momentum. Even ships that were merely passing, on the route to China, were intercepted off Diamond Head.

It was an extremely dangerous practice — Whitney's boat once capsized just as he had hold of the rope and he was nearly dragged under the ship's counter — but it could be most rewarding. By jumping precipitously on board, he or his shipping reporter, Joseph O. Carter (who was also the paper's accountant), would be the first to see any newspapers the ship might be carrying, and to have interesting conversations with the captain. This last could be particularly useful. For all editors of Pacific port newspapers, and not just Henry Martyn Whitney, a gossipy skipper (or a talkative skipper's wife) was a pearl beyond price.

The two ships that called in with the *Ellenita* story were the clipper *Yankee* and the merchantman *Aspasia*. Both captains, Charles Lovett and Charles Sissons, were familiar figures in town. The *Yankee*, which had brought the San Francisco papers (and had J.C. Spalding in the cabin passenger list), had arrived on the 19th, while Captain Sissons, who had sailed from San Francisco on 30 August, had arrived on the 20th with the mail. The two captains were great friends and rivals, who enjoyed turning the run to Honolulu into a race, and so Sissons was rueful that the *Yankee* had beaten the *Aspasia*, despite her head start — but that was a small matter, compared with the news they both carried and the gossip they had to share.

Obviously, Whitney had no way of checking the authenticity of what Sissons and Lovett — or J.C. Spalding — told him. Nonetheless, he published the details of Captain Hayes' lurid past without question, in his overwhelming need to get the story out. This, it seems, was his usual habit. Charles Hopkins, the editor of the rival *Polynesian*, often derided Whitney's stories for lack of solid facts, calling his writing 'shadowy' and his conclusions 'insubstantial', and in later years Mark Twain (Samuel Clemens) wrote, 'Mr. Whitney is jealous of me because I speak the truth so naturally, and he can't do it without taking the lock-jaw.'

But, whether flimsy hearsay or not, the story had 'legs', as a modern journalist would say. Not only was 'The History of a Consummate Scoundrel' reprinted all about the Pacific, but it triggered the Captain William Henry Hayes legend.

*

Having published the grubby background details, the *Pacific Commercial Advertiser* had certainly not finished with Hayes. In that same 24 September issue, a story was reprinted from a copy of the *Daily Alta California* that Captain Lovett had brought into the office. The item, originally dated 30 August 1859, was headed 'THE FLIGHT OF THE ELLENITA'.

In this, the complete chicanery of Captain Hayes, 'a smart Jeremy Diddler', was revealed. 'He bought furniture, carpets, provisions, wines, liquors, and in fact, everything necessary to the comfort of a sea-voyage. Unfortunately, however, Capt. Hayes forgot to pay for the articles.' No one was spared — 'His butcher, grocer, market man, and, strange to say, even his lawyers, were victimized to the tune of $500. The only man who felt any doubt of his honest intentions was the man who filled the water casks, and who libelled the brig for his bill, amounting to $80.' But, as Whitney's readers already knew, the ploy did not work, as Hayes took the advantage of a brisk breeze, 'and spreading his sails to the favoring gale, he quietly "drew out" from the harbor, and *cleared the Heads instead of the Custom House*, forgetting the little formality of *"the papers."* As soon as it was ascertained that the brig had gone there was a terrible hub-bub' — but, just as in Port Adelaide (though Whitney's readers did not know that titbit yet), sending out the steam tug was fruitless.

Further details were provided by another paper from the collection brought into the office by Captain Lovett. This was the San Francisco *Herald*, whose editor, it seems, was even more unselective about gossip than Henry Whitney. 'It is said,' the columnist confided, 'that a number of persons had taken passage on the brig and had paid beforehand, but the vessel sailed leaving nearly all of them behind. Captain Hayes, however, carried off the wife and three children of a gentleman who is one of those left. He also carried off a trunk belonging to a Mrs. Armstrong, and containing all that lady's title deeds to property in Sydney. Captain Hayes, however, did not carry off his own wife, that lady having left town the day before he sailed.'

This last was true enough. Four years later, on 10 October 1863, the *Daily Alta California* posted a notice that Amelia Hayes had commenced suit for divorce — 'She says they were married in Australia in 1857, that he deserted her in this city four years ago and she does not know where he is' — and, on 27 February 1864, the *San Francisco Bulletin* noted that the *decree nisi* had been granted.

The rest, however, is open to question, as is the *Herald*'s estimate of the debts Hayes left behind. 'We learn that the following parties have been swindled by Captain Hayes,' this part of the story revealed — 'Mr. Morrison, $800; Mr. Tichenor, $250; ship carpenters, $800; victuallers and grocers, $1200; vegetable dealers, $300; a gentleman, for borrowed money, $300; legal advice, $100; a bill which his lawyer promised to pay, $114; money borrowed from his lawyers, $80; plumbers, $500' — which, with a number of unnamed sundries, added up to 'about $4000. The fellow also managed to swindle Mr. Morrison out of some forty tons of beans'.

Four thousand dollars being five times the worth of the entire ship, the editor's informants were exaggerating with a vengeance. The *Daily Alta California*'s estimate of $500 was much more likely.

*

The *Herald* was also wrong in the final detail. 'It is supposed by those who appear to be the best informed,' the item concluded, 'that he will steer for Tahiti, where he will lay in a cargo of oranges for the Sydney market.' Tahiti, however, was not part of Captain Hayes' plans, as the *Polynesian* noted on the very same day that the *Advertiser* published the *Herald* story. 'By letters from Maui we learn, however, that Capt. Hayes and the brig had arrived safely at Kahului on that island at some day previous to the 19th inst. (say the 16th), where the Captain represented himself as having arrived in distress, leaking, and as bound to New Caledonia.'

Hayes then purchased stores from local provisioners, to the extent of about $600, 'besides entering into sundry little speculations *sub rosa*, of which the Custom House Collector at Lahaina is reported as having very much disapproved; so much so that the Sheriff of the island set out for the scene of the worthy Captain's operations in order to remind him that Kahului was not a port of entry, that the new tariff had reduced the duties on liquors so much that it was hardly worth the risk to smuggle, and finally to invite the Captain to make the personal acquaintance of the Collector, and to insist — with all the urbanity of a Sheriff — but to insist on the vessel being brought to Lahaina.

'At this part of the Captain's adventures, the reports become rather confused,' the editor of the *Polynesian*, Mr Hopkins, admitted, but his rival, Mr Whitney of the *Advertiser*, was fully up to sorting it out. According to him, while Captain Hayes had every 'design of taking on board some fresh provisions, and probably of smuggling a few goods', he was foiled by 'the gallant Sheriff of that island, Peter H. Treadway, Esq.', who mounted a horse, galloped across the island to Kahului, and arrested 'the rogue upon a warrant for the violation of the revenue laws'.

Captain Hayes, while undoubtedly taken aback, was gracious about it, asking only that the Sheriff accompany him on board, so he could give some orders to his mate. Once there, 'various pretexts' detained them from going back on shore again, presumably involving Hayes' famous hospitality, with the upshot that Mr Treadway was persuaded to spend the night on board, after Hayes agreed to ride with him to Lahaina the next day. 'Early in the morning, however, the Captain announced to the Sheriff his determination to resist the arrest, alleging it was illegal, and declaring that he should go to sea immediately, and gave the Sheriff his choice to go ashore or remain on board. Being unaccompanied by any force, he was obliged to submit, and having been landed, was subjected to the mortification of seeing the *Ellenita* squaring away before a fresh wind.'

No blame could possibly be attached to the Sheriff, Henry Whitney declared — 'Uncle Peter' had behaved as any normal man would. 'Where Hayes will go next remains a problem,' he mused then. Could it be Kauai? 'It is hardly likely that he will eventually dare to show his face again in Australia or China.'

Like his counterpart on the San Francisco *Herald*, Whitney hazarded a guess that it would be Tahiti, or maybe South America. 'Hayes is a man of little education,' he concluded, 'and of but little talent except for rascality. He is very plausible and gentlemanly in behavior when he has an object in appearing so, and seems to have the dangerous faculty of impressing strangers with the belief that he is an honest man. He is minus one ear — said to have been bitten off in a fight. His most intimate friend and accomplice is a man by the name of Robert Parkinson, who navigates the vessel for him, and plans the rogueries that Hayes carries out.'

And, in the final sentence, Henry Martyn Whitney made history yet again — by being the first to call William Henry Hayes a pirate. 'Whatever may be said in extenuation of his crimes, he is now to all intents a pirate,' he wrote, 'and we trust may meet the reward his conduct so justly deserves.'

CHAPTER 6

The Wreck of the Ellenita

It was the fault of the beans. The load shifted, the beans blocked the pumps, and the ship was doomed. 'The *Ellenita*, brig, 318 tons, Captain W.H. Hayes, foundered on the 16th of October, in latitude 12-48 south, longitude 172-25 west,' announced the *Sydney Morning Herald* on 4 December 1859. Down she went, leaving twenty-six souls stranded in the middle of the ocean, seventy miles (one hundred kilometres) from Samoa, with just one boat to save them all.

According to the evidence of some of the survivors, both passengers and crew had done their utmost to keep the old brig afloat, but when the water washed up to the deck beams, they gave up trying to pump the ship dry and set to building a raft instead. Under the direction of Captain Hayes, they constructed a platform by nailing planks across the main trysail boom and a spare topmast, and launched it over the rail after securing water casks on top. Water lapped so freely over the platform that a deck had to be made out of cabin doors and partitions, but at last the contraption looked steady enough for provisions to be loaded, and for some of the braver men to clamber on board. Other people took places in the launched boat, all of which lightened the brig considerably, so Captain Hayes and four seamen stayed on board to throw anchors and other weighty stuff away. Their hope was that the *Ellenita* would stay sufficiently afloat to tow the boat and the raft at least part of the way to the Samoan Islands.

All was in vain. The brig went down by the head, sinking so fast that it was a scramble to save the captain and men who were still on board of her. Night fell on the chaotic scene, the men on the raft paddling madly to keep up with the last sighting of the boat. Morning dawned to find that they were still in company, but a lot of the supplies had been washed off the raft, while the boat held just a few demijohns of water, and no provisions at all. At that stage, Captain Hayes took firm charge, ordering everyone out of the boat and onto the raft except for himself, the mate and one seaman, to make space for the women and men with families. When one of the male passengers refused to move, he threatened to throw him overboard. Cowed, the fellow scrambled over to the raft, and Hayes then set to organising the provisions, taking a good share of what was there.

No objection was made by those on the raft, because as they said later, they 'thought he was going to stay by them', but disillusionment was due. At noon, Hayes took a sight of the sun, told them their position, 'and something about the bearings of some place, and then said he was going to leave us; he accordingly left us without compass, or chart, or epitome, or any kind of navigation tools except a quadrant'.

The boat set sail and scudded swiftly out of sight, carrying off Captain Hayes, Robert Parkinson, one oarsman and nine passengers — Mrs Armstrong, Miss Cornelia Murray, Mr Clarke with his wife and three children, and Mr Bunting and his son. On the raft there were three seamen, the cook, the steward and nine male passengers, one of them a boy. Their water barrels held about seventy gallons of fresh water, and Hayes had spared them one barrel of bread, but it was so wet 'that salt water could be squeezed out of it'.

The weather was very rough, with waves constantly washing over the deck, carrying away blankets and clothing, along with the quadrant. On the fourth day they saw land, but it was a long way to windward and was gradually lost to sight. That night was even rougher than the nights before, the sea rolling the raft so madly that as the men rushed from one side to the other, trying to keep it on an even keel, it threatened to capsize. 'All this time the sharks were very numerous around us, which no doubt helped to keep the people excited.'

Men began to lose their minds, 'and talked of going to hotels to get a good meal. In going to their supposed hotel two of the men walked overboard two or three times but caught hold of the raft and got on board again'. They set a small sail and steered south 'until the men got too weak to stand to the helm'. On the eighth day, they caught a shark, 'which was a great relief, as it was fresh, and our provisions was getting very low. It was caught by tempting it alongside, by tying a ham bone to a small line, and throwing it towards him; he followed it close up to the raft, when a bowline, or noose, was slipped over his head'. Dragged on board, the shark was sliced up 'still kicking', and eaten raw after its blood was drunk.

Water was getting very low and the men were all suffering from terrible thirst. Some drank their own urine, 'the Steward especially'.

To add to the horror, the raft was beginning to break up, pieces snapping off and drifting away until there was not enough room for them all to stand on the deck. An empty water barrel was cut open to make a kind of shelter, and the two men who were most badly off stood inside it — until others objected at what was seen as their superior comfort, which led to open fighting. Not only did the men have agonising salt-water boils, but they were hallucinating badly — some thought they could hear cocks crowing, while others imagined people talking and the ringing of bells. Then, on the fifteenth day, the steward died, 'perfectly insane'. The corpse was left to lie a while, and then, with a prayer, they threw it overboard, attracting another shark, which was caught and eaten just like the shark before.

The very next day, they saw land — dead to windward. Over the next two days, they gradually neared it, and on the third morning, just as the raft was being pulled away by an offshore current, some natives swam out, hauled the raft to the reef, and helped the castaways to the beach. They were on a tiny atoll off Wallis Island, now known as Uvea. Next morning, the natives carried them in canoes to the main island, 'where we were kindly treated by the French missionaries and natives, until the arrival of H.M.S. *Elk*, when we were taken on board, and every kindness shown us by the captain, officers, and crew'.

The *Elk*, they learned, had been looking for them. The *Ellenita's* boat had arrived at Samoa with all safely on board, and Captain Hayes had reported the drifting raft. Since then, the *Elk* had been cruising from island to island, warning the natives to keep a watch for the castaways — 'Had not the natives been told to look out for us,' testified the raft survivors, 'there would have been no one there.'

*

'The "new year" began last Sunday,' wrote the editor of the *Sydney Morning Herald* in an accounting of the seven days from Saturday, 31 December 1859 to 7 January 1860. 'On that day there was such a reunion of friends and relatives in Sydney — the survivors from the foundered *Ellenita* — as, if described by a novelist, would have been pronounced too hard a strain upon the imagination.' By the strangest of coincidences, the Hamburg brig *Antonio*, which had brought Captain Hayes, his mate and the boat passengers from Samoa, and the *Elk*, with the survivors from the raft on board, both dropped anchor in Sydney on New Year's Day. 'A happy new year must it, indeed, have been,' rhapsodised the writer, 'to those who, by God's blessing, met once more after so fearful a separation.'

Never was a man so wrong. Captain Hayes featured in that paper twice more that week, both times not at all to his credit.

*

On 6 January 1860, the *Sydney Morning Herald* reprinted Henry Martyn Whitney's *Advertiser* story, 'The History of a Consummate Scoundrel'. It had arrived via its reprinting in the *San Francisco Evening Bulletin*, a copy of which had been carried into port by none other than Captain Allen's brig *Deva*. Though with the alternative title 'THE STORY OF A SCOUNDREL', it was the same as Whitney's original, word for damning word. And, the following day, the *Sydney Morning Herald* carried a report of Hayes' arrest — for indecent assault.

'William Henry Hayes, late master of the brig *Ellenita* (foundered at sea), appeared in surrender of his recognisances,' the second item began, 'he having been apprehended under warrant granted on the information and complaint of Cornelia Murray.' The newspaper's court reporter did not have much sympathy for Cornelia, calling her 'a somewhat plain-looking girl', but at least her testimony was printed in full. She, after stating that she was 'fifteen years and seven months old, unmarried, have a father in Sydney, my mother I believe is in California', described meeting Hayes for the first time on the brig, having boarded with her two brothers as a steerage passenger. The captain had seemed pleasant enough. After a few days at sea he had summoned her brother Robert, and gallantly observed that the steerage was not a nice place for a young girl, 'among so many vulgar men'. Accordingly, he proposed that Cornelia should move to the cabins, where she could help Mrs Clarke with her children.

'I consented to go into the cabin,' she said, 'and on or about the 3rd or 4th of September, my brother removed my bed from the steerage to the cabin floor.' The cabin turned out to be the captain's, but still Cornelia went to bed, Hayes not being in the room. Then, in the middle of the night, she regretted her lack of caution. 'I was wakened up by feeling something heavy across my breast, and said, "Who is there?" I felt the hand of the captain, who said, "Hush, do not make a noise, be still."'

At that, Cornelia lunged up, but he caught her about the feet, and assured her that the only reason he was lying beside her was that the ship was rolling so, and he only wished to talk. Then, when Cornelia threatened to scream, he became angry, saying that if she did scream, it would be the last time she ever would. A struggle ensued, and then Hayes abruptly gave up and returned to his own berth. Cornelia, after sitting the rest of the night on a box, asked her brother to move her bed back to the steerage.

The court didn't show much sympathy, either, especially when Cornelia admitted under cross-examination that she had allowed a young man in the steerage to lie on her bed with her — and that, yes, she did take her meals in the cabin after the so-called assault, and that, apart from that one night, 'she was always treated kindly by defendant'. And Mrs Clarke, in whom Cornelia had confided, had taken no issue with Hayes at the time. As Cornelia also admitted, 'Mrs. Clarke quarreled with the captain after the vessel foundered', and it was probably because of that, that she took Cornelia with her 'to inform Mr. Williams, the Consul'. Within a day, the charge was withdrawn and the case thrown out of court, but the gossiping did not stop.

*

Three days later, on 9 January, a rival Sydney newspaper, the *Empire*, reprinted Whitney's 'History of a Consummate Scoundrel' story, but not word for word, as the *Sydney Morning Herald* had done. Instead, the piece was embellished with a great deal of editorial comment, plus details of what had happened since Hayes had left Lahaina.

The headline ran 'THE CAREER OF A REMARKABLE SCOUNDREL, UP TO THE LATEST DATE', while the article commenced with the same kind of excuse for printing gossip that Whitney had used — 'For the information of our readers in Sydney, and New South Wales generally, we have the satisfaction of informing and of warning them that there is now, or was a day or two since, in this colony, one of the most systematic and unmitigated scoundrels that it has ever had the fortune to be possessed of.'

Evidently the writer had met Captain Hayes (or had talked to someone who had met him), as he then launched himself into a description — 'a man of some six feet high, about 15 stone weight, and of rather plausible, bluff exterior, which with many, it would seem, has enabled him to pass off, until a settlement came, as a very honest, jolly seaman; and he is a man who at times spends his money, or the money in his possession, very liberally, which, considering the very strong probabilities connected with its acquisition, is not very difficult to account for.

'The success of this enormous mercantile humbug (he having possessed himself probably to the amount of £20,000, or to the value thereof, if not twice as much, in the last eight years, without any equivalent but impudence and promises) is the more singular from the fact that he is a man of the most meager education, and possessing no particular qualities, except for cunning.' Plus the advantage, as the writer went on to say,' of 'an unlimited command of impudence, and a somewhat more than average degree of physical power of which fact he is partial to giving discourteous intimations to the unfavourably disposed'.

This description penned, the writer then quoted Whitney's précis of the life of Captain William Hayes, up to the sale of the *C.W. Bradley junior*. Then he launched into his own indignant description of Hayes' escape from his creditors in Adelaide. Being labelled insolvent, he said, 'by no means damaged' Captain Hayes' 'ardour in the pursuit of cash', or his passion for an 'uproarious life', because the American was able to keep up his habit of buying on credit, 'the storekeepers and others generally believing his statement that he was a flourishing and wealthy mariner; when suddenly, to the surprise and disgust of his friends, the news spread of his having decamped'. The story of the chase in the steam tug followed, but the real drama — that Goularte had fooled the creditors, and Hayes was on the schooner, not the brig — was completely missed. Instead, the writer gave way to imagination, describing Hayes dancing about on the deck making 'pantomimic gestures' and shouting derision, as dusk fell and the brig tacked away.

For the story of the *Otranto* and the six weeks in Honolulu, the editor of the *Empire* returned to the Whitney version. The trick played on the Sheriff of Lahaina was also related much as it had been told in the Honolulu newspapers, but then came an embellishment of the 'indecent assault' on Cornelia Murray, the writer claiming that she had been attacked twice, the second time 'when the vessel was sinking, and the water was coming above the lower deck'. This was followed by a breathtaking claim that the *Ellenita* had been deliberately scuttled, 'having foundered apparently at a most convenient moment', leaving Hayes in charge of the only boat, with the passengers' cash and jewellery secreted about his person.

'Whether this gentleman, who seems as yet with impunity to have committed more scoundrelism than the aggregate of crime which in former days has sent many a hundred men to the gallows, will renew his performances in Sydney by way of relieving us of a ship as a rover, or will kindly vary the entertainment with another wife, or will try his hand at an "escort" is a matter of conjecture (for of course now he has a soul above horse-stealing, and such pettifogging transactions), but it is more than probable he will confine himself for a time to his favourite peculiarity — an extended system of credit,' the writer concluded, adding, 'Should any further noteworthy action of Mr. Hayes come within our knowledge and it cannot be supposed for a moment that a gentleman of his talents would allow them to be idle, we promise our readers the earliest and latest intelligence.'

*

So, who was this longwinded commentator with an appetite for embellishing what was already a good story?

Samuel Bennett was a career newspaperman who had taken over the *Empire* — originally founded by Henry Parkes, later Sir Henry Parkes, Premier of New South Wales — after it had failed with liabilities of £50,000, in June 1859. He was, it seems, an abrupt sort of person, his obituary in the *Sydney Morning Herald* in June 1878 describing him as having 'a certain brusqueness and austerity of manner'. However, the item also described Bennett as being a careful researcher. Perhaps he was misled by his informants, or there may have been a personal motive in such a heavy-handed interpretation of the facts. Or, as he claimed, he merely wanted to bring the details up to date. But it is most likely that Samuel Bennett simply wished to out-do Henry Whitney in Honolulu by publishing an even more sensational story.

If he had lived up to the reputation that Bennett had given him, Hayes would have marched into his office and threatened him with a horsewhipping. Instead, this 'remarkable scoundrel' wrote a wounded letter and sent it with four testimonials to his honesty — but not to the editor of the *Empire*. Instead, Hayes addressed the envelope to Bennett's rival, John Fairfax, the owner of the much more substantial *Sydney Morning Herald*, and the founder of a media empire.

A markedly honest man who made a point of always settling his debts — in 1852 he had returned to his home town of Leamington Spa, England, to repay the liabilities he had left behind when he migrated to Australia as an insolvent — Fairfax ran his paper 'upon principles of candour, honesty and honour', adding, 'We have no wish to mislead; no interest to gratify by unsparing abuse or indiscriminate approbation.' Accordingly, he was fair-minded enough to publish the letter — apparently in full — on Thursday, 12 January 1860.

Considering that the *Straits Times*, back on 20 August 1859, claimed that though the American could read, he 'writes very imperfectly', Hayes demonstrated quite a flair with the pen, unless someone did it for him. 'Much as I am pained by the perusal of this libel,' he commenced with a flourish, 'I feel some pleasure in the reflection that I have living personages in this city who can, on oath, when necessary, contradict the gravest charges — which fact, coupled with my own conscious innocence, support me in my trying adversities.' Hayes then accused the original writer (Whitney) of 'bitter malice', the 'unrelenting cruelty of the whole article' being apparent from the very start. And most of it was a tissue of lies! For a start, 'My father was not an innkeeper', and though he was poor, this was the first time Hayes had heard that poverty could be considered a crime. The horse-stealing story was also false — 'in 1852, I was in Calcutta!' And, as for that second marriage, 'if in San Francisco a gentleman was foolish enough to set up this so-called married woman in a retail liquor saloon, it must have been after I left, and for his own purposes, not mine!'

At this stage, interestingly, Hayes denied any ownership of the *Otranto*. Instead, he claimed that he had been given the command 'by recommendation to the owner'. She had been sold in China, he said, by John Purvis and Sons. 'In this they exercised their own discretion, and paid me my wages — 1780 dollars. The *Otranto* was never seized, nor was a single dollar raised on bottomry. I then purchased the *C.W. Bradley jun.*,' he went on, adding that he raised a mortgage of $3000 for a term of twelve months. 'This vessel cost me just double that sum, and the mortgagees, thinking she was so old as to run the risk of condemnation, urged me to sell her when I reached Adelaide, which I did — honestly placing her in their agents' hands — who sold her, and paid their principals.'

And the story of the tailor? False from beginning to end! 'It is also false that the action brought by me in Adelaide was lost as fraudulent.' His claim to ownership of the *Estrella* (unnamed) after lending the money to keep Goularte afloat was upheld, he said, but the sale of the ship paid nothing more than the seamen's wages, 'the law swallowing the balance'.

Then Hayes attended to all the libels concerning the *Orestes* — the $2000 was in fact just £80 (equivalent to $400), 'which a passenger did invest in grog', and which that passenger (unnamed) sold himself, to his own profit. 'Another falsehood — my wife procured a divorce. This is cruelly false both to her and me; I never ill-treated her, as those who know her best can testify.' The only money entrusted to Hayes was '50 dollars deposited by the cook'. And as for the wreck — 'am I to be charged with crime because I was unable to preserve money from the shipwreck when I nearly lost my life — my ship actually uninsured?' The so-called jewellery was nothing more than a few trinkets, bought for the aforesaid wife — and, as for the writer's claim that 'I would not dare again to show my face in Australia or China', that was patently untrue.

'And now,' Hayes went on with unmistakable complacency, 'for the satisfaction of the ungenerous writer, while I have denied what is false, I will confess what is true. I did do the Sheriff of the Sandwich Islands, and would do so again under similar circumstances.' Hayes had put in to fix a leak, and certainly not to smuggle goods, and had been unaware that Kahului was not a 'proclaimed port' of entry to the islands. And, as he had only a cargo of common vegetables (including those beans), he 'did not choose to be arrested'. The 'jolly sheriff' had enjoyed a 'jovial evening', along with his friends, and had even helped work the ship out, 'being an old sailor'. Indeed, 'he did better duty in my ship as a sailor than ever he did as a sheriff', and it would be good to meet him again. Or so Hayes confided, 'never forgetting our cordial shake of the hands, the drink he took before he left me, parting the best of friends'.

And, with that, he concluded with another flourish, soliciting 'the favour of the insertion of the letters enclosed herewith', a favour that the *Sydney Morning Herald* granted, printing them immediately beneath.

*

The first was signed by a name that had not appeared in connection with Hayes since his first arrival in Adelaide — B.T. Taylor, one of the two cabin passengers on the voyage of the *C.W. Bradley* from Singapore to Australia. Who this gentleman was, or what he was doing in Sydney, is impossible to tell, but he certainly sailed with Hayes on the voyage from Singapore to Adelaide, as his name was on the passenger list.

Despite having witnessed the bouts of brutal discipline that seaman Hines had described, plus the dubious presence of the Chinese woman, Taylor turned out to be quite a friend, and apparently an old one, too. Not only did he confirm that Hayes had handed over the *Otranto* to John Purvis and Co., but he revealed that Hayes bought the *Bradley* on impulse. It was a sudden change of mind, it seems, as he and Hayes had planned to sail to New York on the *Yankee Ranger* — an American ship that was indeed listed in the port of Singapore in March 1856, when the *Bradley* (then *Santubong*) was up for sale. According to the *Straits Times*, the *Yankee Ranger* was headed for London, not New York, but her home port was certainly the latter.

Taylor also confirmed that the *Estrella* (still unnamed), was claimed via the bottomry bond that Hayes had signed, but 'owing to the heavy expense of a crew for that time, and other charges brought against the ship, Captain Hayes in the meantime became reduced in circumstances, so that he was not able to purchase the ship, for the reason that he could not furnish means to pay the crew's claims'. And, as for the *Bradley*, it was 'sold on a mortgage, which was given to a house in Singapore'. Then he added a spicy detail — that it was the mortgagers who told Hayes to leave Singapore in a hurry, as the bark was rotten, and they wanted to avoid a legal survey. 'Captain Hayes advised them to send their mortgage to Australia, which was done; and, on the mortgage being produced, Captain Hayes willingly delivered up the ship.' And with that, and having made his oath, B.T. Taylor signed off.

A more straightforward affidavit was signed by one of the women who had been in the *Ellenita*'s boat. 'This is to certify that I, Catherine Armstrong, was a cabin passenger on board the ill-fated brig *Ellenita*,' she wrote, 'and, seeing the report that there was a wife and family on board, whose husband was left behind, is not true, as there was but one lady with a family on board, and that was a Mrs. Clark with three children, whose husband was on board with her.' A less credible postscript followed her signature, saying, 'P.S. — I was well acquainted with Captain Hayes and wife; I visited them, and that they were very happy.'

The third testimonial was signed by H.E. Nealds, who certified that he was in Melbourne when Hayes arrived from Adelaide, and that the *Orestes* was the 'only vessel he had anything to do with' while there, and the gossip about the ship he 'sold' to the gang of miners was quite unfounded. 'I never heard anything against Captain Hayes' character, only that he was very strict with his crew, and would punish them if they deserved it.' Captain Nealds was a well-known local shipmaster, with many years of experience commanding brigs and schooners about the coasts of Australia, and so, even if he were one of Hayes' cronies, he was a credible, if succinct, witness.

The same cannot be same of the last, a Charles W. Jackson who claimed to have known Hayes in Cleveland. 'I knew Captain Hayes as master of sailing vessels and steamers,' he wrote. 'He was considered a first-class commander and a very popular man.' And, what's more, he had not been married — or not to the writer's knowledge. 'I never heard anything against Captain Hayes' character until I saw it in the *Sydney Morning Herald*,' he concluded.

*

While all this was being assembled into print, Hayes was arrested yet again, this time for his more easily proved practice of bilking other people of their money. According to a notice in the *Sydney Morning Herald* on 13 January, criminal charges had been brought by Abner W. Kempton, master mariner. While at Apia, Samoa, the two captains had become acquainted, and when Hayes had learned that Kempton was looking for work, he pretended that he was the owner of a ship lying at Port Adelaide. He would gladly put Kempton in command, he said … but, in the meantime, he was rather short of cash.

Kempton loaned him £53, and came with him on the *Antonio*, expecting to take over command of the fictional ship. And, now that he had learned that the ship owed its existence to Hayes' imagination, he wanted that money back. The case for criminal charges was dismissed, the court having no jurisdiction, but Hayes was imprisoned at Darlinghurst for non-payment of that debt and others, as he also owed Charles E. Bunting (another passenger on the *Antonio*) £20, and £100 to Joseph Hemming, one of the passengers on the ill-fated *Ellenita*.

He was behind bars for just days, however, as he was released after filing for bankruptcy, the required notice having been posted in the *Sydney Morning Herald* on 23 January 1860 — 'The following estate was surrendered and accepted: — William Henry Hayes, of Sydney, master mariner. Liabilities, £173. Assets: value of personal property, £15. Deficit, £158. Mr. Morris, official assignee.' Striding out of the jail, penniless again, but apparently quite unbowed, William Henry Hayes sallied north, headed for his next adventure.

CHAPTER 7

Launceston

It was none other than Mrs Sarah Ann Allen who recorded the next encounter with Hayes, and a bizarre encounter it was too.

The Allens blundered into the now-notorious Hayes during the second week of August, 1860, when Captain Thomas Allen and his wife were attending the famous horse races at Maitland, New South Wales. A few miles up the Hunter River from the coal-port of Newcastle, Maitland was a lively town, known for its social scene — horse races in particular — and the prosperity of its populace. Many of the top-hatted gentlemen who gathered in convivial groups at the racecourse, smoking, comparing horse-flesh and betting, had done well out of squatting — settling on a piece of land and breaking it in for grazing sheep, horses and cattle — or by supplying goods and livestock to those who had established farms and stations in the fertile upriver dales.

According to what Sarah Ann Allen described to her nephew, A.T. Saunders, they 'met Hayes dressed as a nigger minstrel'. As Saunders recounted years later, in 1913, 'Hayes told them he and the others of the troupe were doing fairly well', so the impression that he was a banjo-playing member of a minstrel show is indelible. However, Captain Hayes' occupation at the time was not quite such a comedown. The advertisements currently posted in *The Maitland Mercury and Hunter River General Advertiser* named the travelling entertainers as 'The Alhambra Waggish Marquee' and W.H. Hayes was described as the Marquee's agent. Accordingly, he was much more likely to be wearing the suit and top hat of a businessman than he was to be garbed in the white cutaway jacket, white pipe-stem trousers, floppy bow tie and blackface of a 'nigger minstrel'.

The Alhambra Waggish Marquee was, in fact, a circus, 'waggish' at that time meaning frolicsome, merry and enjoyable. And the notice promised an entertainment to suit, one that was both interesting and varied.

The Alhambra Waggish Marquee Will Open at West Maitland, on the First day of August (for the Race Nights only), at the rear of the Olympic Theatre.

The talented troupe consists of Chinese Tumblers, Spanish Cautorshines, and New Zealanders, and your old favorite —

PABLO FANQUE

Also, several New Feats, too numerous to mention. This talented troupe will give one performance at Raymond Terrace on the 30th, and Morpeth on 31st.

PABLO FANQUE, Manager

W.H. HAYES, Agent.

During the mid-nineteenth century circuses were extremely fashionable, and Pablo Fanque is one of the most famous names in the history of the big top. Born William Derby in Norwich, England, about 1796, Pablo Fanque was the first black circus proprietor in Britain. Whether he came from a slave background is unknown, but his history certainly made no difference to his reception, as his circus was immensely popular, dominating the British entertainment scene for more than thirty years.

The Fanque who employed Hayes as his agent in New South Wales was not the Pablo Fanque of British fame, however. Instead, it was his nephew, William 'Billy' Banham. Like Fanque's son, Edward — who also toured Australia and New Zealand, but was a show boxer, not a circus performer — Billy Banham used the Pablo Fanque name with permission, because he was talented enough not to let the image down. The original Fanque, famous for his contortions on horseback ('cautorshines' in Hayes' idiosyncratic spelling), was also a tightrope walker — what they called a rope dancer — and Billy Banham Fanque had been well taught, as his tightrope-walking acts toured Australia to rapturous reviews. In Maitland, back in January 1860, the paper declared that his performance 'fully justified the flattering opinions expressed in references to his agility and cleverness'. As the reviewer added with patent awe, 'He is extraordinary.'

How this 'extraordinary' circus manager met Captain Hayes is lost to history. Billy Banham Fanque was in Sydney in July 1860, as he appeared in a benefit for 'Master Risley' at the Royal Victoria Theatre, and his agent at the time was S. Wade. Evidently he replaced Wade with Hayes, and took him to join the troupe at Maitland, a favourite stamping ground because of the crowds drawn by the race meetings.

There, the ground behind the Olympic Theatre was rented, the big top set up, and the advertisements and bulletins duly posted by Hayes. 'There was a large attendance of spectators,' reported the correspondent to the *Sydney Morning Herald* on 9 August 1860, the second day of the races, 'the course being thronged with ladies and gentlemen on horseback and vehicles of all descriptions, besides a goodly number of pedestrians, all of whom were evidently on pleasure intent. There were a great many booths on the course, the proprietors of which appeared to drive a thriving trade. There was also a merry-go-round, and Pablo Fanque's Walhambra, which was also well patronized.' Unfortunately, the weather was cold and cheerless, but otherwise the scene was enchanting, and the publicans' booths well attended, as were the theatre and Marquee that night.

Fanque was still in town on 30 August, as an advertisement placed in the Maitland paper noted that it was hoped he would make an appearance at the Olympic Theatre, in a benefit for the stage manager, Mr G.R. Morton. From there he took the Alhambra Waggish Marquee upriver, via a performance staged in a hamlet named Muswellbrook, to the little inland town of Tamworth, New South Wales. There, he ran into trouble. As the *Empire* of Sydney reported with gusto on 20 September, Fanque was thrown into jail, being accused of theft. 'The "Waggish Marquee" and "gigantic" troupe, of which this gentleman is the sole manager and proprietor,' the item elucidated, 'was advertised to appear in Tamworth shortly, so that his appearance was looked for by some — ourselves in particular — with interest. It appears, from what we can learn, that a charge of stealing some wearing apparel at Muswellbrook appeared against him in the *Hue and Cry*, and this is the offence of which he now stands charged. Pablo states that he had been brought up before the Bench at Muswellbrook on this charge and the case was dismissed; but whether this is the case or not we are unable to say.' If he truly were innocent, then this was a case of 'great hardship', as Pablo had been in jail for seven days, and still a Magistrate had not arrived to try him, the nearest being sixteen miles away.

It was the end of the Alhambra Waggish Marquee. When he finally got out of jail, Billy Banham Fanque and what remained of his troupe joined another circus, Ashton's, which billed him as 'the First Rope Dancer in the World'. They toured Queensland, where Fanque received the usual rave reviews — his act 'would be difficult to excel', wrote the *Maryborough Chronicle* in January 1861.

But William Hayes was not with them to share the applause.

*

Instead, Hayes had returned to Maitland. Not only was it close to the busy seaport of Newcastle, but it was a great place to ingratiate himself with the local gentry.

One of these was Samuel Clift, a man who had done very well for himself. Born in England about 1791, he had followed the trade of a carpenter, but in 1817 was handed down a fourteen-year term at the Northampton Assizes, for the crime of holding some forged bank notes without a good excuse. He was sent to New South Wales on the transport *Neptune*, and after arriving in Sydney moved to the Hunter River valley. About 1820, he settled on a Crown grant of forty-four acres on Wallis Creek, where he built a neat little cottage that still stands, one of Maitland's cherished historic buildings. It is a sign of his growing prosperity that he imported twelve panes of expensive crown glass for a large window on the ground floor.

Because of the lawlessness at the time, he and his wife Ann, with their growing family of children, used to access the single bedroom on the upper floor via a ladder and a trapdoor, pulling up the ladder behind them. Within a few years, though, he felt secure enough to install an ornate cast-iron spiral staircase.

When he met William Henry Hayes, Clift was aged about seventy. He had moved out of the little cottage long before, progressing through a series of increasingly grand houses. As well as building these himself, he had extended his land-holdings greatly. A prosperous man about town, celebrated for his fine horses, sheep and cattle, he was known for being willing to employ men and women who were down on their luck. But, while Hayes was definitely going through a bad patch, the American's jovial, reassuring demeanour, and the many rousing tales he could tell of seafaring in the Orient, also made his company attractive.

*

On 24 February 1861, the Sydney bark *Launceston* arrived in Newcastle from Melbourne, under the command of Captain Charles Robertson. For no stated reason, she was put up for sale. Clift either bought her on Hayes' behalf, or loaned Hayes the money to make the purchase himself, with the result that when the ship was reported in Sydney on 27 March, Hayes was in charge, and also acting as the agent. Then, on 13 April, the *Launceston* weighed anchor again, Hayes declaring his destination as Bombay.

The next notice of him is in the issue of the Singapore *Straits Times* for 7 September 1861, where there is an unmistakable note of panic. Wrote the editor, 'Considerable excitement has been occasioned in the mercantile community, by the supposed reappearance of Captain Hays, of Singapore notoriety.' The paper had received a circular from Batavia (now Jakarta), Java, dated 30 August 1861, which carried tidings of such importance that he printed it at once, as did the editors of papers all about the Pacific, once they had received the news.

'We conceive it to be advisable to place you in possession of some proceedings which have lately taken place here,' the notice began, 'and which are charged with the gravest interest to mercantile and underwriting classes.' About the beginning of that month 'an English barque called the *Launceston*, and commanded by Captain W.H. Hayes, arrived at Sourabaya, from the colonies, with a cargo of coals'. The captain had delivered the freight to the consignees, Fraser, Easton, and Co., and then, as was usual, had looked for a charter back to Australia. The ship passed the compulsory survey, and was chartered at the rate of £8 a ton, then sent to Semarang to load with sugar and coffee, and from there to Dadup, 200 miles (320 kilometres) southeast of Batavia, to top up with rice. And the agents at Dadup, accepting Hayes' assurance that he did not want to call at Batavia for despatches, agreed to send her directly to Newcastle.

But then, as the bulletin described, rumours came to their ears — 'that a certain Captain W.H. Hayes had been publicly announced in the Singapore papers as a notorious marine swindler, who had already absconded with two ships and cargoes, and had always succeeded in making his escape'. Someone, it seemed, had remembered reading the sensational revelations that had been published in the *Straits Times* almost exactly two years before, and was warning 'the mercantile classes and others in Java and the Dutch settlements' about the 'villainy' of this particular captain.

But was this Captain Hayes the same as the first Captain Hayes? That was the burning question. The agents and the insurers made a call at the office of the British Consul, where a consultation was held. The ship's papers were found in perfect order, and although Hayes was unable to produce the British master's ticket that would have guaranteed his competency to command a British ocean-going ship, he was definitely the owner. Accordingly, the British Consul declined to take any further steps. Turning to the Dutch authorities had the same result, so the agents made another approach to the British office, this time with a different proposition. They asked the consul to write a letter to Hayes requesting him to take his papers to Batavia, where he could 'clear himself of imputations made against his character'. And the consul agreed.

Caught aback by this new development, Captain Hayes wavered. First he promised to sail to Batavia, and then he changed his mind. Deciding that attack was the best means of defence, he declared his strong intention to proceed on his voyage without waiting for any money, 'the cargo he had on board being sufficient to pay his full freight'. Unfortunately for him, however, he stated this in writing, and when the men from Fraser, Easton, and Co. had a look at the letter, and compared the script with the signatures on the ship's papers, 'it was evident that they were not written by the same person'.

At this stage, the second mate and one of the men deserted. Hayes duly reported their absence, and after they were captured by the police, they 'declared that they would rather jump overboard than proceed with the ship'. This was common enough, particularly with captains as strict as Hayes, but it clinched the matter. Having made up their minds that he was indeed the rogue described by the *Straits Times*, but not having enough evidence to bring criminal charges, the men from Fraser, Easton, and Co. 'resolved that a proposition should be made to Captain Hayes to discharge the cargo which he had already on board against payment of his full freight, at the expense of the insurance offices'.

The insurers, for obvious reasons, were most unhappy about this, especially when Hayes agreed to the arrangement, so wrote the aforesaid bulletin, the one that was sent to the editor of the *Straits Times*. 'We do not believe that any man with a clear conscience would have submitted to an arrangement so inconsistent with his honour and self-esteem,' they thundered in writing. The letter then concluded with the pious hope that 'Captain Hayes, of the *Launceston*, may have sufficient regard for himself to furnish the Australian authorities, on his return to Sydney, with decided proof of his integrity and honesty, in which event, apology will be due to him'.

Instead, Hayes sailed off — with the cargo. The very next day, 31 August 1861, another letter, written by another merchant house in Batavia (Hunter, Houghton, & Co.), revealed that instead of discharging his freight, Captain Hayes had flown. 'He has received of his agents £500, and his cargo is worth about 100,000 guilders, 60,000 of which only is insured.'

CHAPTER 8

Cincinnati

The *Straits Times* story was reprinted in the *Newcastle Chronicle* on 19 October 1861, and in the *Maitland Mercury* three days later, which must have given Samuel Clift pause for reflection. As the *Maitland Mercury* observed, 'The *Launceston* sailed from Newcastle, the vessel having been purchased by Captain Hayes, as we are informed, with money advanced to him by a wealthy resident at Maitland, who, however, it is said, took no security for the amount.'

Whatever the precise situation, it does not seem to have made any difference to the friendship. When William Hayes returned to Maitland he presumably brought the money from the sale of the ship and cargo with him, because his welcome was warm. Indeed, he was able to invest in yet another ship. On 22 August 1862, an advertisement appeared in the *Newcastle Chronicle* — 'For the Otago Gold Fields. The A1 Barque *CINCINNATI*, 700 tons, W.H. Hayes, Esq., Commander, will sail for Otago on or about the 28th instant, and offers unrivalled accommodation for passengers. For freight or passage, apply to the Captain on board, or to DIBBS, THORNE, AND CO.'

The bark *Cincinnati* (actually 443 tons) had arrived in Newcastle on 12 August, from Otago, New Zealand, commanded by Captain Fitzsimmons. Considering that this was just ten days earlier, the sale to Hayes (or his sponsor) had been negotiated remarkably swiftly. And the editor of the *Newcastle Chronicle* was nothing less than approving, commenting the next day, 'THE CINCINNATI — This splendid vessel, we perceive, by reference to our advertising columns, has been laid on direct for that land of ophir — Otago. Independent of her superior passage accommodation — and which will doubtlessly availed of — she is commanded by a gentleman, (Captain Hayes), who, independent of his nautical skill, has, by his courtesy and social qualities, won the respect and kind regard of those who have been fortunate enough to come in contact with him.'

For all kinds of reasons, it was not going to be hard to find passengers. Quite apart from Hayes' 'courtesy and social qualities', Port Chalmers, the entry to Dunedin and Central Otago, was currently the most popular destination in the Pacific. Back in May 1861, an experienced Australian prospector by the name of Gabriel Read had discovered gold in a gully that was given his name, a rich find that impelled thousands to vie for passage to the south of New Zealand. The diggings of California, Canada, Victoria and New South Wales were emptying out as hopeful miners swarmed into the diggings of Gabriel's Gully.

The people Hayes took on board were not gold prospectors, however. Harking back to his days with Pablo Fanque and the Alhambra Waggish Marquee, he filled his cabins with those who meant to make money not from mining, but from entertaining the miners instead. They were actors and musicians billed as 'The Buckingham Family', being the nine children of the famous George Buckingham.

*

The family's progenitor, comic actor George Buckingham, was most probably English in origin, and may have been a convict who had worked out his sentence. Whatever, he was both talented and energetic. In May 1838, he opened the first theatre in Adelaide, and in February 1842 he acted in the earliest performances in Melbourne's first theatre, the Pavilion. He then managed the Melbourne theatre until the authorities closed it down in 1843, an action that led to a decision to take his talents across the Tasman Sea, to the burgeoning town of Auckland, New Zealand.

The first mention of him there is on 23 December 1843, when he hired Wood's Royal Hotel, renamed it the Royal Victoria Theatre for the occasion, and advertised a 'laughable Farce' called *The Two Gregories*, which was accompanied by singing and dancing. This was remarkably swift organisation, as he and his wife, Ann Jane, with their two children — Ann Jane junior, who had been born in Sydney in July 1838, and George Harvey junior, born in Adelaide in 1840 — had arrived in town just two days before, on the brig *City of Sydney*. But energy and enterprise was typical of George Buckingham, both then and in the future.

The local editors were very pleased to see him. The *Daily Southern Cross* observed on 6 January 1844 that 'Mr. Buckingham, the late manager of the Melbourne theatre', was quite an acquisition to the colonial scene, as he 'was an established favourite in Port Phillip, and the Melbourne journals have one and all passed very high encomiums on his managerial career'. As the writer commented, 'The good folks at Auckland may congratulate themselves on the prospect of abundant amusement being afforded them by Mr. Buckingham.'

On 24 February 1844, the same paper noted that he had opened 'a very neat little Theatre' — the Fitzroy, one of the earliest purpose-built theatres in New Zealand. The editor did not expect good attendances, however, considering the uncultured 'state and stage of our Colony', and he was proved depressingly right. By November, George Buckingham had given up the hopeless venture and opened a coffee house and grocery. This was by no means the end of the Buckingham theatrical enterprise, though, as he became a favourite guest performer at concerts, amateur theatricals, civic dinners and balls. And, meantime, his family was growing, with the births of Rosetta (familiarly called Rosa) in 1844, Walter in 1848, Conrad Sydney in December 1849, and Henry Douglas in September 1852.

Within a few years the older children were starting to sing and act well enough to appear alongside their father. As a reviewer remarked on 4 December 1849, a comic song rendered by 'a son of Mr Buckingham (a boy of about ten years of age)' was 'loudly applauded and encored'. However, it was not until 4 November 1853 that the *Daily Southern Cross* was able to hail an upcoming concert to be staged by 'Mr. Buckingham's Family'. The venture went well, with the Governor and his lady among the large audience. 'The vocal and instrumental pieces were gone through in a highly creditable and pleasing manner,' wrote the reviewer eleven days later, 'especially the popular song of "The good time"', which was 'merrily performed' by the younger Master Buckingham, and 'kept a numerous and respectable audience in a roar'.

The warm reception of this, and of the three concerts that followed, encouraged George to take his family on a theatrical tour of New South Wales, and so he and his wife and their six children sailed for Sydney on the brig *Moa*, on 20 February 1854. Again, the experiment worked well. Within weeks, on 25 April, the editor of the *Daily Southern Cross* was able to report that 'our fellow citizen', Mr Buckingham, with his 'talented family', was 'delighting the good folks of Sydney, drawing crowded houses and winning golden opinions from the press of the great Southern Metropolis'.

On 11 September, they returned to Auckland on the brig *Algerine*, Buckingham having signed a three-month contract with W.H. Foley, the proprietor of the Theatre Royal in Auckland, to act in a series of comedies with Mrs Foley. Unfortunately, the Foleys' management system clashed with Buckingham's ideas, and the papers gave Mrs Foley all the warm reviews, which did not suit Buckingham's self-image at all. By October, the Buckinghams were back to performing their family concerts, and Ann Jane junior, though just sixteen years old, was staging solo recitals and teaching piano. None of it paid well. The quarrels with Foley ended up in a court action that Buckingham lost, and despite the happy advent of yet another son, Alfred William, born in September 1854, Auckland had lost its gloss. A return to Australia beckoned.

It took quite a while for George senior to settle up his affairs, but finally, on 2 April 1856, the Buckingham family boarded the Sydney-bound *William Denny* — headed for that encounter with Captain William Henry Hayes.

*

A great deal happened between the Buckingham family's arrival in Sydney in April 1856, and August 1862, when Hayes advertised passage to Otago on the *Cincinnati*. Their tour was focused on New South Wales — in April 1857 they were in Sydney, where a third daughter, Emily Esther, was added to the family, and on 29 January 1858, when the family was in the town of Armidale, Ann married Samuel Glogoski, of Posen, Prussia (Poznan, Poland). Variously known as 'Herr Glogoski', 'Signor Glogoski' and even 'Professor Glogoski' (being a teacher of music and dancing), Samuel was as resourceful as the family he was marrying into, playing the violin for assemblies, staging quadrilles, and raising funds by tuning pianos, if necessary. Altogether, he was quite an acquisition.

But, from then on, matters turned much for the worse.

*

From Armidale, the family moved back to Sydney, to play at Toogood's Saloon, where they billed themselves as the 'Largest Operatic Company out of England'. Ann Jane junior, now 'Madame A. J. Glogoski', starred as 'the charming Ballad Singer', accompanied by her husband, 'Signor Glogoski, the Prussian Violinist'. Brother George was the 'Buffo Singer', while fourteen-year-old Rosetta was another 'talented singer'. Ten-year-old Walter performed as 'the Old Musketeer', and nine-year-old Conrad sang Irish ditties as 'Paddy Malone'. The stint with Toogood, however, ended as badly as the arrangement with Foley had in Auckland, George Buckingham's temper being so short.

In July 1858, just four months into the contract, he was brought up in court to answer what *Bell's Life in Sydney* facetiously called 'Inhuman Assault'. As the writer went on to describe, 'George

H. Buckingham, a tall fierce-looking individual, apparently an Englishman', appeared before the Bench 'to answer the charge brought against him of assaulting that enterprising, liberal, and accomplished gentleman, Alfred Toogood, Esq., landlord of the Rainbow public house, for administering an impetus with his sinister podestal to Mr Toogood's dexter ribs'.

The effects might be grave, as the journalist observed, for the plaintiff 'appeared in delicate health', and was forced to come into the court 'leaning upon the arm of his affectionate attorney'. A further comic note was added when Mr Toogood, being a very short man, was helped to stand on a side table, so that he could match the height of the defendant. In his deposition he also revealed interesting details of publicans' arrangements with visiting entertainers — the Buckingham family received no salary, instead being given half the price customers paid for 'spirits, wines, cheroots, and swankey', and one-third of the price of lemonade. Whether there had been any quarrel over the accounting went unmentioned, as the testimony moved straight on to an aggrieved description of the assault. While stepping past the little man, Buckingham had kicked him in the side. The publican was so startled, he said, that he 'suffered his nice sense of honor and his keen susceptibility to momentarily disarm his urbanity and prudence, insomuch that he threatened to knock the defendant down if he attempted to repeat the attack'.

George Buckingham found this very funny. As the reporter recounted, instead of showing proper penitence, he, 'au contraire, treated the matter with shocking levity'. Unsurprisingly, he lost the case, but the Bench, very amused, merely sentenced him to a fine of 'ONE SHILLING STERLING'. As the journalist quoted in conclusion, 'So much for Buckingham!'

George Buckingham's size, strength and sense of humour would have been very useful in the family's dealings with Captain Hayes. Instead, tragedy struck twice. On 19 April 1861, George's wife, Ann, died of dysentery at their home in Campbelltown, New South Wales, 'leaving a husband and nine children to mourn her loss' — the ninth being another son, Arthur Stewart, who had been born in June 1860 when the family was in Wollongong, New South Wales. And very shortly after that, George himself disappeared. Whether he died or merely left the country is unknown. Whatever the reason, the nine children were now on their own.

*

Presumably, it was Ann's husband, Samuel Glogoski, who made the decision to carry their act to the goldfields of Otago, New Zealand. The arrangement with Hayes appears to be aboveboard, as not only had Captain Hayes mended his image in Newcastle and Maitland, but he seems to have been doing his best not to put a foot wrong. He departed with due legality, taking his clearance from the Customs House on 3 September — 'for Otago, with 613 tons coal. Passengers — Mr and Mrs Glogoski, and two children, Mrs and Miss Buckingham and servant, Masters Buckingham (3) and Messrs Dalton, E. Conn, and G. Buckingham'.

At this stage, he seems confused about the identity of his passengers — the two children listed with Ann and Samuel Glogoski must have been her two youngest siblings, five-year-old Emily and two-year-old Arthur, while the 'Mrs' Buckingham did not exist. 'Miss Buckingham' was Rosa, now aged eighteen, and the three 'Masters Buckingham' were Walter (fourteen), Conrad (twelve) and

Henry, who was almost ten, while George was listed separately. But Hayes was soon to know them all very well indeed.

When the ship sailed from Newcastle six days after that, on 9 September, the list in the *Maitland Mercury* was altered, but only to include Captain Hayes as a passenger. A shipmaster who often filled in on a temporary basis, Captain Hyde, was now the master. This was most probably because Hayes, being American, did not have a British shipmaster's certificate, though Hayes himself would still have been in charge. Then there was an unexpected development. At the same time that the *Cincinnati* was lying in the stream at Newcastle, a claim was made in a number of papers that 'The notorious Captain Hayes, with the barque *Cincinnati*, visited Sydney, and after engaging passengers for Dunedin, and receiving their money, sailed away without a single passenger.'

Considering that the ship was reported with fourteen passengers (or thirteen, if Captain Hayes is not counted), this is at least partly in error — but what about those who were supposedly left behind? The mystery was solved in a report from the Water Police Court, published in the *Sydney Morning Herald* on 6 September. Joseph Wardlaw, gold-digger, had brought an action against a ship chandler by the name of John Frederick Lincker, on the grounds that 'he had contracted with defendant, as agent for the master of the ship *Cincinnati*, for a passage in that vessel from Newcastle, in this colony, to Otago, New Zealand'. Lincker, he said, had advertised for men who wished to work their passage to Otago, but Wardlaw and his eight comrades had declined to do that, preferring to pay Lincker £5 each for the fare.

Prevaricating, Lincker had taken the money, but only on the understanding that Wardlaw and his eight friends would sign the ship's articles at the rate of one shilling a month, to avoid the Passengers Act. Naturally, because of the devious nature of this arrangement, there was no receipt, it being a spoken agreement. The only paper was a memorandum from Lincker to Captain Hayes, instructing him to take on Wardlaw and his eight comrades as passengers, though they would be listed as crew. But when Wardlaw and his friends arrived in Newcastle, Hayes flatly refused to go along with the arrangement, saying that he had received no money and expected them to work if they went on board. And, as there was no accommodation for passengers, the boys would have to rough it. When they turned down this unappealing option, he had simply instructed them to go to Lincker for a refund, and sent them away.

Lincker, for his part, swore that he had indeed given Hayes the money. That made no difference to their Worships, who 'ordered that defendant pay the passage money £5, passage of complainant to and from Newcastle £1, expenses at Newcastle 9s., boarding and lodging in Sydney £1, with costs; in all £8 4s'. Wardlaw was the only one who was paid, however. His eight comrades, no doubt driven by their own reasons, had preferred not to make an appearance in court. Lincker, embittered, listed two more vessels for Otago, the captains of which 'have now proved themselves true to their advertisements'. So, seemingly, he was the source of the libel.

*

The theatrical troupe had a miserable time in the Tasman Sea, Captain Hyde reporting to the *Otago Daily Times* on 24 September, the day they arrived, that they had been struck by a heavy sea on the 12th, 'which carried away a considerable portion of her bulwarks on both sides, two of the ship's whaleboats, and a carriage which was on deck'. After that, the ship leaked so badly that Captain Hyde had steered for Auckland, 'but as she made less water while running before the wind, he altered his course and came through Cook's Straits'.

Having learned all this, the shipping reporter tackled Captain Hayes, showing him a Melbourne paper with the item about the abandoned passengers — said passengers 'had declined to accept the accommodation which it was originally agreed they should have on board', the American curtly informed him, and with that the conversation was over.

In the same issue, the *Otago Daily Times* lauded the arrival of the *Cincinnati*, saying that as well as the much-needed coal she was bringing, she 'has also about twenty passengers, including the members of the Buckingham family, whose arrival is an acquisition to the entertainments of Dunedin'. They staged their first concerts locally, however. While still in Port Chalmers, they took over a local bowling saloon and turned it into a concert hall. The *Otago Daily Times* noted that 'several members of the Family possess both talent and skill', affording 'excellent entertainment' to the locals, and forthwith advertised that the 'celebrated' Buckingham Family was engaged to play at the Theatre Royal, Dunedin.

Dunedin was an exciting place to be, at the time. Since the discovery of gold by Gabriel Read in May 1861, the settlement had trebled in size, with builders, shopkeepers, taverns and theatres doing a booming business. Over that weekend of 12 October, as the paper reported, 'no less than twelve hundred persons' arrived to crowd the streets, adding to the general spirit of optimism. Few of them attended the Buckingham Family's performances, however. The man who had employed the troupe — actor and theatre manager, Clarence Holt — must have been very disappointed with both the takings and the reviews. While the newspaper's commentator 'admitted that as an Irish "character" singer, Mr Buckingham possesses a great deal of humour', and 'Master Walter has a rather nice voice', the entertainment, as a whole, 'is not of a class that it is desirable should be often repeated at the Theatre Royal. Elsewhere,' he decided, 'the Buckingham Family would probably receive a fair amount of support'.

The Buckingham Family took the hint. Mr Holt staged a benefit concert to help them on their way, and then the troupe headed for the goldfields. And Captain Hayes, having sold the old *Cincinnati* to the firm of Cargill and Co. for use as a coal hulk, went with them. Somehow, over the stormy passage from Australia, he had charmed the family into taking him on as their manager.

*

They first headed to the Taieri diggings, the Buckingham Family having been hired by a Mr Davis, the proprietor of a hotel called the Prince of Wales in the bustling town of Hindon. There, so many hotels and taverns had been built that they jostled against each other, so he planned to beat the competition with attractions staged in a theatre he had annexed to his tavern.

As so often happened, their arrival brought controversy. As part of his arrangement with young George Buckingham, Davis had paid the coach firm of Quick and Co. to carry the entire troupe — Ann and Samuel Glogoski, Rosa, George, Walter, Conrad and Henry, plus the two small children — 'at the usual rate of fare for each passenger', which included 14 pounds' weight of luggage per person. This allowance was not nearly enough, there being an excess amounting to 180 pounds of baggage, which Davis neglected to pay until 8 January, when Quick took him to court. However, according to a report in the *Otago Daily Times*, 'Mr Davis's new theatre is crowded nightly' and the Buckingham Family was much appreciated by the weathered miners (who particularly applauded Master Walter's fantasias on the cornet), which gave Mr Davis some compensation for his trouble.

From there the troupe and their mountain of luggage proceeded to Dunstan, up the Clutha (called the Molyneux River back then). It seems the party left precipitately, as on 15 January 1863 letters for the Glogoskis were included in the list of unclaimed mail at Hindon. It is not on record whether Quick's coach line carried them or not, but if Quick declined, Cobb & Co. would have filled the gap.

Whichever the carrier, the journey was bound to be a revelation, even for a troupe that had roughed it in the diggings of New South Wales. To get to Dunstan, the carriages and drays had to travel a rutted trail north of the river to the mountain range called the Knobbies, climbing out of the summer heat of the gorges to a bleak plateau where it was likely to be snowing, and then working through mud, potholes and rubble. As was usual, the gentlemen would be requested to dismount at frequent intervals to lighten the coach and even help push. Famously, the stagecoach driver would yell 'Lean to windward!' at precipitous corners, to keep the carriage on an even keel. Creeks and rivers were either forded or crossed on rafts made of boats tied together. This was stark, spectacular, utterly inhospitable country, the land where much of the first of *The Lord of the Rings* movies was filmed, many years later. Anonymous fortune-hunters died here, caught in the open by storms or freezing temperatures.

All that negotiated, the driver headed for the Dunstan range of mountains, until at last his passengers overlooked the steep and dangerous descent to the river, and the scattering of miners' tents that ran alongside it. Down there, back in August 1862, two heavily bearded men with seamed, weathered faces had dug eighty-seven pounds of gold at the junction of the Kawerau and Clutha rivers. One was an American by the name of Horatio Hartley and the other was an Irishman, Christopher Reilly. When they had registered their cache at the Dunedin treasury, it had earned them a reward of £2000 for their discovery of a new goldfield.

A new rush had commenced — a gold rush so vigorous that the Buckinghams' coach had passed endless lines of trudging men, bowed down under their swags, their pannikins and gold-washing pans jingling and rattling with every movement. Down in the Dunstan Gorge, a small tent town had sprung up at the famous junction of the two rivers, called, unimaginatively, the Junction (now known as Cromwell). Eight miles above this was a little township — known briefly as Hartley Town, but soon to be famous as Dunstan — which had sprouted proper buildings, and was the business centre of the diggings. And there, with typical briskness, the Buckingham Family set up their own establishment in a large tent, which they called the United States Hotel. And, according to a letter written to the *Otago Witness* on 24 December, they 'secured good audiences'.

'We are well up in the way of amusement,' wrote the same Dunstan correspondent on 12 January 1863. 'We have a theatrical troupe, the Buckingham Family.' Dunstan, despite having been established in a hurry, was surprisingly civilised, with timber-built stores, offices and hotels going up cheek-by-jowl, forming a substantial main street.

A cricket club had even been established. On 23 January, the writer to the *Otago Witness* recorded a civic dinner, with 'an excellent band' which, under the supervision of George Buckingham, 'enlivened the proceedings by playing a number of appropriate airs'.

On the same date he revealed that 'New diggings have been discovered in the neighbourhood of the Arrow' by a party of Germans. This new find was just a short distance from Arrowtown (then called Fox's, or Fox Town), a gold-rush centre that had sprung up after a digger named Fox had struck it rich in the terraced gorge where the river ran. Business there was particularly lively, not just because of the constant talk of new finds along the Arrow River, but because the miners were flooding into town to stock up for the winter. Opportunity beckoned, and so, after selling the site of the United States Hotel, the Buckingham party took the particularly dangerous and precipitous trail to the Arrow River.

They quickly settled in — 'At the Arrow,' wrote the correspondent to the *Otago Witness* on 29 February, 'Miss Harriet Gordon and Mr. J.P. Hydes, assisted by the clever Buckingham Family, are drawing good houses, and offering really first-class evening amusements.' Again, this was in the family's own establishment, which this time was in a sod-and-calico building, instead of a tent, and called the Provincial Hotel.

Puzzlingly, a second hotel was constructed straight across the narrow street from the Provincial, to be managed (and perhaps solely owned) by Captain Hayes. It was called the Prince of Wales Hotel & Theatre, and Hayes lived there with Rosa Buckingham, who was now calling herself Mrs Hayes. There is no record of a marriage — which would have been bigamous, anyway, as Amelia Littleton Hayes was still waiting for a *decree nisi* in California. Rosa did not care for that, as not only was she pregnant, but she was living the high life of the wife of a big spender.

There was some lively competition between the two theatres. How acrimonious it was is impossible to tell, though it is likely that it was staged for publicity. However, it was to lead to one of the most enduring yarns that are still told about Captain William Henry Hayes.

*

The tale first appeared in the *Otago Daily Times* on 8 August 1896, thirty-three years after the event. It was written by a man by the name of J.A. Miller, who appears to have spent much of his life at sea. He claimed to have been hired by Hayes, that 'bad yet a remarkable man', to stitch the roof of his hotel in Arrowtown.

The walls were sod, he said, and about eight feet high, and enclosed 'a space of about 60ft by 30ft' that was covered by a frame-and-calico roof, and then, according to the narrator, called 'THE UNITED STATES HOTEL'. Miller and his mate — a man who had been in California in 1849 — were given the job of sewing the calico because they had been sailmakers in the past. Hayes did not treat them dishonestly, Miller writing, 'My mate and I received every shilling that was due to us', but Miller's mate was vividly aware of their employer's notorious background. Not only, as it proved, had he read Henry Martyn Whitney's 'History of a Consummate Scoundrel', but he remembered one sentence in particular: *He is minus one ear — said to have been bitten off in a fight.*

'Nearly opposite the United States Hotel in Foxtown was the Provincial Hotel, run by a family of talented young people known as the Buckingham Family, and doing a roaring trade,' Miller wrote. 'The chief attraction in the family was a talented young lady of more than ordinary personal attractions and accomplishments, amongst which was a gift of voice so powerful that she sang "Bonnie Annie Laurie" and other songs to the accompaniment of a full brass band' — a low blow, considering that the Buckingham Family advertised their programme as being 'chaste and elegant', and implausible, too, there being no record of a 'full brass band' in the gold-rush town at the time.

'By some means,' Miller continued, 'Hayes enticed her away from her family to his hotel, it being said that he married her.' The family, he claimed, did not like this at all, so the situation was ripe for wreaking revenge. 'In the meantime it had leaked out that there was a reason for the captain wearing his hair of such extraordinary length, and that the reason was the want of an ear. The missing ear had been left in California, where at a game of poker Hayes had been suspected of cheating, when one of the players pinned his hand with a bowie to the table, several cards were discovered up his sleeve. A melee ensued, and others who had lost heavily to Hayes suggested lynching. The upshot, however, was that Hayes was deprived of an ear.'

The story of the amputated ear having been told all about Arrowtown (presumably by Miller's Californian mate), the Buckingham Family 'were not slow to turn it to account', as Miller went on. 'The several barbers in Arrowtown at the time were offered a £5 note to cut off Hayes' hair short should he come to patronise any of them.' That opportunity to commit 'the foul deed' was not slow in coming, and so Hayes' secret was revealed.

'Like the ignorant fool that he was, Hayes went about with a flannel bandage round his head, blustering, threatening to shoot and knife all and sundry in a promiscuous sort of way. However,' continued Miller with obvious relish, 'worse was to come.' The Buckingham Family decided to turn the story into a comic farce, called 'The Barbarous Barber' and charge the outrageous admission price of ten shillings. Hayes and his 'partisans' tried to prevent the show, by surrounding the entrance of the Provincial Hotel, but the place was rushed by an eager crowd, and by the time the curtain rose, the place was packed. 'The character of the barbered victim was taken by a man named Spiers, holding some repute as a sword and general dancer. He made up to perfection, and acted the character with astonishing fidelity.'

The crowd enjoyed the fun, and Hayes 'swore and blustered, and threatened libel actions galore, but nothing came of it'. Instead, Captain Hayes disappeared from Arrowtown, 'and I heard no more of him until he turned up in Lyttelton, where he kept a hotel'.

*

The truth or otherwise of this rousing yarn can be judged from the actual newspaper report, which appeared in the very new local paper, the *Lake Wakatip Mail*, on 6 May 1863.

'As a bit of local gossip,' wrote the editor, 'I may mention that a new local farce, entitled "The Barbarous Barber," has, for the last three nights, been performed at the Provincial Concert Hall. It certainly is one of the most extravagant extravaganzas ever witnessed, in fact its chief merit is its absurdity.' Then, for those who did not know the background, the writer provided the details — 'Be it known, then, that between two concert rooms, those of the Provincial, and the Prince of Wales, a pretty severe opposition has for some time been raging.' This had come to a crux the previous

Wednesday night, when a performance by a troupe called 'Our Own Minstrels' was scheduled to take place.

It was usual in those days for theatres to employ barkers — leather-throated men who stood outside the entrance, shouting out the virtues of the shows that were being staged inside. To advertise 'Our Own Minstrels', the landlord of the Provincial Concert Hall had hired the Arrow bellman (town crier), who was a veritable 'Jemmy Lungs', according to the *Mail*, while a local barber with a particularly loud voice ('*The barbarous Barber*') was engaged by Hayes at the Prince of Wales Hotel. 'Fierce raged the contest, and great was the applause, when these two belligerents came to (bell) arms' but at last 'the scraper of beards was obliged to own himself beaten and gave in, whilst Jimmy Lungs stood at the door of the Provincial Concert-room, and loudly invited people to enter, decidedly to the detriment of the room opposite.'

The farce that had been conducted in the street continued in the courts, as Captain Hayes took objection to something Jemmy Lungs had said, and so it was revealed that the Arrow bellman's real name was Sagoski. 'W.H. Hayes, being sworn, deposed: I am the landlord of the Prince of Wales Hotel, resident on the Arrow,' the paper reported on 13 May. 'On the night of the 30th the prisoner was ringing the bell for the landlord of the Provincial Concert Hall. Not satisfied with doing all in his power to forward the interest of the house for which he was engaged, he brought into question the good name of mine, designating it as (and warning the people against) the half-crown swindle.'

And what was a 'half-crown swindle', pray? That was what the Bench wanted to know. Nothing, however, was made clear. The constable who was called reckoned he did not hear any abusive language at all. 'I was busy at the time and did not notice what was said.' John Roberts, one of the Our Own Minstrels, had been at the door, and had not heard anything abusive, either, just a simple warning against a half-crown swindle, for which he had no explanation. Then Sagoski hazarded a guess that the secret might lie in the fact that the admission to the performance of Miss Harriet Gordon, being held that night at the Prince of Wales Hotel, was two shillings and sixpence. But, as Hayes promptly pointed out, the admission to the Provincial Concert Hall was exactly the same amount. Baffled, the Bench dismissed the case, no costs allowed.

Back at the Provincial Hotel, as the newspaper related, George Buckingham had taken swift advantage of the buzz the vocal battle had caused to write a farce about it, called *The Barbarous Barber, or the Lather and Shave*. He himself played the barber, and as the editor of the *Lake Wakatip Mail* commented in that 6 May story, 'the tortures which he inflicts upon his (not over patient) patients is highly amusing'. The barker was played by the bellman himself, the same Mr Sagoski, 'and the part of Mr Potts, a gentleman slightly inclined to corpulency, was taken by Mr Geordie Spiers'. As a farce, it was a riot, 'heartily enjoyed by the audience'. The writer feared, however, that it would take a more serious turn. 'Regarding its personality, and the motives which brought it into existence, the less said the better; it is never a pleasant duty to be obliged to condemn, and in this case, I am sorry to say, it is impossible to praise.'

So what was the exact nature of the farce? Was the character of 'Mr Potts' a caricature of Hayes? It is impossible to tell, particularly in view of the news item that followed immediately after this. 'A private ball was, on Friday evening, given by Captain and Mrs Hayes at the Prince of Wales Hotel,' it ran. 'About 100 ladies and gentlemen were present, and I am glad to add that it passed with great *éclat*, dancing being spiritedly kept up till daylight did appear.'

The advertisements in the same paper are equally unrevealing. George Buckingham did not advertise the farce at all, merely giving notice that they sold 'Wines, Spirits, &c., of the best brands' at the Provincial, and that there was a concert every evening, 'Talented artistes engaged.' While Hayes did not mention what kind of liquor he had on stock, he advertised 'Vocal and Instrumental Music every Evening by talented artistes', and promised that soon 'the inimitable Thatcher and Madam Vitelli' (both extremely popular attractions, one for her singing and the other for his satirical ditties) would 'make their first appearance in this township at the Prince of Wales Hotel'.

The promise, however, was never kept. Instead, sometime after 20 May, Hayes and the Buckingham family departed from the Arrow, headed for greener pastures — to the Southland town of Invercargill.

*

Wrote the editor of the *Southland Times*, in the issue for 29 May, 'The Buckingham Family gave an entertainment last evening in a capacious building, recently erected in Dee-Street. The house was well filled, and the performance went off with *éclat*.' The performance had staying power, because as late as 20 June, the Southland correspondent to the *Lake Wakatip Mail* enthused that 'amusements are becoming a little more frequent than in the byegone days', when the only recourse in dull evenings was the whisky bottle. The Buckingham Family show was still popular, despite the wretched weather and the miserable concert hall. 'This building is about to be extended and fitted up as a *bona fide* theatre by Mr Frederick Seyler, of Melbourne. From his well known ability as a caterer for public amusement elsewhere, I anticipate the undertaking will prove successful,' the writer concluded, a prediction that seems to have come about, because it was not until 23 August that the family moved on.

This time they travelled by sea. Hayes went to Riverton, a small port a few miles to the west of Invercargill, and chartered a schooner called *Three Sisters* for three months, to carry the family first to Bluff, and then to the northern provinces of New Zealand. They did get as far as Bluff, where the local correspondent of the paper recorded that the social scene had picked up mightily, the Buckingham family having arrived 'in the *Three Sisters* from Riverton, they propose stopping amongst the Bluffites for a week and entertaining them with their musical powers nightly'.

But the arrangement did not work out. Instead of going north after their week in Bluff, the troupe headed back to Riverton, where the family (except for Rosa, who about this time was delivered of a daughter, Adelaida) staged performances in the Criterion Concert Hall. The proprietor, Mr Hoskins, must have been as delighted as Mr Seyler had been, as the *Southland Times* for 15 September reported crowded houses, the audience particularly appreciating the burlesque of the Highland Fling.

Captain Bendell, owner of the *Three Sisters*, was not nearly so thrilled. Instead, like so many men before, he had to chase Hayes for his money. In retaliation, Hayes sued *him*, for non-fulfilment of contract. On Saturday, 29 August 1863, J.N. Watt, Esq., on the Bench, heard Hayes' deposition. 'I was to pay £35 per month; also to provision the vessel for the family, master and crew; the £35 to be paid monthly in advance. Before leaving Riverton I made arrangements with Captain Bendell to pay the master of the schooner two days after arrival at the Bluff or Invercargill.' Yet, despite all this, as he angrily commented, the master of the schooner had not done the job.

For once, Hayes did not get away with his bluff. The owner of the schooner, evidently a canny Scot, had given Captain Lawson, the master of the *Three Sisters*, a letter instructing him to proceed no further if he had received no money within two days, or if Hayes had neglected to insure the vessel. Neither had been done, so instead of taking the troupe north, Lawson had handed the whole affair over to the court. The letter was duly produced, along with a valueless charter agreement, which absolutely no one had signed, and despite Hayes' blustering, the case was lost.

The Buckingham family went north anyway, landing in Christchurch, where George was recorded playing at the Royal Princess Theatre in January 1864. The Glogoskis settled in the town, and in April Samuel Glogoski advertised Quadrille Assemblies, the music being provided by 'A full String Band'. Captain Hayes was not with the family, however. Instead, he had returned to Newcastle, New South Wales.

CHAPTER 9

Black Diamond

This time, Hayes' return to his old stamping ground was marked by dissension. The first indication of his arrival was an advertisement on the front page of the *Newcastle Chronicle* for 9 December 1863. 'I, THE UNDERSIGNED, MINOR KING,' it commenced in capitals, 'hereby declare that, personally, I know nothing derogatory to the character of CAPTAIN HAYES, and if I have said anything publicly or privately against his character, I REGRET IT. Dated this eighth day of December, MINOR KING, Newcastle.' King was an American mining engineer who had patented an improvement to rotary quartz-crushing machines in December 1858, and as he gave his origin as San Francisco, it is possible to guess what kind of gossip he was spreading around and which led to him being forced to back down and recant, by the threat of court action.

Other Newcastle citizens, once they had realised that Hayes was back in town, hastened to stake their claims on debts that he had failed to pay before he sailed off in the *Cincinnati*. One was a publican, Robert Newman, who sued for the money owed for a case of gin delivered to the ship. Hayes said, first, he was definitely not on shore the day he was supposed to have ordered the liquor, and then that the money was owed by someone else — Mr E. Conn, the owner of the vessel. However, he lost the case.

Then Hayes was up in court again, as the owner of yet another craft, the schooner *Black Diamond*, which was first advertised for sale in the *Sydney Morning Herald* on 5 December 1863. This 'well-known schooner' was one hundred tons burthen, and could carry 55,000 feet of lumber, according to the notice. In April, Hayes went to Sydney to buy her, and on 7 May 1864 he dropped anchor back in Newcastle — in time for yet another encounter with the seafaring aunt of A.T. Saunders, Sarah Ann Allen.

Thomas Allen, who now commanded the bark *William Watson*, arrived in Newcastle on 20 May, to moor up 'stern to stern' (as Saunders put it) with the schooner *Black Diamond*, which turned out to be commanded by none other than their old acquaintance. Aunt Allen 'saw he had a "wife" on board, and that the wife was a very young woman and had a nice little baby. Hayes spoke to Captain Allen, and wanted very badly to bring his wife and child to see Mrs Allen, but she declined'.

Hayes had much else on his mind, as he was having trouble with the crew. First, one named Wascoe sued him for non-payment of wages, and then the steward did the same, and after that four men jumped ship. When they were recaptured, and hauled up before the Bench on 17 June 1864, they declared that they had a good reason for deserting from the *Black Diamond*, the schooner not being seaworthy. In return, Captain Hayes vowed that he had had the vessel surveyed by a Captain Robertson. According to him, Robertson had suggested some 'trifling repairs', and had declared that once they were done 'he should personally have no objection to go to sea in the vessel'. Robertson, when summoned, 'indignantly denied' having said any such thing. Baffled, the Bench adjourned the hearing — and Hayes hired four replacements, 'took advantage of a favourable wind springing up, and dropped quietly out of the harbour and stood to sea. His destination appears to be involved in much mystery', the *Newcastle Chronicle* went on. 'The captain, when before the Bench, stated that he was bound for Brisbane, but those who profess to be better acquainted with his movements, state that he will make for the Islands of the Pacific.'

As it happened, Hayes did steer for Brisbane, dropping anchor opposite the Customs House in the dark of night on 27 June — quite a feat, since it was the first time he had navigated the tortuous Brisbane River. His next destination was supposed to be Nelson, in the north of the South Island of New Zealand, but he was blown by a terrific gale to Auckland, where he arrived on 3 July. 'The gale lasted three days,' he told the *Daily Southern Cross*, 'during which she lost her fore-topsail, foretopmast staysail, and main staysail.' As usual, Rosa was not mentioned, let alone how she and the baby fared during the storm.

After staying in the harbour for twelve days, while various seamen took the chance to jump ship, Hayes cleared for Nelson on 15 July and vanished the following night — leaving a mountain of debts in his wake. 'A brigantine called the *Black Diamond* arrived in this port a fortnight ago, with coals, from Newcastle,' reported the *Daily Southern Cross* three days after his disappearance. 'She was under the command of a Captain Hayes, and the quantity of coals he brought in the miserable-looking craft which he succeeded in navigating over from Newcastle was very small, not amounting to more than £100's worth. These were sold through his agent and the balance coming to him, some £30 odd, handed to him about the middle of last week.'

Hayes had assured those who were supplying goods and services that he would not be sailing until the 19th, 'and in the meantime his creditors expected to get their money'. Some of them had been impatient (or suspicious) enough to dun him on Saturday, but Hayes had 'politely excused himself', pointing out that the banks were closed. They would have to wait until Monday, he said — 'Monday came', and the ship was gone. The *Black Diamond* had 'sailed during the still hours of the night'.

The list of defrauded creditors is startlingly reminiscent of those who were owed money after the equally sudden departure of the *Ellenita* from San Francisco. There were the shipwrights who had mended the storm-battered schooner (who were owed £20-odd); ironmongers, ship chandlers, clothiers, 'a passenger by the *Black Diamond* for borrowed money, £9 or £10; and some other amounts, including the cost of the water which was put on board the vessel'. And the list was by no means exclusive, as the writer gloomily concluded. A meeting of creditors was to be held that day, and 'it will probably be found then that there are many more'. Unlike their counterparts in San Francisco and Port Adelaide, they realised the futility of sending a steamboat after Hayes. Instead, they consulted each other and their lawyers, and brooded.

The news item was repeated all over Australia and New Zealand, under various headings, the *Maitland Mercury* glumly introducing it with the words 'CAPTAIN HAYES AGAIN'. The most interesting commentary was an editorial in the 23 August edition of the *Otago*

Daily Times. As the writer pointed out, 'The short and easy method of avoiding debts by taking advantage of the first fair wind for sea, has been more than once adopted in Port Otago.' The ploys used by debt-dogging shipmasters had often been strange and inventive, and had equally often met with definite success. One case in point was that of the 'well-known Captain Hayes', who had recently 'taken his departure with a small craft, the *Black Diamond*, possession of which he had by some means obtained, and to have done this without the ordinary courtesy of bidding good-bye to friends ashore, who with water, stores, &c., supplied him during his stay'.

But, while contemptible, this kind of debt-dodging was by no means uncommon — and hence the popular term for it, quoted in the editorial's heading, 'SETTLING CLAIMS WITH THE FORE-TOPSAIL'.

*

The next piece of news was startling enough for Hayes' serial debt-dodging to be forgotten for the moment. Coincidentally, it appeared in the *Nelson Examiner and New Zealand Chronicle* on the same day that an entertainment by Mrs W.H. Foley was advertised, 25 August 1864.

'FATAL ACCIDENT AT THE CROIXELLES', ran the heading. Because of damage that needed fixing, Hayes had dropped anchor in Croixelles (now spelled Croisilles), a lovely bay in the northwest of the South Island, close to Admiralty Bay and thus familiar to Captain Cook from his voyage in the *Endeavour*. Being sheltered, it was perfect as a haven where the *Black Diamond* could be recaulked to repair any number of leaks.

On 19 August, William Askew, who owned a nearby station, called by, and when he told Rosa that a friend, Elizabeth Rankin, wife of a local baker, was staying at his house, Rosa asked if they could pay a call. Mr Askew obligingly loaned Hayes his yacht, and off they sailed on what was expected to be a pleasure jaunt. The baby, Adelaida, went with them, along with Rosa's fifteen-year-old maidservant. Curiously, Rosa's oldest brother, George Buckingham, was one of the number. It is not known if he was with the *Black Diamond* during the whole voyage, or if he came on board in Auckland or at Croixelles, but it seems more likely that he had joined Rosa and Hayes in Newcastle, and was with them the whole of the voyage.

Whatever the situation, it spelled his doom. Pleasure turned to tragedy when the craft was struck by a sudden squall. The sails snapped aback, then flogged madly, and over she went, spilling them all into the water.

The maid died first, right beside the rapidly sinking wreck. George Buckingham was last seen striking out for some shoals. Hayes called out to him to take the baby, but George did not hear. So Hayes put the baby over his shoulder, grasped Rosa, and struggled to get to shore, using a pair of floating oars. 'The little child Captain Hays kept on his right shoulder for some time,' the news report ran, 'until, feeling assured that it was dying, he said, to his wife "Rosy, Rosy, sissy's gone," but meeting with no response, he placed the child's face against that of its mother, in order that she might give it a last kiss.' Then he let the little body go.

Rosa's head 'had now begun to droop beneath the water', the *Examiner* continued. Hayes struggled to get her onto his back, and then struck out again, but 'death had visited her also'. After two hours, he could feel himself sinking, so at last he discarded her body, 'and eventually reached some rocks and scrambled up them'.

From there, Hayes staggered about in a daze until, finally coming to his senses, he found a high spot from where he could see the *Black Diamond*.

The seamen lowered a boat in answer to the distant figure's frantic waving, 'only to learn that it was their captain, the only survivor of those who had so recently left them'. As a sign of his ordeal, his legs were swollen and black with bruising. A local settler, Arthur Elmslie, was despatched to Nelson with the news, and a constable came back to organise a search for the bodies. Only the baby's corpse was recovered. George Buckingham's coat was found when the crew of the *Black Diamond* raised the sunken yacht, but his body had disappeared forever.

'The deceased young man,' the Nelson *Colonist* lugubriously added to its reprint of the item, 'was the only support of five young brothers and sisters in Canterbury.'

*

The story was reposted all about New Zealand, the *Daily Southern Cross* of Auckland commenting on 25 August that 'a very calamitous loss of life has occurred in connection with the *Black Diamond*, which our readers will remember was in this port some weeks ago'. Interestingly, that item then revealed that Hayes had been bound for Port Cooper — now known as Lyttelton, and the entry port for Canterbury — but again had been blown off-course by a gale, which forced him into Croixelles for repairs. His bad luck with weather was becoming almost as notorious as he was.

Unluckily for Hayes, the tragedy was also reported in Australian papers, meaning that the schooner's mortgagers in Sydney knew the exact location of the man who owed them money. Local Nelson agents Nathaniel Edwards & Co. were instructed, forthwith, that Hayes was to be dunned for the outstanding sum. If it was not forthcoming, the mortgage was to be foreclosed and the *Black Diamond* seized for a forced sale at the nearest available market.

Captain William Akersten, a well-established Nelson ship chandler, was given the job of telling Hayes to choose between the money and the ship. A master mariner who had also distinguished himself by building wharves and bridges, Akersten organised the operation in detail, being determined not to underestimate the challenge. Five strong men were sworn in as special constables, in front of the Resident Magistrate. Then the 'plucky crew' boarded a whaleboat, which was towed to Croixelles by a little steamboat, P.S. *Lyttelton*. After the tow was cast off, the whaleboat was rowed about the bays and inlets of the harbour until the *Black Diamond* was sighted.

It was three in the morning and everyone on board was asleep. The six men clambered up to the deck as silently as they could, but within a few moments Captain Hayes emerged from the after cabin. Taken aback and angry, he demanded the reason for this intrusion — as the Nelson *Colonist* expressed it, he inquired 'in brief but emphatic language to what he was indebted for the honor of such an early morning call'. Akersten produced his documents and, as instructed, made a formal demand for the sum of money named. Hayes hotly refused to produce the cash — take the ship if you dare, he said. Akersten, rising to the challenge with gusto, turned and ordered his men to man the windlass. Grabbing an axe, Hayes ran to the foredeck to block their way, but after a short scuffle he was disarmed and tied to the pin rail.

'The capture was made complete,' the writer concluded with a flourish. 'The anchor was hove up, sails were set, and, in thirty hours from the time Mr Akersten and his crew left Nelson on the mission of seizure, the *Black Diamond* was lying securely at anchor in Nelson harbor. It is as nice a little bit of "cutting out" as we have heard of for some time and well merits the publicity.'

The schooner — 'a brigantine of 102 tons, old register, 73 feet long, 20 feet beam, and 8 feet depth of hold, and is well coppered and copper fastened' — was put up for sale on 29 September, 'together with her Gear, Sails, Yards, Anchors, &c., as she now lies. Without reserve. Terms cash'. Bidding was poor, the best offer being £275, which Nathaniel Edwards & Co. did not accept. But then, after the auction had closed, a local settler named Kerr stepped up and made a successful offer of £300.

He loaded her with cattle and sent her out under Captain Rhind. Rhind was an experienced coasterman, but turned out to be a worthless drunk, so Kerr's bargain was a bad one. But that made little difference to Hayes, who once again was without a ship.

*

Another heritage of the affair was a lifelong grudge held by William Akersten, the man who had boarded the schooner while everyone on the *Black Diamond* was asleep. He had received public praise for both his successful cutting-out operation and his handling of the recalcitrant captain, so the matter could have been easily set aside. Yet, despite the passing of time, he continued to hold a remarkable antipathy for Hayes, as expressed in a long letter that was published in the *Otago Witness* thirty-two years later, on 27 August 1896.

'As a subscriber to your widely-circulated journal,' he commenced, 'it is my duty to inform you that some of your correspondents are in error as to the time, place, and circumstances attending the death of Captain Hayes' wife and others.' Most people, he went on, believed the story that had been told by Hayes to Elmslie, the man who had reported the tragedy to Mr Luckie, the editor of the Nelson *Colonist*; after all, Elmslie 'was a highly respected man among us, and he stated that he was a messenger from Hayes, and as far as he could he endeavoured to give word for word'.

Then, when Hayes was questioned by the police, his evidence did not vary in any significance from the original statement, so no suspicions were raised. 'The body of the infant was exhumed and reburied, and a verdict of "Accidental drowning" was recorded. And thus the matter passed into history. There were, however, not a few who were not at all satisfied with the matter, and among these was the writer.' William Akersten then described how he cross-examined Hayes himself — in Akersten's own house, though he neglected to explain how Hayes happened to be there.

It had been a challenge, Akersten admitted, given Captain Hayes' famous talents — 'He was an actor of considerable ability, and a mesmerist.' But, the more he listened, the more Akersten felt convinced that Hayes' account was a carefully rehearsed lie. 'I ventured to ask (as a mariner) a question or two in a careful, humane manner,' he went on, but Hayes simply changed the subject 'to the seizure of his vessel, and got angry and swore that had he been aware of my going to seize the vessel would have sent me to keep company with those who were drowned.' At that, Akersten became truculent himself, and told Hayes to either stop his threats or get out of his house, 'when suddenly he became calm and communicative, borrowed a few shillings, and left'.

Captain Hayes, it seems, had won the contest in his usual style, leaving a little richer than when he had arrived. Akersten then made a strange admission — that he and Hayes had known each other in London, something of which there is no other evidence. What is certain, though, is that Akersten kept on repeating his doubts about the true circumstances of the deaths of Rosa, the baby, George Buckingham and the maid, adding yet another layer to the legend of Captain William Henry Hayes.

CHAPTER 10

Wave

The day before the sale of the *Black Diamond*, Hayes appeared in the Magistrate's Court on two charges of non-payment of wages, both of which he lost.

The first action had been brought by three labourers, James Pawson, William Turner and William G.R. Holland, who sued for the money they had earned by 'cutting firewood at the Croixelles, and for doing other work on board the *Black Diamond*, and in connection with that vessel'. The plaintiffs claimed that Hayes had hired them at the rate of ten shillings a day plus meals, but while they had been fed, the money had never been paid. Captain Hayes emphatically denied that these were the terms of the bargain, 'but it was proved by the evidence of the men and of the second mate of the vessel, who heard the agreement made'.

The second case was brought by the chief mate of the *Black Diamond*, a man by the name of John Till. He sued 'the master and owners of that vessel for £76, being account for wages earned on board, and cash lent to the captain'. Nathaniel Edwards & Co., the owners' agents, strenuously objected to being sued for the money owed to Hayes — £31 — and, as it was a private debt, it was struck off the claim. Then, after the sensational revelation that Hayes 'had falsified the log-book by throwing overboard the original book and writing a new one after the seizure of the vessel on behalf of the mortgagee', that case was closed too.

But while it was easy enough for the Bench to bang the gavel and demand that Hayes must pay a decreed portion of the outstanding debts, the American did not have the money to do it. His only assets, according to the notice of sale of the *Black Diamond*, were nine water casks and the twenty cords of firewood that had been cut by Pawson, Turner and Holland. It was impossible to pay the woodcutters with the wood they had cut, as it had to be sold, so they left the court with only a fraction of what the Magistrate had awarded.

William Turner did not take this tamely, complaining about it in a letter to the editor, which the *Colonist* printed on 7 October under the bold heading, 'A SUFFERER BY THE *BLACK DIAMOND*'.

'Will you be kind enough to inform me how it is that a poor man in the Province of Nelson cannot get justice?' Turner demanded, and then went on with his tale. He and another man (Pawson) had sued the captain of the brigantine *Black Diamond* for £17 each, while a third man (Holland) had claimed £7 — 'Judgment was given for two-thirds the claims, two for £11 13s. 4d. each, and one for £4 13s. 4d., the captain to pay the costs.'

But Turner had received nothing like that. 'I was one of the men entitled to receive £11 13s. 4d., I received £4 6s. 0d.! (being my share of the proceeds of the wood, water casks, &c., less 21s. for a lawyer's fee). I applied to the Resident Magistrate to obtain a warrant to arrest Captain Hayes, and prevent his absconding from the Colony until he paid me, on the grounds that Hayes intended to sail by the *Phoebe*, which he did *on Sunday morning*, the day after I had in vain urged on the Magistrate to grant me the warrant. How am I to obtain redress in a case like this?' Turner bitterly demanded. 'The man that I got judgment against for only two-thirds of my earned wages, is allowed to decamp and the Magistrate does not allow me to exercise the only lawful means of preventing it.'

It was patently unfair, but the bird had flown, and there was nothing anyone could do about it. As woodcutter William Turner testified in his letter, Captain Hayes had escaped from Nelson by taking passage to Lyttelton in the second cabin of the steamer *Phoebe*, on the way to the pioneer city of Christchurch, leaving the usual simmering creditors in his wake.

*

Once in Christchurch, Hayes rejoined Samuel and Ann Jane Glogoski, who were supporting the surviving Buckingham children. Though the Glogoskis were still staging their quadrilles, they were willing to consider another theatrical tour, so Hayes took up the management role again. Captain Mathews, the master and owner of a little ten-ton cutter called *Wave*, was hired to carry the troupe to Akaroa (a village in an eastern inlet of Banks Peninsula), and further south as required. And, forthwith, a notice appeared in the shipping list of the *Lyttelton Times*, advertising that the *Wave* had cleared from port on 5 November 1864, her passengers being Mr and Mrs Glogoski, W. and E. Buckingham, J. Strang, J.E. Chalmers, and 'Capt. Hay'.

While Strang was a horse-trader, so was evidently going to Akaroa on business, Chalmers, who had arrived in Otago from the Victorian goldfields in 1863, was an itinerant performer of satirical songs and had joined the Buckingham troupe on a temporary basis. By a remarkable coincidence, one of the two seamen on the cutter was John Till — the same man who was Hayes' chief mate on the *Black Diamond*, and who had sued him for £75, but had been awarded just half of the £45 for lost wages that he had claimed. While the amount he received is unknown, it was much less than he was due. So here, on the same small vessel, was another fellow with a grudge, £45 being a large amount at the time. The usual seaman's pay rate was £2 10s a month, which indicates that Till had served with Hayes ever since the *Black Diamond* was acquired in Sydney, back in April 1863, and was owed wages for sixty-four weeks, so their association was a long one, and the grievance profound.

Yet, to all appearances, the passage to the little coastal town of Akaroa went well. And a successful concert was staged there, the *Lyttelton Times* noting that an 'entertainment was given at the Town Hall, Akaroa, on Wednesday evening, the 9th inst., by a company of performers calling themselves the Buckingham Family. A large audience testified by their applause that they went to be pleased, and were not disappointed. The company are *en route* to Oamaru and Moeraki, in a small cutter called the *Wave*', the writer added, 'and merely made a passing call at Akaroa'.

Hayes, as was so often the case, became a local sensation. Nearly forty-five years later, on 14 March 1919, a correspondent to the *Akaroa Mail* remembered Captain Matt Wight telling him about the arrival of Captain Hayes and the Buckingham Family in a cutter, and the entertainment that followed. Hayes took part in the performance, boasting that he could cut a mutton carcass in two with just one blow of a sword. 'People thought he would cut it down longways, but he just slashed it across the middle, which was not a very difficult feat.'

This undoubtedly raised a roar of derisive laughter, but still the jolly captain was impressive. 'He was a very active man standing over 6ft in height and could spring off the floor in Scarborough's Hotel and kick the ceiling' — or so Wight had recounted. Mariners were naturally strong and agile, it being a prerequisite of the trade, but this was unusually athletic. Hayes was not the fastest of sprinters, however. Rumours about him ran about town, including the story of the missing ear, and, 'Matt Wight asked him one day why he wore his hair so long, and he chased him down the wharf but didn't catch him.'

Off to the south they went, but by 24 November the cutter was back in Akaroa, where John Till took court action yet again. This time, as a sign of his very bad luck in getting his rightful cash, it was to sue the captain of the *Wave*, G.F. Mathews, for unpaid wages. Alongside Till as he stood at the Bench was Frederick Sievewright, the other seaman on the cutter, who also wanted his money. Captain Mathews lost the case, and so the cutter was seized and put up for sale.

The auction was held on Thursday, 1 December, 'under Distress Warrant'. Terms were 'cash at the fall of the hammer', according to the instructions of the Bailiff. Who bought it is not on record, but Hayes replaced Mathews as the master of the cutter — or so the shipping lists noted. Whether he had somehow come up with the cash, or whether Till and Sievewright took the cutter in lieu of the unpaid wages and then hired Hayes to command her, can only be guessed.

Hayes sailed the *Wave* to Lyttelton, where he delivered the Buckingham Family on 10 December. The next year, Ann and Samuel Glogoski, with their young charges, toured the West Coast, billed as the 'far-famed BUCKINGHAM FAMILY'. Coincidentally, on 16 November 1865, they played at the British Lion Hotel Concert Hall in Hokitika on the same night that Pablo Fanque was playing at T.B. Smith's Theatre Royal, just along the street. Captain Hayes was not there to renew his old acquaintance with the rope dancer, though, as he was far away, pursuing other adventures and gaining yet more ignominy.

*

On 15 January 1865, Hayes arrived at Wellington, reporting his last landfall as Picton. There, he dropped his anchor alongside a 77-ton clipper schooner named *Shamrock*. While he was still admiring the other vessel, yet another condemnatory item about him was published, first in the *Marlborough Times* on 20 January and then in papers all about the Pacific.

'THE NOTORIOUS CAPTAIN HAYES AGAIN — A CASE OF ABDUCTION', ran the headline in the Nelson *Colonist* on the 24th:

'Our readers will remember the sad story of a tragic occurrence which took place in the Croixelles on the 19th of August last, and which told of the sinking of Mr Askew's yacht and drowning of four out of the five persons who were on board of her.' As the writer went on to ruminate, the only one not drowned was 'the notorious master of the notorious schooner *Black Diamond*'. The circumstances, as the writer made plain, were dubious. 'No human eye but his witnessed the accident; and pathetic, and melancholy enough was the sad tale he told.' Indeed, it was painful to witness his 'deep emotion when he recounted this incident'. But, since then, his emotional recovery had been miraculous.

The editor of the *New Zealander* was even franker in expressing his opinion. 'The notorious master of the *Black Diamond* has turned up in a new character,' he commenced, in an item published on 1 February. 'It will be recollected that it is not long since he drowned his wife, child, and brother in law, and that he ran away with a vessel from Newcastle, which he had repaired and refitted at the expense of some Auckland firms.' Then, like his counterpart in Nelson, the writer went on to reprint the *Marlborough Times* item, which related that just the previous month, January 1865, the cutter *Wave* had called at Akaroa, and Hayes had spent time, as usual, at Mr Scarborough's Bruce Hotel. And there, as the story continued, he met 'a young girl named Helen Murray, 16 or 17 years of age, a native of Ireland, a well-educated and intelligent girl who had lost her parents'.

The girl's description is so like that of the similarly named Cornelia Murray of the *Ellenita* that the story that unfolded seems eerily predictable. Hayes' plan of seduction was rather different in Helen's case, as he spun wonderful stories of the Buckingham Family and their popular performances, and how he planned to take the troupe to China. She was talented enough to join the troupe, he told her; all she needed was training, and the singer travelling with him, Mr J.E. Chalmers, was just the man to do it.

'The glowing language in which the bright future was represented induced the girl to embark', and forthwith the cutter set off for Lyttelton — at least, that was the stated destination, after which the story became confused. Hayes was not really heading for Lyttelton, the writer claimed, but instead to Pegasus Bay, a beachhead north of Christchurch. There, Mr Chalmers was put ashore, to make his own way to the city, and 'Mr John Till and Mr Frederick Seivwright joined the cutter and she sailed for Nelson'.

This belated arrival of the two men was unexplained, yet Till and Sievewright were either the owners of the cutter or the seamen on board. Till's previous job as chief mate of the *Black Diamond*, and the fact that he had once sued Hayes for his wages, also went unmentioned. Instead, the writer repeated the story Till told him, 'in his words as nearly as we can recollect them'. According to this, John Till noticed that 'Hayes was particularly attentive to the young woman, but that she studiously avoided him, and seemed to have a particular aversion to his company. She had begged and entreated to be put ashore at Pegasus Bay' — or so he said — 'but Hayes would not allow it. They experienced bad weather, and were obliged to take shelter at a whaling station', where the cutter was trapped for two nights and a day. 'Here again the girl tried to get ashore but Hayes would not allow her.' Instead, according to Till's tale, he promised to send her to Lyttelton from Nelson. But once they were back under sail, there was another attack on her chastity.

Helen's near namesake, Cornelia Murray, would have understood and sympathised with her predicament. Helen was worse off on the *Wave* than Cornelia had been on the *Ellenita*, however. 'The apartment in which Hayes slept below, and a similar one for the two men forward, was the only shelter which the cutter afforded,' John Till explained; 'but all Hayes' persuasion and entreaties could not induce the girl to share the one occupied by him.' Accordingly, Helen was forced to remain on deck, 'and one night in particular, when the waves were washing over the cutter, she sometimes clung to the mast, and during a temporary lull would cling to one of the men entreating him to save her'. But instead of gallantly handing over the seamen's forecastle berth, Till and Sievewright left her alone on deck, where the 'days she spent in crying and sobbing, and the nights in terror, anxiety, wet, and cold'.

Hayes' moods were as mercurial as they had been on the *Ellenita*, blowing from seductive inducements to shouting in 'the most disgusting and threatening language'. Then, as the cutter lay off the pilot's house in the Tory Channel, he completely lost command of his temper and 'tore off her clothes' before dumping her into a boat and taking her on shore, where 'he represented her to the pilot as a character that no respectable man would admit into his house'. At this dramatic moment, John Till and Frederick Sievewright arrived at the pilot station and proceeded to contradict everything Hayes had said. John Till, who had had a very good reason for sticking with Hayes, had given up all hope of getting the money that was due, so joined Sievewright in refusing 'to re-embark or sail any further with him'.

With both seamen gone, Captain Hayes was in a fix, but the pilot agreed to crew for him, leaving Till, Sievewright and the girl at the pilot house. The *Wave* 'arrived at Picton on the 13th inst.', where Hayes shipped two men, and sailed again for Nelson, meaning that he was over the horizon before the girl (now rather mystifyingly referred to as Ellen) arrived in Picton, having travelled from the pilot station with Till and Sievewright. 'Mr Till proceeded to the Government offices and reported the case to a Justice of the Peace', but he was too late to demand the arrest of the amorous Hayes.

Worse still, Ellen (or Helen) got as little sympathy from the court as Cornelia Murray had in Sydney. Pointing out that the case was one of common assault and not abduction (as John Till claimed), the Justice of the Peace said it was not worth the trouble of pursuing Hayes, if indeed he could be caught. But, as the Marlborough paper went on, there was a happy ending. A gentleman in Picton gave young Helen (or Ellen) a position in his household that was much more seemly than serving men in a raucous Akaroa hotel.

It was a 'somewhat highflown narrative', as the editor of the *Colonist* reflected after printing this. Nevertheless, once the story reached Wellington, it was widely believed that the news of the failed abduction was the reason that Hayes had flown the coop yet again. For that is exactly what he did, sailing out of Wellington Harbour on 7 February — but not on the little cutter *Wave*.

Instead, Hayes somehow acquired the smart clipper schooner *Shamrock*, registering her on 1 February 1865, and advertising her for the Fiji Islands. 'For freight or passage, apply to the Captain at the New Zealander Hotel, Manners Street,' the newspaper notice ran.

Where Hayes found the money for this new venture is unknown. Legend says that he bought her with the financial assistance of a wily newspaper proprietor, Sam Revens, but if that was the case, it was certainly not noted in the papers. There is also a popular story that Hayes was helped by a Sydney woman of dubious reputation, who was known by the name of Bull Pup — but that is not in the official record either. Whatever the background, John Till and Frederick Sievewright must have watched with very mixed feelings as the *Wave* arrived at Picton with a Captain McIvor at the helm.

CHAPTER 11

Shamrock

Hayes arrived back from the South Seas by 19 May 1865, that being
the date when the Christchurch *Press* noted that the schooner
Shamrock, W.H. Hayes, had come into Lyttelton from Fiji, 'with
oranges, coconuts &c.'.

The next day the same paper revealed that he had actually been
steering for Wellington — 'but off the heads encountered a heavy
gale from the N.W., which obliged him to bear up and run for Port
Lyttelton'. So his bad luck with weather had continued. However,
it was to Canterbury's benefit, as he brought 'a full cargo of fruit,
oranges, lemons, and cocoa nuts, all of which are in excellent
condition'. Another report itemised 6000 oranges, 4000 lemons,
2000 coconuts, ten pigs, and a package of Fijian spears, consigned
to Hayes himself. These last found a keen market, native curiosities
(as they were called then) being so popular.

By 30 May, Hayes was advertising another run to Fiji, but was slow finding a charter. In July, one of his seamen, F. Seymour, deserted, and produced the usual excuse when hauled up in court — that the ship was unseaworthy. And though the Bench treated this with the usual disdain, informing Seymour that he had the choice of returning to the schooner or serving fourteen days in prison, the Magistrate agreed that the *Shamrock* should be surveyed, which held up the departure. In the end, the *Shamrock* did not clear from Lyttelton until 26 July, Hayes naming his destination as the Fijian Islands via the North Island river town of Wanganui (now often spelled Whanganui), with seven passengers for that port on board. He did not sail right away, however — because he was getting married again.

According to the marriage certificate, dated 26 July 1865, William Henry Hayes, aged thirty-three, master mariner and widower, married Emily Mary Butler, aged twenty-one, spinster, at the Royal Hotel, Christchurch. Most sources seem to think that she was a barmaid, but nothing else about her is known for sure, though A.T. Saunders was told that her father was William Butler, the proprietor of a hotel called the Clarendon. The witnesses to the wedding were Albert Cuff, keeper of the Royal Hotel, and John Etherden Coker, keeper of the Criterion Hotel.

Hayes' description of himself as a widower was deceptive, as he had not legally married Rosa Buckingham, but at least this particular marriage was not bigamous. Amelia Littleton Hayes had received her divorce in February the previous year, though it is debatable whether Hayes knew that he was free to marry again. Certainly, there were doubts expressed in Sydney, where Hayes was well remembered. Four years later, on 24 September 1869, the *Empire* advertised a

remarkable farce, staged at the Adelphi Theatre in York Street —
'First night of CAPTAIN HAYES, the Husband of many Wives, an
entirely novel and highly sensational drama, in three acts, of intense
Australian interest.'

*

The *Shamrock* finally sailed from Canterbury on 28 July, headed for
Wanganui with Emily on board, and had a very long passage. It was
not until 26 August that the *Lyttelton Times* took note of a rumour
saying that the schooner had been stranded near the river port, but
that all the passengers and crew had got safely to shore. The *Shamrock*
had been easily refloated, and according to Wanganui local history
Hayes sailed into port flying the Stars and Stripes — quite illegally,
the schooner being registered in New Zealand, but impressively so,
all the same.

Despite this flamboyant display, it seems that the schooner was in
need of repair, because the *Shamrock* was put up for sale where she
lay at Queen's Wharf. Instead, she was chartered by John Jones, an
entrepreneur and farmer, and a local lawyer, H.B. 'Bogo' Roberts,
to carry cattle to Levuka. Both men were cautious, however. John
Jones sailed as the supercargo, and Roberts sent along his son (also
named William Henry), ostensibly to look after the cattle.

If the two Wanganui men were expecting adventure, they
experienced rather too much of it. As described in Jones' obituary
in the *Wanganui Herald*, on 1 November 1917, they 'were witnesses
of a cannibal feast, and not until they were asked to participate did
they realise to their horror that human flesh was being eaten'. The
schooner was in Fiji when a hurricane struck at night on 7 January

1866. And, though both men survived this, on Sunday, 25 March, when the schooner was back off the bar of the Wanganui River, they were put into terrible danger again.

As he was bound for Lyttelton, Hayes chose not to waste time sailing into port. Instead, he sent the passengers and their baggage ashore in the two entirely unsuitable boats, needing two trips to do it. Somehow, the first time the two boats worked their way through the surf, the oarsmen managed to land their passengers successfully, though after a struggle. They then returned to the schooner for the captain, his wife, and the rest of the passengers, but this second foray proved disastrous.

Emily Hayes, clutching the sides of the wildly plunging dinghy in the rear, watched with horror as the leading boat was swamped, dumping its load in the heavy swell. Her husband immediately dived overboard, but while he 'succeeded in saving a Maori woman', according to the news report, 'the other passenger, a Mr Roberts (son of Mr Roberts, solicitor, of Wanganui), the mate and seaman, met a watery grave'. By grim coincidence, William was the second son that Roberts had lost by drowning, 'and curiously enough, both on Sundays'.

Having swum back to his boat and taken Emily to shore, Hayes did not stay around to make a formal report. As the *Wanganui Times* noted on 27 March, 'Hayes and his lady companion remained on shore on Sunday night, went on board and set sail on Monday morning, but made no report either at the Custom house or elsewhere.' The bodies had not been found at the time, and neither had the inquest been held, so Hayes was breaking custom, if not the law. Perhaps he knew that the pilot's testimony would be devastating.

The inquest was held on 29 March 1866, at the Red Lion Hotel. John Jones, the supercargo, gave evidence first. 'Two boats left the vessel with passengers,' he said, 'landed them and then returned to the vessel. The captain did not land in either of the two first boats.' Jones himself was one of those who had got ashore, so was watching from the pilot house as events unfolded. 'The pilot made a signal not to attempt to come the second time,' he went on, adding that as well as flying the signal, the pilot warned the mate, who had headed one of the first boats, that a second landing should not be tried. 'This warning was given to him several times.'

The pilot confirmed that the two boats had landed safely on the first foray, but despite this, 'I thought at the time it was dangerous attempting to land.' Accordingly, after cautioning the mate of the *Shamrock*, he had asked him to tell the captain to fly his ensign as a sign that he had received and understood the message. But, though he watched anxiously, he did not see the flag hoisted. Instead, 'I saw the two boats leave the vessel. The one that was first got into the breakers to the leeward of the bar and it was there the accident happened.' The pilot immediately manned his boat, but the sea was too rough to try any rescue. 'Their boat turned bottom upwards. I saw four men clinging to her.'

Like the captain, the pilot kicked off his boots and dived into the water, but soon both he and Hayes were struggling for their own lives. 'I saw no chance for them but to stick to the boat and I told them several times not to let go the boat or they were lost.' Sadly, however, four men drowned — William Roberts, a seaman named Edward James, John Johnstone (the mate) and a male Fijian crew member. As the pilot went on to say, 'The boats were small square stern boats', hardly fit to cross the bar in fine weather. The men were all sober. 'I asked Captain Hayes why he came in against my signal. He answered that the mate said the bar was perfectly smooth.'

Though Captain Hayes was not there to confirm this, Thomas Ryan, a passenger in the swamped boat who had survived the disaster, did it for him. 'The second mate stopped on board after the first trip saying he was nearly swamped the first time,' he said, but went on to add that though the captain heard this, he believed the first mate's assurance that the bar was 'quite smooth'. A second person Hayes had been able to save from the wreckage — a Fijian woman — had warned him that the surf was very dangerous, too, but of course no one would pay attention to a native, and a female one, at that. And so the only condemnation that the coroner handed down was that the boats were 'totally unfit for the purpose'.

Interestingly, someone who was not asked to give evidence was Emily Hayes. Yet not only was she still in town, but she would have agreed with the coroner. It seems that even though the boat she had been in had survived the torn water over the bar, she flatly refused to get into it again. So instead of sailing off with her husband on the *Shamrock*, she waited until the steamer *Storm Bird* arrived, and then took passage, arriving in Wellington on 9 April. Then she boarded the steamer *Lord Ashley*, which arrived in Lyttelton the day after that.

*

There may not have been anyone waiting on the wharf to meet her, as 10 April was the same day that Hayes' consignment of Fijian clubs, spears, mats and so forth was auctioned. 'At first the attendance was meagre and the bidding slow,' the *Lyttelton Times* reported, 'but shortly after the sale commenced the room was well filled by the townspeople and strangers, and the various curiosities sold fetched excellent prices, and the competition for the best articles was very spirited.' And, the day after that, Captain Hayes was busy in the Magistrate's Court, where he was staging a legal action — one that solves the mystery of why the *Shamrock* had taken almost a month to get to Wanganui after leaving Lyttelton on 28 July 1865.

Captain Hayes sued a chandler, D. Marks, for £16 6s. 8d., the amount he had paid for four tierces of beef, back when he was provisioning the schooner for the voyage to Fiji. Though Marks had guaranteed the quality of the beef, 'when the vessel had been out at sea a day or two, the tierces were opened one after the other, and the meat was found to be putrid and unfit to eat'. Consequently, the *Shamrock* had been forced to put into Port Underwood (in the Marlborough Sounds), to purchase meat to feed the passengers, greatly delaying her voyage.

Several witnesses were called, who all substantiated the captain's claim, so while the butcher who had supplied the meat protested that the rest of the lot was perfectly good, the Magistrate had no hesitation in finding for Hayes. Indeed, he was in sympathy, 'observing that it was a most important matter that ships should be able to depend on the state of the provisions supplied'. If the schooner had been blown out to sea, not only would the passengers and crew be out of food, but the crew 'might very likely have turned mutinous'.

Then Hayes made up his mind to sell the schooner. Whether Emily had any part in this decision is unknown, but if she put her foot down about sailing again on the unlucky *Shamrock*, it worked. On 25 April 1866, the *Lyttelton Times* advertised the upcoming auction of 'the fine, fast-sailing SCHOONER *SHAMROCK* (British Built)'. And, on 4 May, the same paper announced that 'THE SCHOONER *SHAMROCK* has changed hands; she has been purchased by Mr. Dunsford'.

But it did not leave William Hayes without a ship. Mr A.J. Fisher of Dunedin had put up his vessel for sale, and Hayes had the ready to buy her. 'Capt. Hayes, late owner of the *Shamrock*,' the item continued, 'has purchased the fine brig *Rona*; she will in future trade from this port to the Fiji Islands.'

CHAPTER 12

Rona

By the year of 1866, Captain William Henry Hayes had reached such legendary status that crimes committed by others were freely attached to his name. Back in April 1865, for instance, the same agents the mortgagees of the *Black Diamond* had hired, Nathaniel Edwards & Co., had sold another schooner, called *Amelia Francis*. She was bought by two Lyttelton men, Gibbons and Bentley, who put her in the coasting trade. On 1 August 1865, she sailed for Hokitika with a large and valuable general cargo on board, and according to the report, had never been heard of again.

But more was to come. On 1 October 1866, the *West Coast Times* published a report that was fated to be printed all over the land. 'It may be within the recollection of some of our readers,' it began, 'that about nine months ago the schooner *Amelia Francis* sailed from Nelson, bound to this port with a cargo valued at £3000. She never arrived at her destination, and long ago was given up for lost and placed upon the list of missing vessels. She has, however, turned up, but on the other side of the Pacific.' In a word, her captain had bolted off with her to the Pacific islands, where he had sold the cargo and pocketed the money. 'Her master,' the report concluded, 'was mate under the well-known Captain Hayes, of New Zealand notoriety.'

The runaway master was Captain Rhind. He had never served under Captain Hayes. His only connection with Hayes was that he had been given the command of the *Black Diamond*, after the schooner had been sold. But it was easy to believe the newspaper's facile claim, simply because Captain Rhind's escapade sounded so very like Captain Hayes' kind of crime.

Another example is Captain John Daly Hayes (also known as 'Bully'), a settler in Whangaroa, near the Bay of Islands in the far north of the North Island. The son of Captain John Daly Hayes, senior, and Sarah Mary Simpson Daly, John was born in 1842, and married Eliza Harriet Slattery in Russell, Bay of Islands, in 1867. Over the next three years he and his father, commanding the schooners *Hetty* and *Petrel*, were charged with many breaches of the Liquor Licensing Act, as well as quite a bit of debt-dodging.

And, while they were openly accused of supplying spirits to the Maori people, it was also whispered that they traded arms and gunpowder to the Maori tribes during the Land Wars, under the cover of their legitimate timber and cattle trading business. Which led to the longstanding myth that 'Bully' Hayes (meaning Captain William Henry Hayes) smuggled arms to the tribes in the Maori Land Wars. A myth that is definitely not true.

*

Despite all this kind of gossip, a Lyttelton resident by the name of Philips was so keen for adventure that he bought passage on the 'fine brig' *Rona* for a voyage about the Pacific. He expected it to be a pleasure jaunt. And, from the account he wrote for the *Lyttelton Times* (which the paper published on 13 September 1866), his liveliest expectations were amply fulfilled.

'We sailed on 6th June from Lyttelton,' he commenced, 'and after a pleasant run of eight days brought up at a small island called Eehuea' — 'Eua, an island in the Tongan group. There, as he described with gusto, 'we were greeted by a drove of natives in unmistakeable buff, with the exception of a slight sensation of rushes, artistically arranged round their loins; no hats, boots, or anything else'. Evidently, the schooner was laying on and off the island, because after trading with these 'airy individuals' for fruit and curiosities, Hayes asked for a pilot, who turned out to be 'an amphibious piece of architecture, with no clothes whatsoever'. However, he did have wonderful tattoos and a very broad smile, and the ability to guide them safely into Tongatapu — which was a blessing, as on the way in they passed the wreck of the brig *John Wesley*, cast high on the surrounding reef.

A passage for ships' boats had been cut through the reef at Nuku'alofa, so Mr Philips enjoyed a very pleasant ride to shore, where he was gladdened by the sight of the British ensign flying bravely from a flagstaff, and enjoyed being received by an escort of 'about fifty Turkey Cocks, which, however, are very tame and particularly well dressed'. Casting off these gaudy attendants, he and Hayes called at the Tongan king's palace, where 'we were met and welcomed by a hearty shake of the hands by Mr. Moss, king George's factotum'. This was an Englishman, David Jebson

Moss, who was the king's adopted son. The Tongan king, being shrewd enough to understand that he needed an adviser to help him negotiate dealings with Europeans, had resorted to this to make sure of getting a trustworthy one. Moss, who was very proud of his Tongan name — Tupou Ha'apai — carried out 'all the official work, from writing a letter to giving you three months in the "House of Blazes" as the "Chokee" is called'. Not only was Moss polite and obliging, but he 'dispenses advice gratis to all who need it'.

From there Hayes took his guest to meet the British Consul. This was Joshua Cocker, a Yorkshireman who had sailed to Tonga for adventure, and who performed consular duties (including writing formal reports) with no recognition or recompense whatsoever, simply because of his idealistic nature. He imported the first cow and bull, the sight of which sent the terrified Tongans scampering up the trees. His wife, Elizabeth, brought a sewing machine, and taught the Tongan women how to use it. Philips found him 'a thorough good sort of man, not an iota of pride about him, and makes you as welcome as if you had boarded him in Yorkshire'.

The schooner headed next for Rarotonga, but Hayes had his usual bad luck with the weather — 'talk of contrary winds if you like, we had them with a vengeance, and nearly came back to Lyttelton again'. Instead, they arrived at Sunday Island, where they found just two European inhabitants. 'The first thing they asked was, "Is the American war over? Who has gained the day?" and glad they seemed to hear the result.'

Back to the Cook Islands the schooner steered, landing at Atiu, 'where we were boarded by no less than three uncrowned kings, who were graciously pleased to shake hands with us, as also did the princes of Wales'. Captain Hayes, evidently amused by his passenger's wide-eyed appreciation of all he saw, then warned him to watch out for 'mermaids' who were swimming out to the schooner. 'These mermaid arrangements are decidedly spirited, and if you have not manners enough to greet them with, they will welcome you with a hug that would do credit to a bear.' Luckily, Emily Hayes was not on board. She had opted to stay in Lyttelton, with the very good excuse of looking after her baby twin daughters, Laurina and Leonora, who had been born on 2 May 1866, just one month before the *Rona* sailed.

The schooner lay off the island for some days, trading for yams and fruit while the freshwater casks were filled, 'and from thence to the island of Rarotonga, which has a nice little harbour, exactly big enough to fit the *Rona* and no bigger, not even room beyond for anything larger than a ship's boat, all deep water'. They were welcomed by a 'jolly Englishman' who called himself 'Captain Cook', and served as Hayes' interpreter. There was no fruit available save oranges, because a recent hurricane had destroyed the trees, and after loading these the anchor was weighed and the *Rona* set off for Lyttelton, where they arrived on 11 September 1866.

Not only was Mr Philips delighted with his adventure, saying, 'I would here advise all those who have time and opportunity, to pay a visit to these South Sea Islands, as they are well worth seeing,' but he had no hesitation in adding, 'I would strongly recommend them to take a passage with Captain Hayes in the *Rona*, who, I feel sure, will make them as welcome as he did me; for I am sure I could not have been better cared for had the vessel been my own.' According to the shipping reporter, the *Rona* had carried two extra passengers into Lyttelton, one being 'Squire Flockton' and the other 'Miss Jane

Venua Atu'. Unfortunately, Mr Philips had nothing to say about either of them, and what Emily thought of 'Miss Jane Venua Atu' is also unknown.

*

Hayes hired a wine and spirit merchant named Fleming to act as his agent in port. As one of Fleming's clerks, James Kearsley, remembered in a communication to the *Auckland Star* many years later (23 October 1935), Fleming was reluctant to accept the business at first, having had previous acquaintance with 'the famous buccaneer', but was persuaded to dispose of the *Rona*'s cargo of oranges, which went well. 'The packing and shipping occupied a week or more, so that we had a lot of the captain's company,' Kearsley wrote. 'He was a very jolly man, full of humour; was not much over 40 years of age, good looking and well built. His wife lived in Lyttelton, and was a tall lady-like person about 30 years.'

During the month the *Rona* spent in port, the cook-steward, Edmund S. Aches, was knifed during a drunken fight in one of the boats. 'Included in the crew,' as Kearsley remembered, 'was a Fijian boy of about 19 years, and on a Saturday evening this lad, accompanied three or four sailors and the cook for a run of a few hours on shore, most of which was spent in public houses.' After the crewmen had got back into the boat, there was a bit of an argument, after which 'the boy asked the cook for the loan of his knife, which the latter handed to him, and with it the boy stabbed the cook to the heart'. Death was instantaneous, and so quiet that the other men did not realise what had happened. But then 'the boy began to cry, and said, "Poor cookey dead"', and so the tragedy was revealed.

According to the report in the paper, the culprit — Henry Ives, 'a half-caste belonging to the Fijis' — tried to conceal his guilt by changing his clothes, and cleaning the knife before hiding it. Soon, however, he burst into tears, and confessed the crime, though only through an interpreter. The inquest began on 17 September. Even though there had been just a handful of men in the boat, testimony was demanded from all the members of the *Rona*'s crew, a polyglot lot that included a Fijian named Francis, 'a native of Manilla' named Frank, 'Bob Purre, a native of the Sandwich Islands', and a Fijian seaman by the name of Lorenzo De Cruz. Then, most inconveniently for Hayes, all the witnesses were bound over to appear at the next session of the Supreme Court, which was not until December.

Hayes solved this problem by simply ignoring the directive. As Kearsley remembered, 'he quietly slipped out of port, after having taken his wife on board, together with her furniture, etc.'. The date was 3 October. Hayes had declared his destination as Guam, and he had left just one seaman, James Wright Anderson, to give evidence. The counsel for Henry Ives, H. Wynn-Williams, was furious. Years later, in August 1903, he wrote a vigorous letter to the Christchurch *Press*, denying that Ives had confessed to the crime. Because of the chaos, nobody knew for sure what had happened, and 'Ives, it was perfectly obvious to all who heard the case, had no intention of killing the cook'. The jury had the sense to bring a verdict of manslaughter (which carried a sentence of three years with hard labour, in lieu of hanging), but no thanks to his captain and his fellow crew. 'They said he was only a — Fijian nigger,' Wynn-Williams wrote; 'and they declined to assist him in any way.'

Instead, they had sailed off in the *Rona*, leaving the poor man to his fate.

*

Hayes' destination was deceptive, the *Colonist* of 25 December noting that, 'The schooner *Neva*, which arrived at Auckland on 11 December, reports that the notorious Hayes was at Rarotonga, collecting a cargo of fruit, which he intended to bring to Hokitika after calling at the island of Tongataboo, after filling up with pigs for the same market.' And, sure enough, the people of Hokitika had scarcely time to brace themselves before the *Rona* came in, just three days after the notice. Her manifesto, as the *West Coast Times* announced on 29 December, was '50,000 oranges, 200 pigs, 100 cockatoos, 200 citrons, 200 pineapples, a large number of cocoanuts, and a quantity of curios'.

Hayes was not long in town, weighing anchor again on 2 January 1867, but the locals remembered him vividly after he had gone. An enduring yarn was that when Customs officers were searching the holds of the *Rona*, and one lit a match to see better, Hayes casually remarked to a bystander that if the fellow knew what was down there he would be a lot more careful. H.L. Michel was a child when the brig arrived, but for the rest of his life told the tale of how he learned to play bowls on board the ship, by rolling coconuts along the deck. But there were no grave sins to report. As the editor of the *Colonist* reflected when the paper printed Michel's reminiscence, in January 1914, 'Hayes is said to have had a trick of slipping away from port without paying his bills, and this was about the full extent of his piracy at Hokitika.'

The Auckland papers, acutely aware that many of their loyal readers were merchants who had been cheated when Hayes came in with the *Black Diamond*, were a lot less forgiving. As the *Daily*

Southern Cross commented on 15 January 1867, for 'obvious reasons', Hayes would avoid dropping anchor in Auckland, being unwilling to 'renew his acquaintance personally with various Auckland tradesmen'. After leaving Hokitika, however, he was forced to do exactly that, having run out of important provisions on a passage that had been badly delayed by the weather. His best hope was not to be recognised. Consequently, as the shipping reporter of the Auckland *Herald* noted, when he arrived in the harbour he hoisted no number, hoping to pass as 'a perfect stranger'.

Instead of going ashore to buy the foodstuffs himself, Hayes sent his first mate, a man by the name of Hall. At about eleven in the morning, as the *Herald* went on, two boats were seen pulling away from the brig, and after crossing the harbour 'two gentlemen and a lady' landed at the Queen Street stairs. One of the gentlemen presented his report at the Custom House, one 'which but for the circumstances detailed below, would have gone forth to the public as a correct one: — "The brig *Hayward*, 250 tons, Capt. Hall, from Adelaide, bound on a trading voyage to the South Sea Islands, put in for provisions"'.

Unfortunately for both Hayes and Hall, an officer with the Customs smelled a rat. A boat was manned, and off across the water he sailed, intent on boarding and searching the so-called *Hayward*. No sooner had his boat neared the brig than he saw her hastily getting under weigh — 'this further gave rise to suspicion, chase was at once given, the vessel overtaken and boarded by the authorities.

'They had scarcely gained the main deck,' the report ran on, 'when, judge their surprise, they found the stranger not to be the *Hayward*, Captain Hall, but the *Rona*, Captain Hayes (of *Black Diamond* notoriety) from Hokitika.' Frustratingly, though his men searched the vessel thoroughly, the Customs officer could find nothing amiss — 'her papers were examined and found to be all correct'. Hayes, questioned about the false report of his brig, was both surprised and aghast, exclaiming that 'Captain Hall was his chief officer, and that he ought to have known better than to have given the vessel a false name, as he (Captain Hayes) had sent letters up to town by him to influential merchants here who knew better'.

So why had he weighed anchor with such haste, just as the Customs boat was coming up? Because 'he had only the cook and another man left on board, and the vessel was dragging too near shore'. But, as the reporter went on with relish, 'Before, however, the Customs authorities left the brig they turned out eight able-bodied seamen, stowed away forward.' As the *Daily Southern Cross* remarked, Hayes mustered a strong crew, making the ship quite crowded, since he had his wife and two children on board.

At that moment the two ship's boats were seen returning to the *Rona*, so the Customs boat sallied out from the brig to accost 'Captain Hall' and upbraid and reprimand him 'for making false declarations', at which he confessed everything. And a search of the two brig's boats yielded nothing, either. While they were loaded with provisions and ship chandlery goods, Hall had receipts to prove that he had paid cash.

'Captain Hayes is well known here among our Auckland merchants and others,' the *Herald* report concluded, but, 'this time he has escaped scot free, there being no infringement of the Customs' Regulations, the clearance and register being all correct.' Foiled, the merchants and officials of Auckland were forced to watch the *Rona* sail away, bound — as the *Daily Southern Cross* put it — 'in continuation of his voyage of adventure'.

A few days later, on 26 January 1867, the *New Zealand Herald* communicated a rumour that 'the notorious Captain Hayes' had visited Cabbage Bay and taken 12,000 feet of sawn timber on board. Without a doubt, however, this was Captain John Daly Hayes. William Henry Hayes was far away, headed for the tropics. Though the many men to whom he owed money did not know it, New Zealand had seen the last of the notorious captain.

*

The inter-island trading schooner *Neva* was the next vessel to bring news of the *Rona*. Captain Young, accosted by the shipping reporters as he dropped anchor on 25 May 1867, revealed that the missionary bark *John Williams* had been cast up on the reef at Savage Island (Niue) — 'the wreck being afterwards purchased by the celebrated Captain Hayes, of the brig *Rona*, for $600'. Hayes had made two voyages of rescue, carrying castaways from Niue to Samoa. And after that he had delivered four of the missionaries to their stations on other islands.

One of the missionaries who sailed with Hayes was James Chalmers, a charismatic young Scotsman who was pious without doubt, but who had chosen the foreign field because of his lively sense of adventure. On 4 January 1866, at the age of twenty-four, Chalmers had boarded the missionary ship *John Williams*, accompanied by his wife, Jane, and had sailed to Australia. From Sydney, the *John Williams* had sailed to the New Hebrides (now Vanuatu), but the ship ran onto a rock, so had to return to Port Jackson for repairs, with all the men on board pumping for their lives and the ship.

Getting the *John Williams* fixed did not bring the end of bad luck. The ship sailed to Niue, where the party arrived in early January 1867, expecting to spend a couple of days before heading for Samoa. But, as Chalmers wrote in a letter to the missionary society, dated 4 February 1867, 'On the 8th ultimo, about 11.30 p.m., our much loved and thought of *John Williams* became a total wreck on the reef that surrounds this island.'

Because of a developing swell, it had been impossible to load all the provisions for the onward journey, so some of the mission party had stayed on shore. Chalmers was among those who were still on board, so was there to record, 'About half-past seven, just as we were going to evening worship, the ship was noticed to drift astern.' The whaleboat was lowered, and then the pinnace, and after that the gig, but row as they might, the oarsmen could not tow the ship out of the landward swell. Instead, 'she continued to go astern faster than ever'. Closer and closer the doomed ship came to the lashing surf, while as many as possible of the seventy souls that were on board were off-loaded into the three boats. 'She very soon struck with a fearful crash.'

The rain was coming down in torrents as the boats forced their way along the shore, heading for a wet refuge at the battered mission station. Reaching this crowded haven, the missionaries huddled together. The Chalmers couple was stranded far from Rarotonga, where they hoped to establish a station. 'Do not for a moment suppose that we feel discouraged,' he wrote, however, 'we have no intention of turning back, and leaving our mission work. God forbid!' God was his strength, and his trust was in the Lord.

They were six weeks on Niue before a Samoan Trading Company schooner arrived, and Chalmers and his wife, with the mate of the

John Williams, some of the crew and another missionary couple, were able to take passage in her to Apia. 'We were kindly received by all in Samoa,' Chalmers wrote in his autobiography, which was published in 1902. 'The consul did all he possibly could.' And part of this ready assistance was the organising of passage to Rarotonga for Chalmers and his wife — on the brig *Rona*.

Chalmers met Captain Hayes for the first time when the *Rona* came in with his first lot of castaways. 'Soon after we arrived at Samoa,' the missionary wrote, 'Captain Williams and his wife, and the remainder of shipwrecked missionaries and sailors (only the second mate and a few sailors remained behind), were brought to Samoa in the *Rona*, a brig of one hundred and fifty tons, owned and commanded by the notorious Bully Hayes. On the arrival of the captain the wreck was sold, and Hayes bought it with all belonging to the ship that had been saved.'

After returning to Niue to pick up the rest of the crew and the remaining baggage, Hayes came back to Apia, where he 'was chartered to take us to Rarotonga, and Mr and Mrs Saville to Huahine'. And thus commenced an interesting couple of months, spent in the company of a man of dubious reputation but with as much charm as Chalmers himself. 'Hayes seemed to take to me during the frequent meetings we had on shore,' Chalmers remembered, 'and before going on board for good I met him one afternoon, and said to him, "Captain Hayes, I hope you will have no objection to our having morning and evening service on board, and twice on Sabbaths. All will be short and only those who like to come need attend."' At which Hayes most gallantly replied that he had no objection at all, saying, 'my ship is a missionary ship now, and I hope you will feel it so. All on board will attend these services', he vowed, which astonished Chalmers not a little, for all he could weakly reply was, 'Only if they are inclined'.

The two missionary couples embarked, and the *Rona* set sail. 'We were well treated on board,' Chalmers went on. 'Hayes was a perfect host, and a thorough gentleman. His wife and children were on board; and although we had fearful weather nearly all the time, yet I must say we enjoyed ourselves. Instead of going to Rarotonga first, we had gone so far south that we could easily fetch Tahiti, and so we stood for it, causing us to be much longer on board; Hayes several times lost his temper, and did very queer things, acting under the influence of passion more like a madman than a sane man. Much of his life he related to us at table; especially such things as he had done to cheat governments.' How true these tales were is debatable, Hayes being a natural entertainer. How accurate Chalmers' memory was, after all those years and the many tales about Hayes he had heard, is also questionable. What is definite is that he — like many other men — thoroughly enjoyed those yarns.

After leaving the Rev. Saville and his wife at Huahine, the *Rona* steered for Mangaia, in the Cook Islands, where James and Jane Chalmers, with Captain Hayes, were stranded on shore by rough weather, which blew the ship out to sea. Five days later, the *Rona* was seen at last, but with sad news. Two men had been lost while out in a whaleboat during the storm — 'one a native of the Sandwich Islands, who was second mate, and the other a native of Ireland, named Hughes, who was working his passage from Huahine'.

Despite this tragedy and reports of awful weather, Mr Gill, the missionary on Mangaia, decided to sail with them to Rarotonga. They could visit Aitutaki on the way, to pick up the missionary there, Mr Royle, so that they could hold a missionary conference when they got to Rarotonga. Chalmers enjoyed that unexpected landfall, too, as the welcome at Aitutaki was so exuberant. Loaded down with presents (including a bull and cow), they proceeded to Rarotonga. The happy voyage was then crowned by 'a very kind letter from Hayes, thanking me for the services I had held on board the ship, and for my kindly demeanour towards him, saying, "If only you were near me, I should certainly become a new man, and lead a different life"'.

It was obvious that Hayes needed reforming. A few days later, while the brig was still anchored at the port of Avarua, Rarotonga, 'he nearly killed his supercargo with a bag of dollars which I had given him as the last payment of the charter for the voyage now successfully completed'.

*

Hayes loaded with oranges and then sailed, reporting his next destination as Hokitika — though he was unlikely to call at Auckland on the way, according to the editor of the *Daily Southern Cross*, 'being wanted by the police on urgent business'. His real destination, however, was not anywhere in New Zealand, as the Auckland papers gradually found out.

The oranges had been loaded for California, said the master of the *Hercules*, when that ship arrived at Auckland. Then, when the island trader *Neva* arrived, that captain was also positive that Hayes was headed for San Francisco. It is likely that both men got this idea from a store manager named Salmon, who ran the trading post in the port village of Avatiu, for the Tahitian firm of Branders. Salmon, who had been cheated by Hayes during a previous call, had wreaked his revenge during this visit. His wife, a local high-ranking lady, had brought him a lime grove as her dowry, and so he had been able to tempt Hayes with the prospect of a part cargo of lime juice, which had a very good market in San Francisco, the hub of American ocean-going clippers — but instead of filling the kegs with lime juice, he filled them with salt water. Then he had hammered short lengths of bamboo into the bungs and primed these with juice, so that when Hayes tested them, he thought he had the real stuff, and duly paid for it.

But there is no record of Hayes trying to sell the fake cargo in California. According to the *Daily Alta California*, the closest the *Rona* ever came to San Francisco was Tahiti. In San Francisco, just as in Auckland, Adelaide and Honolulu, Hayes owed a lot of money to a lot of angry merchants. As he openly admitted at a later date, it was dangerous for him to drop anchor there — just as it was in Australia or New Zealand. 'It is not probable that Captain Hayes will visit a New Zealand port again, a warrant having been issued against him by the Whanganui Bench some time ago for fraud as a baillee on a solicitor in Whanganui,' the *Daily Southern Cross* meditated on 15 May 1868, after reporting that Hayes now confined himself to trading between Tahiti and islands of the South Pacific.

So this, it seemed, was the last of this newsworthy man. But then, just days after this item appeared, the schooner *Jeannie Duncan* arrived in Lyttelton from Fiji, with news so sensational that Hayes hit the headlines yet again.

*

The story was first broken in the Christchurch *Press*, on 19 May 1868 — that Captain William Henry Hayes was dead. Killed! Murdered during a duel!

As the paper reported, Captain Shepherd of the *Jeannie Duncan* had arrived in Lyttelton with information 'of the murder of Captain Hayes, of the brig *Rona*, formerly trading to this port. It is stated that a dispute arose between Captain Hayes and his mate, the mate challenged his captain on shore to fight a duel immediately; on stepping out of the boat the mate drew a revolver and shot Captain Hayes dead on the spot. The mate then took charge of the vessel and proceeded to sea'.

'BULLY HAYES', headlined the *Wanganui Herald* on 26 May: 'This character, who is as well known all over the colony as he is in Wanganui, has met with an untimely death.' Then, after summarising what had appeared in the Canterbury paper, the writer meditated, 'Capt. Hayes, it will be remembered, had a great deal of the pirate in his disposition. He commenced his career in New Zealand, so far as can be learned, by carrying away a young girl from Akaroa, and his subsequent brutal conduct towards her, while she was his captive, is sufficiently known to the public. He was next heard of in the North, where his craft was boarded by the Custom-house officers off Rangitoto, at the entrance to Auckland harbor; but he was allowed to slip his cables, and nothing has been heard of him until he reached the Fijis.'

It is noteworthy that this is the first time that Captain Hayes' nickname — 'Bully' — appeared in print, though evidently it was generally known. One day later, the editor of the Nelson *Evening Mail* wrote, 'The schooner *Jeannie Duncan*, which arrived at Port Cooper, from the Fiji Islands, on Saturday last, brought intelligence of the murder of an individual of most unenviable notoriety through these colonies, Captain Hayes, better known as "Bully Hayes."'

It was as if the news of the notorious captain's death had freed the writers from editorial formality.

*

Naturally, everyone wondered about the identity of the fellow who had rid the ocean of this rogue. The editor of the *New Zealand Herald* speculated that it might have been a master mariner named Coffin. 'Our last advice from Rarotonga stated that Mr. Coffin, formerly here in the schooner *Neva*, had shipped in the *Rona* with Captain Hayes, but it is possible he may have left before reaching the Fijis and another person shipped in his place.' Captain Young of the *Neva* confirmed this, the *Daily Southern Cross* reporting that though he had received no intelligence of the murder of Hayes, Coffin, most certainly, had 'shipped, as previously stated, as mate of the brig *Rona*'. Otherwise, all Captain Young could tell them was 'that Captain Hayes, when leaving Rarotonga, took his wife and child with him, and was bound for the Navigators' Island' — that is, Samoa.

Then the general musing was rudely interrupted by the arrival in Lyttelton of the *Mary Ann Christina*, which had sailed from the Fijian islands on the same day that the *Jeannie Duncan* had left. When the master, Captain Simmonds, was examined by the shipping reporter of the *Lyttelton Times*, on 25 May, he simply shook his head — 'informs us that he does not think there is any truth in the report of the murder of Captain Hayes. It was stated on the Island that he had bought the wrecked missionary ship *John Williams*, had got her off the reef, and had taken her to Valparaiso'.

No one knew whether to believe him or not, it being only Simmonds' opinion. As the editor of the *Daily Southern Cross* remarked, 'Conflicting rumors, as our readers are aware, have been circulated respecting this notorious personage; some reports asserting his death at the hands of Captain Coffin, others purporting that he was yet alive, but where he existed no one at the time knew.' The *Sydney Morning Herald* was certain that Hayes was alive, asserting on 25 June that the report of his death was deliberately circulated 'with the view of preventing further inquiries about him'. As the writer went on to reckon, he had hauled the wreck of the *John Williams* off the reef, jury-rigged her, and was sailing her to Valparaiso to be repaired.

Absolutely not so, vowed Mr R. Turpie, the erstwhile chief mate of the *John Williams*, in a letter the Sydney *Herald* printed on 27 June. 'Allow me, sir,' he penned, 'to correct any such impression on the minds of your readers respecting the *John Williams*. I can affirm that when she was sold to Captain Hayes she was a complete wreck, and there was no possibility of her again being floated. When sold she was only worth burning or breaking up for the sake of the metal in her construction.' While the wreck had since vanished, there was no possibility that the hulk could be on the way to Valparaiso.

And Hayes was certainly murdered, declared the *Wanganui Herald* on 7 July; not only was he dead, 'but we are now informed that the duel was fairly fought according to the laws and duelling, and that the Captain fell'. They had firsthand information, the writer went on — 'A Mr Joyce, lately arrived in Lyttelton from the Fijis, in the cutter *Lapwing*, says he conversed with a gentleman who was an eye-witness of a duel, at Tanna, New Hebrides, between Captain Hayes of the brig *Rona*, and his chief officer; both parties landed revolver in hand, stepped fifteen paces from each other, back to back, turned round, fired without aim; the captain's shot missed, while the mate's took deadly effect.'

But then wild and romantic speculations were dashed — by a letter from the man himself! Written at Tahiti, and carried to Auckland by the new master of the *Neva*, Captain Harrison, it read:

155

Captain of the Neva will please report the brig Rona, at Rarotonga on the 3rd September, bound from Savage Island to Queensland with cargo and passengers, and that Captain Hayes is not dead as reported in the Auckland papers but is still alive and kicking.

So, as the editor of the *Daily Southern Cross* sighed on 13 October, 'This extraordinary individual, we learn by the arrival of the schooner *Neva* at Auckland, from the South Sea Islands, is, beyond all doubt, alive; at any rate was so when the *Neva* left.' The 'extraordinary individual' had been busy, too. As Harrison's report went on to reveal, 'Captain Hayes has purchased the brigantine *Samoa*, and appointed Mr Hall, his late chief officer of the *Rona*, as captain. Captain Hayes' absence from the Islands is accounted for, according to his own statement, by his having made a trip to Vancouver's Island. It appears that on his return he touched at the Savage Islands, and conveyed a number of natives to Tahiti, where he disposed of them to the planters.'

Not only was Bully Hayes 'alive and kicking', but he now employed two vessels in the disreputable 'blackbirding' trade.

*

Hayes' proud ownership of two island traders was to last just a handful of months. On 11 October 1869, the *New Zealand Herald* reported that they had received the information 'that the brig *Rona*, in charge of the notorious Captain Hayes, foundered at sea off Manihiki, and that the schooner *Samoa*, also the property of Captain Hayes, has been totally wrecked on the reef at Manihiki'.

Both ships wrecked — at the same small island, in the middle of the vast Pacific? Such bad luck seems incredible, even with Hayes' past record of terrible weather and foundering vessels. However, just ten days later, the *Sydney Morning Herald* — which, like all the Australian press, had been avidly following his adventures — published a detailed and 'extraordinary' account of the double loss. 'On the 23rd of March last,' the report began, 'the brig *Rona*, commanded and owned by Captain W.H. Hayes, sailed from Huahine, Society Islands, bound for California. At the same time sailed from the same port the brigantine *Samoa* (also owned by the same Captain Hayes), bound to the Navigator's Islands and elsewhere.'

For the first ten days, the *Rona* sailed in light breezes, but 'when in latitude 7 deg. S. fell in with a heavy gale of wind from the S. E., which lasted for four days', and then veered north. On 4 April, it was found that the brig was leaking badly, 'till the pumps could hardly keep her free'. Hayes steered first for Hawaii, but the wind came dead ahead, 'therefore stood for the Island of Manihiki', with all hands pumping hard all the way. Despite every effort, the water gained on them, until by 1 May there was six feet of water in the hold, rising fast. 'On the next morning, May 2nd, ten feet of water in the main hatch; ship settling down forward. At this time the vessel was abandoned, the weather being still very bad, with heavy rain squalls. The people were divided between the long-boat, commanded by the captain, and the quarter-boat, which was taken in tow.'

And so, for the next twelve days, the two linked boats crept over the ocean, with twenty-one miserable souls on board. First they landed at Rakahanga (called Reirson's Island then), but the atoll could not sustain them for more than a few days, so 'they proceeded to the Island of Manihiki, where Captain Hayes, to his astonishment, discovered that his other vessel, the brigantine *Samoa*, had gone to pieces upon the coral reef, a month before'.

He also found his erstwhile chief mate, Captain Hall, and the crew of the wrecked *Samoa*, living in the castaway camp they had established. 'Thus, two vessels belonging to one owner left one port at the same time — the one bound on a long voyage to the eastward, the other to the west, and in a few weeks both captains and crews met upon a remote and seldom visited island after the loss of both ships,' recounted the writer of the *Sydney Morning Herald*. What the conversation might have been like was left for the readers of the *San Francisco Bulletin* to guess for themselves, that paper noting (on 20 November) that the loss had been due to 'the carelessness of the mate', as there was no storm at the time. Luckily, Hall had been able to salvage all the cargo, and when Hayes arrived he was busily trading it to the stations on shore.

According to the *Sydney Morning Herald*, the captains and crews then built a cutter out of the timbers of the *Samoa*. The *Bulletin*, on the other hand, stated that there was a large boat on the island that had been left by Hayes during a previous voyage, and this was 'cut in two, lengthened', and then decked over with planks from the wreck. 'She was schooner rigged,' the *Bulletin* went on, 'and when completed measured nine tons. When launched she was named the *Tannu*, after the name of the native village in which she was built. It took some three months to build her.'

By whatever the means, they set off for Apia — 'On August 4th Captain Hayes took on board his goods, and on the 5th he sailed for Navigator Islands, having on board himself, his little daughter of three years, Mr Hussey, mate; Mr Sterndale, Mr Alvord, and Mr Strickland, white men; Henry Coe, half-caste, son of the United States Consul at the Navigator's; Joseph Jordan and his sister Mary, son and daughter of Joseph Jordan, of Huahine, Society Islands;

Allen Strickland, his mother, and three little brothers; Henry Williams, half-caste; nine native men, three women and one girl belonging to Savage Island, making in all twenty-eight souls, put up and huddled together on board a nine ton leaky boat, besides a very large Newfoundland dog and a very little poodle, to go a distance of some 800 miles, besides towing the *Rona*'s longboat astern.'

The grim voyage took two weeks. The makeshift vessel arrived in Apia on 20 August 1869, 'after a long and perilous passage', to report not just the loss of both ships, but the death of the United States Consul for Fiji, Mr Kentlege Pritchard, who had boarded the *Rona* in Tahiti, after negotiating passage for California. 'He had arrived on board in ill health, and gradually sank and died on the 15th of April.' The poor man had succumbed to brain fever while everyone on board was battling to save the schooner.

CHAPTER 13

Atlantic

It was only natural, perhaps, that the loss of the *Rona* and the *Samoa* should be received with some glee in certain quarters. 'CAUGHT AT LAST', headlined the Wellington *Independent* on 16 November 1869. 'The notorious Capt. Hayes, of *Black Diamond* and *Rona* notoriety, who was "wanted" in several ports of New Zealand besides Auckland, has seriously come to grief.' The traders who had been bilked could have some satisfaction in knowing that Hayes was again without a ship.

At the same time that this was published, however, Hayes was sailing the tropics again, this time in the 72-ton schooner *Atlantic*, a sturdy vessel built in New Zealand of durable native pine, and rated at 125 tons burthen. How he acquired her is unknown, the first record of him in connection with the schooner being his departure from Apia on 12 October 1869. Stevens, in his history of blackbirding, says that Hayes stole the *Atlantic*, while from other sources it seems that he hired the schooner from Montgomery Betham, a 37-year-old Englishman who had spent time on the goldfields of Australia, and who about 1866 had been sent to Samoa to represent the trading firm of Henderson and Macfarlane. What is certain is that once he had another deck beneath his boots, Hayes returned to the blackbirding trade.

The recruitment of island labour had begun in 1863, as a direct result of the American Civil War. With no supplies of cotton arriving from the Southern States, the mills of Bradford, England, were grinding to a halt. Other sources of cotton — Egypt, India — were unreliable, and so the establishment of cotton plantations elsewhere was an attractive proposition. Queensland, Australia, was considered ideal, as were Samoa and Fiji. All that was needed was a low-cost source of plentiful labour, as cotton is a labour-intensive crop, and a Sydney merchant by the name of Robert Towns was the man who found a solution.

Originally an English sea captain who had carried cargoes to Australia as a venture, Towns was a hugely successful entrepreneur. Over just a handful of years, he made his mark in an amazing number of spheres, from wharves to whaling, from directorships in banks to sponsorship of Seamen's Bethels. He did not confine himself to Sydney, speculating in Queensland to such an extent that a booming settlement — Townsville — was named after him. Since 1844, he had been sending out his Brisbane-based ships in the trepang (sea slug) and sandalwood trade, focusing on New Caledonia and the New Hebrides (Vanuatu), and so he thought he knew how to find the cheap labour needed.

After buying land forty miles upriver from Brisbane and having it planted with cotton, he sent his schooner *Don Juan* to Melanesia to recruit natives to weed and harvest the fields. This was as early as May 1863, but it seems that there might have been competition already, or else that he was afraid of giving a rival the idea. In his letter of instructions to his recruiter, Henry Ross Lewin (who was also the second mate of the schooner), Towns added, 'You had better call at Leifoo before Hayes gets there, and leave before he arrives.'

The *Don Juan* got back to Brisbane on 15 August 1863, the *Queensland Guardian* reporting that the schooner carried 'seventy-three South Sea Islanders for Captain Towns' cotton plantation'. Originally, the number had been seventy-four, but one of the natives had died of seasickness. 'The agreement made with these men is, that they shall receive ten shillings a month, and have their food, clothes and shelter provided for them.' Many of them had worked for Towns before, collecting trepang in the lagoons and tending the 'batter houses' where the slugs were cured, smoked and dried. They trusted Towns, and with good reason — the master of the schooner, Captain Greuber, had been instructed that they were to be treated kindly, with no force of any kind to be used. The natives were given two pairs of trousers and two shirts each, and on the plantation they were fed well on rice, meat, pumpkin and potatoes. Additionally, the promise that they would be returned home within a year was kept. Though strict, Towns was fair and humane. The men who abused the system came after him.

Ross Lewin, the man Towns had entrusted with the first recruitment, was one of the first, and by reputation one of the most cruel. By 1866, he was in his own business, and soon became known as the worst man-stealer in the Pacific. At Tanna, the missionaries told Captain George Palmer of H.M.S. *Rosario* that he seized natives out of their canoes, and in 1869 he was tried (though acquitted) of raping an island woman. A popular ploy with him was to pose as a missionary — Bishop John Patteson being a favourite — so that he could kidnap natives who approached the ship in search of a sermon or a prayer. He charged £7 per head for the 'cargoes' he brought in to work the sugar cane fields of Queensland, and soon made enough money to settle on Tanna and tyrannise the natives there.

Another notable character was Dr J.P. Murray of Melbourne, who owned the schooner *Carl*, registered in Fiji. One day in the year 1871, when Murray saw H.M.S. *Cossack* coming down fast, he went down into the hold where sixty islanders were trapped, shot them, and then had the bodies thrown overboard. After arrest, he turned Queen's Evidence, testifying against the captain, mates and crew to save his own skin. Many charges of murder were brought by the commanders of the ships-of-war patrolling the Pacific. Great numbers of natives were recruited honestly, as the islanders, tired of the social restrictions imposed by the missionaries, were keen to go in search of fun and money in Samoa, Queensland, Tahiti and Fiji, but so many captains and mates abused the system that an anti-kidnapping Act was passed in 1868. Though largely toothless, it was followed by other legislation as public outrage simmered.

Unsurprisingly, many blackbirders were killed by natives, too, either in retaliation for their own crimes or for those committed by recruiters earlier. Lewin himself was murdered by a Tanna native — in revenge for shooting a boy who had stolen a bunch of his bananas.

*

When collecting a cargo, it was common practice for the captain to stay on board and send his recruiter (usually one of the mates, though it might be the supercargo) to the beach in a boat. Four heavily armed seamen went with him. After the boat was safely ashore, and turned with its prow to the sea for a quick getaway, a second boat was sent out, also manned with armed seamen. This one stayed a little offshore, to cover the recruiting boat in case of attack. If the operation was legitimate, an Australian Government Agent was there, to supervise the recruitment process. It seems, however, that the natives were more commonly tricked into the boats, before being herded to the ship.

Blackbirding was not new to Hayes, though he was unusual in that he liked to go ashore and do the recruiting himself, relying on charisma and hollow promises. Back in December 1868, George Miller, the British Consul in Tahiti, wrote to Lord Stanley, 'There has been introduced by the brig *Rona*, of Lyttelton, W.H. Hayes master, about 150 natives of Savage Island under contract for service.' However, as Miller went on to describe, 'They have not, to my knowledge, complained of having been deceived in their engagement or ill-treated during the voyage hither.'

Consular agents were often ambivalent about the business, as they were planters themselves, or dealt with planters in a trading capacity, and were always conscious of the need for cheap labour. Consequently, when the *Westport Times* reported on 31 August 1869 that they had received intelligence from Fiji that 'Bully Hayes, of unenviable notoriety, is carrying on a trade with labourers from Tanna and other islands', the main concern was that his 'unfair dealing with the natives' meant that he had 'injured the market for others'.

Hayes' new venture with the *Atlantic* may have been backed by Montgomery Betham, the agent (and perhaps the owner) of the schooner, as he was a plantation owner in need of workers. It was triggered, however, when a man approached him with a proposition to obtain and supply native labourers for various planters in Fiji. Incredibly, this was none other than Frederick Henry Sievewright —

the same man who had crewed the cutter *Wave* on the passage from Lyttelton to Akaroa in November 1864; the same man who, with Hayes' erstwhile chief officer, John Till, had sued Captain Mathews, the owner and master of the *Wave*, for unpaid wages; the same man who, again with John Till, had accused Hayes of kidnapping and molesting Helen (or Ellen) Murray.

Considering this background, it must have been an interesting voyage. It also had a melodramatic outcome.

*

The first news appeared, very belatedly, in the *Sydney Morning Herald* on 5 March 1870, and just as a brief sentence — 'We learn from private letters that the notorious Captain Hayes is under arrest at Samoa for kidnapping.' Captain Hayes being so newsworthy, it was rapidly reprinted, the scantiness of the details leaving thousands of readers in suspense. They had to wait until April for more, but then Captain Nicholls of the *Jeannie Duncan* arrived in Auckland with gossip.

As he told the reporter from the *New Zealand Herald*, he had talked to a man in Levuka, Fiji, who had told him that the *Atlantic* had put into Apia for water, her supplies being low, with 130 natives on board. 'It became known that some of these men had been kidnapped, and Capt. Hayes was taken prisoner, and the vessel seized,' he gossiped, then added, 'The man who acted as trader for him escaped from prison.' This was Frederick Sievewright, but as his name was not published, no one remarked on the strange coincidence.

It would not be surprising if the newspaper editors had trouble believing him. As the Nelson *Colonist* commented, 'The irrepressible Captain Hayes, of *Black Diamond* notoriety, has once more turned up in the capacity as a kidnapper, after various reports of his death by violence, shipwreck, and sundry other causes.' Hayes' 'notoriety' being what it was, however, the gossip was repeated throughout the New Zealand and Australian press. Then the Melbourne *Argus*, in an item published on 4 October, revealed a further development — not only had Hayes been arrested for blackbirding, but the man who had arrested him was a Samoan chief! 'The notorious Captain Hayes,' it read, 'whose exploits in the Pacific are well known, has fallen into the hands of a Samoan chief, who captured his schooner (the *Atlantic*) and took him and his crew prisoners.'

*

The *Atlantic* had dropped her anchor in the harbour of Pago Pago, on the Samoan (now American Samoan) island of Tutuila, on 14 December 1869. There was nothing to tell that high drama was nigh, her arrival being so peaceful that the resident missionary, Thomas Powell, paid little attention. But next evening, as Powell testified later, when he and his wife were sitting quietly in their parlour, their native servants rushed into the room to report that there were islanders from the islands of Manihiki and Pukapuka on board the schooner, men and women 'whom the captain had kidnapped'. Then, while Powell was trying to make sense of their excited chatter, their chief, Mauga, made a dignified entrance. Not only did he announce that the tidings were true, but then revealed that he and his people were going to liberate the captives. Horrified, Powell tried to dissuade him, feeling certain that bloodshed would result, but the chief's mind was made up.

No sooner had Mauga gone, along with his retinue of warriors, than Sievewright knocked on the mission house door. He wanted to report a crime, he said, and the natives had told him to see Mr Powell. Not only had Captain Hayes stolen 20,000 coconuts, and £100 worth of mats from the people of Manihiki, but he had carried away 'some ten or more of the people of that island against their will'. Pressed for details, Sievewright listed '10 Boys, 2 women and 1 man' — but that was not all, because Hayes had also kidnapped nineteen Pukapuka people (fourteen girls, four men and one boy), along with their chief by recruiting them 'under false pretences'.

While Thomas Powell was absorbing this, a man named Moete arrived, representing the Manihiki party. The captain had sent them ashore to wash their clothes, he said, and his orders had been to come back to the ship when they were finished, so what should he do? Puzzled, Powell asked why they should obey, if they had been stolen from their island? Surely it would be best to stay on shore?

Emboldened, Moete left at once, to pass on this good advice. Unfortunately, as the missionary found out later, the rest of the natives had tamely returned to the *Atlantic*, meantime. The Pago Pago chief, Mauga, was on the beach, however. He told Moete to pretend to follow Hayes' instructions, and once he was back on the ship to wait for a signal. When that came, he was to urge all the natives to jump overboard and swim for the shore.

The signal was made, and the natives poured over the rail and dived into the sea. Three or four had to be left behind, though, as they were either too weak or too frightened. To make sure they were freed, Mauga's warriors seized the ship's boat, which was tied up on the beach while the mate, Mr Hussey, and a gang of men were filling freshwater barrels. Until Captain Hayes released the remaining natives, they would hold the boat hostage, Mauga announced.

Evading his own capture, Mr Hussey tore up to the mission house for advice, but Mr Powell refused to listen — 'I said,' he testified, 'I had nothing to do with it.' Instead, he informed Hussey that if he wanted someone to complain to, he should go to Chief Mauga. No sooner had Hussey rushed off again than Powell saw Captain Hayes jump down into a canoe and force the Samoan occupant to paddle him to shore. It was obvious he was in one of his infamous rages, so the missionary retreated to his house. But no sooner had he left the beach than he heard 'a great confusion of voices, and then the report of two pistols'.

Hurrying back, Powell found Mauga in a state of great merriment. Seeing that the captain had two pistols in his belt, the chief had shouted out to the canoe paddler to upset his craft and dunk his passenger so thoroughly that his gunpowder would be soaked. Raging and dripping as he staggered to his feet, Hayes had hauled one of his two six-shot revolvers out of his belt and pulled the trigger, only to be mortified further when the pistol misfired. Then the young men rushed at him, seized the two guns, and emptied both into the air. And, rage as he might, Hayes could do nothing about it, as he was held fast by two mighty warriors. And to complete his humiliation, Mauga formally arrested him.

Powell, while watching Captain Hayes being escorted to confinement in Mauga's house, was accosted by Fred Sievewright again. This time the trader had a message from Captain Hayes, demanding the missionary's support in the face of this outrage — 'This I declined to do, saying that I wished to keep aloof from the affair.' Instead, the missionary recommended referring the matter to Matthew Hunkin, who was the British consular agent for Tutuila, and lived in Leone, up the coast.

Mauga, told about it, heartily concurred. No matter how high his status, a Samoan who had arrested and confined a European was in a very delicate position, and so passing on the responsibility seemed a very good idea. Accordingly, he wrote a short but eloquent message to the British agent: 'I Mauga write this my letter to you, and I say, you come here, for great trouble is in this land. 29 Manihiki and Pukapukan have been stolen away by the Captain. You come quick, then we shall find out the rights of it. What about this Captain will it not be right to make him fast and send him to Apia. There was one person nearly killed by the six mouthed gun belonging to the Captain.'

Matthew Hunkin read the message very reluctantly indeed. Like Powell, he did not want anything to do with the controversy, so excused himself by saying that Hayes had been flying American colours as the schooner had passed Leone on the outward voyage. So the American consular agent, Thomas Meredith, was duly summoned. He was from Liverpool, England, not anywhere in America, which was common in those days, when consular posts were sought after by all the traders and chandlers, the job giving them improved access to the captains who came into port for stores. But it meant that his situation was as tricky as high chief Mauga's.

As Meredith testified later, he arrived at Pago Pago to find the schooner *Atlantic* hauled up on the beach with a native guard on standby, and Captain Hayes, his mate and most of his crew imprisoned. During a long private consultation, Hayes emphatically informed him that he 'had been ill treated by the Natives', who had no excuse to seize his ship. Then, much to Meredith's surprise, he protested about being represented by an American vice-consul, arguing that the *Atlantic* was British-built and British-registered, and that the matter should be handled by the British. In short, Hayes

169

did not want anything to do with him — not because of Meredith's dubious nationality, but because Meredith was a copra trader, and one of the many men who was owed a lot of money.

Meantime, the British consular agent, Matthew Hunkin, had received a letter from Frederick Sievewright — an old letter, apparently, as it was dated 15 November 1869, at Manihiki. It was also a very odd letter. 'I address you from here in anticipation of being left on shore at this place or Pukapuka,' this strange missive began, 'in consequence of my knowledge of the scoundrelly manner in which people of this island have been kidnapped. We arrived here twelve days back for the purpose, as I understood of taking on board portion of a wreck of the *Samoa* and to obtain labourers (in an honest manner I imagined). I now find that the people were desirous of making a feast on a neighbouring island.'

To this end, as Sievewright went on to describe, they had collected 30,000 coconuts, 'they having been told by the capt: he would take their nuts and their families in his vessel, & that after the feast was over he would again take them on board and return them to their homes. The people gladly availed themselves of the Captain's offer and nearly all embarked. I may mention that between the time of our arrival and that of the vessel's departure the capt had purchased over £100 worth of native produce, to be paid for on the way to Atta'anga comprising mats, hats &c'.

While this part of the letter may indeed have been written before the schooner left Manihiki, it is obvious that it was continued after sailing, as Sievewright went on to say that once 'the vessel had got sufficiently far from land to prevent any possibility of these poor natives swimming ashore', Hayes had informed them that he was not going to Rakahanga, but to Pukapuka instead. Then, once at

Pukapuka, he recruited a gang with false promises — but for work in Samoa, and not on the plantations of Fiji.

Naturally, Sievewright, who had commissioned Hayes to recruit labour for Fiji, was furious. Resentfully, he went on to describe the arrangement made with the Pukapuka people: 'I had whilst ashore here drawn out at his dictation two agreements for these people to sign after going on board one of which bound them to serve for *six months* at *7 dollars* and the other for *five years* at *2 dollars* per month. His interpreters in his intercourse with the natives being Joseph & Mary Jordan.'

From there, he went on to confide that he was in fear of his life. 'With respect to myself I was at the captain's mercy! — and had no means whereby I could make known the Capt's object to the natives without incurring the risk of being left here or at Pukapuka where I do not believe a white man could live six months on the diet peculiar to the place. Even now the Capt suspects I intend reporting his conduct and I have therefore to write for fear my surmises with respect to my being left ashore be too correct.' And, with that, he ended:

'I am, sir, Your obedt servant, Fred H. Sivewright.'

*

Driven by curiosity as well as a belated sense of consular responsibility, Hunkin took his canoe to Pago Pago, where he arrived on 18 December, at about the same time as the American vice-consul, Thomas Meredith. No sooner had he stepped out onto the beach than he was summoned by Mauga and the other chiefs, who were all very anxious for a conference. Pausing only to order Captain Hayes to send on board for the ship's papers, Hunkin complied, to find that Mauga had assembled all the Pukapuka and

Manihiki people to tell their side of the story, and justify Mauga's action in arresting a European shipmaster. And so, forthwith, he examined them one by one, with the help of two translators Hayes had in his crew, one being Allen Strickland, who was a half-caste Pukapukan, and the other Joseph Jordan, a man from Huahine.

While the ship's papers, when they arrived, confirmed that the schooner was definitely British, and that he, Matthew Hunkin, was the consul responsible for the matter, what he heard did not help make up his mind about whether Hayes was guilty or not. It was evident that the Pukapukans had been properly recruited, though they were very vague about the precise details of the arrangement. Their leader, chief Pilote, confirmed this, saying that he had come with them of his own free will, to make sure that they were well treated in Samoa.

The Manihiki party — made up of ten boys, two girls and a woman — also had a chief as their spokesman, the same Moete who had run to Thomas Powell for advice. Moete was definite that they had been lured on board the schooner and forced to stay below while the *Atlantic* sailed away. And then, while Hunkin was digesting this, he received a long statement from Frederick Sievewright, one that not just confirmed what Moete claimed, but made further charges (underlined for emphasis) that were even graver.

As Sievewright testified, he had arrived in Apia in September, with orders for Captain Hayes to procure labourers for plantations on the island of Naitoba, in Fiji. 'As the laws regulating the introduction of foreign labourers into Fiji are very stringent I was desirous to see the manner in which these people were engaged,' he went on. Accordingly, he had sailed on the *Atlantic*, which left Apia on 12 October, and had arrived at the island of Manihiki exactly one calendar month later.

He, with Hayes and Joseph and Mary Jordan, had gone on shore,

Sievewright being under the impression that Hayes intended to recruit men there. Unfortunately, the schooner was driven out to sea, so the quartet was stranded on the island for the next few days, and it was during this time that Sievewright had learned that the locals had plans to take boats to a neighbouring island, Rakahanga, and had stockpiled 20,000 coconuts as a present for the people they were visiting. 'It was proposed by Capt Hayes that as their boats were very small and liable to be upset to take the cocoanuts *and the whole of the people* of the settlement in the schooner to Rakahanga, adding that he had done a similar kindness for them on a former occasion.'

At the same time, Hayes was buying fine mats and hats on credit, building up a debt of about £500. For the Manihiki people, the lack of payment was troubling enough, given Captain Hayes' reputation for dodging creditors. Even more worrying was his determination 'to get the whole of the female population on board and his deflow'ring a child of tender years'. Accordingly, though the village elders decided to consider the captain's offer of carriage to Rakahanga, it was on the condition that males only would go on the schooner, the women and girls being left behind.

When Captain Hayes was told this, he protested that it would look very odd to arrive at a party without women, and offered 'to give each female a new dress on going aboard, and thus make a good appearance on landing at Rakahanga'. This made the elders even more suspicious. However, they made no objection as the coconuts were stowed in the hold, and when Hayes, Sievewright and the Jordans boarded the schooner, some of the locals went with them, the idea being to collect the money for the hats and mats. These people, however, were sent on shore again, as Hayes said he wanted to pay the women who had woven the mats in person. And, when the boat came back, it held 'two little girls, one middle-aged woman, eight boys and several old men'.

Sievewright gave no explanation for this odd assortment of people. Instead, he went on to describe Hayes' next action — 'the eight boys and two girls were ordered down into the cabin and the old people ashore the young people crying bitterly and begging hard to be permitted to go ashore, their appeal was in vain. The middle aged woman had her son aboard as had also an old man; these two begged to be permitted to take their children but without effect: — The old woman finding her appeal was useless said then if you take my son take me; the same desire to accompany his son was expressed by the old man.' The woman, 'not being past working', was allowed to stay, but the old man was forced down into the boat.

'The boat belonging to the native teacher was hoisted aboard and given to a white man resident at Bukapuka,' Sievewright wrote. 'The Mats, Hats &c were not paid for. There was also one man named Moete who accompanied us: upon our arrival at Pagopago he gave such information to the natives as led them to seize the vessel. There was a woman named Akerere who went on board at the same time as Capt Hayes, M. Jordan, J. Jordan & myself.

'Fred Sievewright, Pagopago, 18th Dec 1869.'

*

Quite apart from the serious charge of sexual abuse of a child, this testimony raised as many questions as it answered, such as how Moete had materialised on board. There was also the matter of the agreement the Pukapukan workers had signed — was it fair and legal? Or had the Pukapukan men and women been captured by stealth? For Hunkin, this posed a problem.

As it turned out, there were two versions of the contract. The missionary, Thomas Powell, wrote informally to his friend, Consul Williams, to tell him that after Hayes was arrested and taken away, Sievewright had come to the house with a bundle of wet papers for him to read. They belonged to Captain Hayes, he said, and when Powell objected, saying they were private, Sievewright argued that Hayes had given them to him, and therefore 'it was not a breach of confidence to shew them to me'.

So, though still feeling reluctant, the missionary read the pages as they were pried apart and handed over. As he went on to describe to Williams in heavily underlined phrases, one of the documents was 'an agreement on the part of the natives of Bukabuka and Manihiki engaging with the firm of Betham & Moore to go to one of the Fiji Islands (Niatamba) to work for *Five Years* at the wages of *$2 per month*, and it was stipulated that if any one of them should be ill, *the wages were to be stopped* during the illness'.

This, without doubt, was a scandal.

*

Understandably, the missionary and his wife greeted the American with caution as he stepped up onto their veranda, next day. Politeness prevailed, however. 'In the afternoon of this day Captain Hayes came up and introduced himself,' Powell continued in his letter to Williams. 'He spent some three hours & took tea with Mrs Powell & myself. He referred to the affair of taking his vessel, and said, "Somebody has put their foot in it." He said something to the effect that he would not deny that the people of Manihiki were unwilling at first to come, but that afterwards they agreed.'

Early the following morning he was back at their door, this time with a favour to ask — he 'requested permission to write out some documents, saying there was so much noise in the chief's house; I immediately furnished him with pen & ink', Powell testified, and after that he and his wife left the American alone, sending in his breakfast instead of inviting him to the table. Despite this, Hayes gave the missionary one of the papers to read — 'It was apparently a verbatim copy of the agreement of the Bukabuka people to work for Messrs Betham & Moore which Mr Sievewright had shewed me on the 15th in a wet state,' wrote Powell, 'but there was this difference that for "*Five Years*" on Niatamba of the former document was substituted *Six months* on Upolu in this new document and instead of the $2 per month of the former was substituted 12 fathoms of cloth per month for the men and 10 for the women.'

So which version was the true one? That indeed was the question.

*

Matthew Hunkin made up his mind to help Mauga out by taking official possession of the schooner. As the Reverend Powell wrote to the *Samoan Reporter*, Mr Hunkin 'decided on seizing the *Atlantic* in the name of Her Majesty'. That done, the problem was what to do next. Obviously, the matter had to be referred to the British Consul in Apia — Powell's friend, John Chauner Williams — but the only vessel capable of carrying the charged man, the natives and the documents to Apia was the *Atlantic*, and once the schooner was over the horizon, there was no guarantee that Hayes would not take back control and abscond.

Mauga and his advisers held a deep discussion, then sent for Hunkin so they could have a conference, in which they proposed that the schooner should be sent to Apia with a native crew, while Captain Hayes remained a prisoner in Pago Pago. When Hunkin objected to keeping him on the island, they pointed out that if he went, the Pukapuka people would have to go too, a prospect that terrified them, as they were convinced he would seize back the *Atlantic* and carry them to bondage in Fiji.

Matthew Hunkin wavered. Then he was faced with another complication, because the crew of the *Atlantic* staged their own protest, saying that they felt certain that Captain Hayes would abscond with the schooner if given a chance. This was most disconcerting — 'The crew knew Capt Hayes, I did not,' as he wrote in his letter to Williams. And all the written evidence would be on the same vessel, so if Hayes vanished, that would also go missing. 'Thoughts of this kind were now agitating my mind,' he wrote. The foreign residents, some of whom had good reason to know that Hayes was a duplicitous man, were weighing in with their opinions too, 'and the evidence was certainly strong against him'.

So Hunkin gave in. 'In the presence of Mr Thos Meredith U.S. Vice Commercial agent I gave the vessel in the charge of the mate Mr Hussey who accepted it and I requested that Capt Hayes would come with me in my boat on the following morning to Leone to which he very readily agreed.' Captain Hayes became Matthew Hunkin's prisoner-at-large in Leone, while Mr Hussey obeyed instructions 'to proceed as soon as possible to Apia', and put the schooner and the despatches into the hands of the British Consul, John Chauner Williams.

*

The *Atlantic*, with the mate, Mr Hussey, in command, dropped anchor in Apia on 24 December 1869. And the instant the anchor was dropped, Mr Hussey rushed on shore, marched into the office of the British Consul, and told John Chauner Williams all about it.

Williams, extremely disconcerted at these dramatic revelations — which were totally new to him — was not at all happy with Mauga and the vice-consul in Tutuila. Once Mr Hunkin had decided that there was a case to answer, he should have sent Captain Hayes, along with the labourers he had engaged at Pukapuka and the people he had kidnapped from Manihiki, so that an inquiry could commence at once. That he had neglected to do so meant that Consul Williams was forced to seize the *Atlantic* for the third time, and go himself to Tutuila to fetch Captain Hayes and the native witnesses.

This third official seizure infuriated Mr Betham, who was not just the agent for the owners of the schooner, but was also owed a lot of money by Hayes. First, a written demand for the *Atlantic* arrived, and then Betham stamped into the office. High words were exchanged, interrupted first by Frederick Sievewright, who said he had come with the schooner to avoid being attacked by Captain Hayes, and then by Emily Hayes, who arrived to demand a bill of exchange that her husband had on board. Then, while Williams was still countering all this, Mr Hussey, the mate of the schooner, arrived back in the office. He asked for his discharge, as he did not want anything more to do with the affair, which, he said, was a ruination to his health. Sighing, John Williams hired a local shipmaster, Captain Hamilton, to take the *Atlantic* back to Tutuila.

New Year's Day, 1870, was spent boarding the schooner, at the commencement of a tedious voyage to Leone that was impeded by contrary winds. Marching on shore on the 5th, the consul irritably pushed aside Captain Hayes '& the other foreign residents' in order to approach Matthew Hunkin and demand to know why he had acted the way he had. 'Mr Hunkin explained fully to me all he had done & why he had seized the vessel again,' William finally wrote, and then, after instructing the consular agent to put it all down as written evidence, Williams set off to Pago Pago — a four-hour journey from Leone, with Hayes, Betham and Hunkin trailing behind — to get another version of the story from Thomas Powell.

Mr Powell received the party with his customary politeness. But when it came to giving his own testimony, he objected — 'He did not wish his name to be mixed up with this affair,' wrote Williams. Impatiently, he informed the missionary that his evidence was needed for justice to be done, and Powell complied, producing a long, detailed testimony, though hedged with the final sentence, 'I cannot vouch for the correctness of *every word* in the above statement but the narration of *facts* is correct, to the best of my recollection and belief.'

Having obtained this, Williams, 'in conjunction with Mr Betham & Hunkin, went to Mauga the Chief — I stated the object of my visit & cautioned him to give up all the Islanders he had in his charge'. Mauga proved to be the most cooperative man around, handing over the Pukapuka and Manihiki parties, who were equally amenable, though very bewildered.

The Pukapuka people were sickly and weak, Williams noted with some alarm. However, he did not realise that he was effectively signing their death warrant.

*

The wind had turned, meantime, so the *Atlantic* did not arrive back at Apia until the 9th, which was a Sunday. This made it difficult to know what to do with Captain Hayes, particularly as there was no prison. Williams coped by demanding his parole, and then sending him home to his family. The islanders were housed in the compound where all foreign natives lived, and then he tackled the business that had piled up on his desk.

On 11 January, the day before the commencement of the inquiry, he was interrupted by Frederick Sievewright, who slunk into the office with 'a letter stating that his life was in danger & that he wished to go away in the *Dantzig* for Fiji'. He had been approached, he said, by a perfect stranger, who had advised him 'that an attack will be made on me after the close of the present examination not openly but when time and opportunity may present themselves. Judging from the cowardly and unprovoked attack made on me in a previous occasion and since', as he had written in this second strange letter, he had no trouble believing this warning, and so he wished to take advantage of the kindly offer of escape that had been made by the master of the *Dantzig*.

Williams emphatically refused permission, but Sievewright ran off on the *Dantzig* anyway, meaning that the only formal evidence the consul received from him was the long affidavit he had written at Pago Pago and given to Hunkin, along with a copy of the same statement that Sievewright had made and given to Mr Powell.

Naturally, Captain Hayes opposed it as evidence, Sievewright being absent. Then, when Mr Hussey took the stand, the inquiry seemed to be going all Hayes' way, as his erstwhile mate was so staunchly loyal. Had any of the Manihiki people been forced on board the schooner? No, Hussey replied, there was no violence whatsoever. In fact, no more than five minutes after the anchor had been weighed, they were singing and dancing on deck. Dancing? Yes, and lots of it, too. And, as for them being shut down in the hold, there were no doors, so how could they be trapped? Consul Williams did not believe a word of this, writing in his journal that Mr Hussey's statements were 'not in accordance with the truth', but nonetheless he had to allow it.

Then the proceedings were brought to a sudden halt, as Hayes threw an apoplectic fit. 'I was sent for last evening about half past five to go to see Capt Hayes who was in a fit,' Williams wrote on 24 January. J.G. Alvord — an American actor who had been a passenger on the *Rona* when she sunk, and had, understandably, stayed in Apia (where he functioned as an auctioneer) after the makeshift rescue craft had arrived there — had fetched him in a panic. As Williams went on, 'I found him suffering great pain of the stomach & left side violent fit put him into a blanket bath & gave him an emetic of ipecac by Eight he was a little easier.'

It was impossible to believe Hayes was faking, as he was so very ill. 'I saw Capt Hayes he is better this morning but weak,' the day's entry concluded, 'we shall not be able to have any court.' The stress of the trial was preying on the captain's mind, it seemed, because two days later there was a deterioration — 'at half past ten in the night I had to go to see Capt Hayes he was taken with another fit & pains in the side in the region of the heart applied a large mustard poultice'.

Any sympathy the consul might have felt for Hayes dissolved on 28 January, when the inquiry was resumed and Williams found that the American was plying the native witnesses with alcohol. As well as that, the Pukapuka people were dying — 'Four Pukapukans have already died & others are ill from the change of living,' wrote Williams two days later. On 14 February, he went to the foreign compound to see them and came away very worried indeed — 'I went to see them, poor things, they are miserable 8 or 9 more looking bad and ill with cough, sinking.' Obviously, they were unfit for work, so he could not find them jobs, and there was no way of sending them home.

Added to that, he was certain that witnesses from Hayes' crew were all telling lies, while Handley Sterndale, Captain Hayes' friend and erstwhile companion on the *Rona*, was not just whipping the Manihiki people in revenge for their accusations, but slandering Moete's reputation too — 'he is like the pot saying to the kettle you are black'. Hayes himself tried to persuade Williams that Moete had been fined several times for misdemeanours, which the Manihiki chief indignantly denied.

Exactly a calendar month after the inquiry had begun, it came to a close, but without a decision, even though both Hayes and Betham pestered Williams for an opinion. The consul was in a quandary, writing on 24 February 1870, 'Capt Hayes was very anxious to know when I should give my decision, but I must hold off. He reminded me of my obligations as a Mason, of course I cannot hold when Justice is to be served, but I am really in a fix, for if I make known that I must send the vessel & him to Sydney I fear he will make his escape.' For the first time, he felt some sympathy for Matthew Hunkin in Tutuila. The plain fact was that there was no local shipmaster with the resources to confine someone as desperate as Hayes on the long passage to Sydney and prevent him from seizing back the schooner. Accordingly, the British Consul was forced to wait for the arrival of a British ship-of-war.

He dithered too long. On April Fool's Day, 1870, Captain Hayes absconded.

CHAPTER 14

Pioneer

The story of Bully Hayes' remarkable escape was broken by the *Daily Southern Cross* on 28 September, written by an editor who found the news amusing. 'Captain Hayes is a name which has become notorious throughout the colonies,' he began, going on to meditate, 'His exploits have been so many and various that no one who is at all acquainted with his history would be surprised at hearing of his again distinguishing himself, were it not for the fact that he had been reported dead. The captain, however, with that versatility for which he is so remarkable, is no sooner reported dead than he reappears in another quarter.'

Constant reincarnation was not Captain Hayes' only skill, according to the yarns — 'He would be a very bold man who would vouch for the smallest particle of the many extraordinary stories that we are told of Bully Hayes.' The latest was that 'he kidnapped a number of natives from one of the islands, and took them in a schooner to Fiji, where he expected he would be able to dispose of his cargo at a good figure without being subjected to the indignity of having to answer awkward questions. The natives, however, contrived to forward a complaint to the American Consul, who seized the vessel, admitting Captain Hayes to parole pending inquiry.

'But,' the story ran on, 'a new complication now arose. A firm with whom Hayes in bygone times had contracted some liability, took the opportunity to step in and demand payment of their little bill. To appease these insatiable creditors, Hayes was compelled to hand over his chronometers as security. Days passed on, and at length an American barque anchored off the place. Thereupon went he to the creditors, and in that genial off-hand manner for which he is so distinguished, requested that he might be allowed to take the chronometers on board the barque in order to regulate, and, if possible, sell them. In a moment of weakness the too confiding creditors consented.'

The 'American barque' spread her sails the moment Hayes was fairly on board, 'and our informant states that they had been ever since anxiously looking for the return of Hayes or the chronometers'. Instead, with sublime cheek, the master steered for a plantation owned by the 'lamenting' creditors, where Hayes, in the guise of a representative of the firm, took £2000 worth of cotton on board, and then sailed off again. 'The firm then chartered a schooner, and manned her, with the object of going in chase of the captain; but, after a cruise of three weeks, gave up the search.' Chasing another lead, they steered for an island where they had a second plantation, expecting Hayes to call there, again with no result.

But, as the editor had commented, it was hard to distinguish fiction from fact in the stories told of Bully Hayes. A man who told a different tale of the famous escape was George Herbert, the thirteenth Earl of Pembroke, who at the age of twenty cruised the South Pacific in the *Albatross*, with his physician for company. In 1872, a year after getting home, he published a book of his adventures called *South Sea Bubbles by the Earl and the Doctor*, which did not mention Bully Hayes at all. He did say something interesting, though — 'When you go to sea, you must either believe *all* the yarns you hear without unravelling them, or none at all.' Twenty years later, when he wrote the foreword to a book by an adventurer by the name of Louis Becke, he retold one of those yarns just as he reckoned he had heard it, leaving his reader to do the unravelling.

'When in October, 1870, I sailed into the harbour of Apia, Samoa,' as the Earl commenced, he not only made the acquaintance of Mr Louis Becke, who was running a cutter between Apia and Savaii, but he found the place 'seething with excitement over the departure on the previous day of the pirate Pease, carrying with him the yet more illustrious "Bully" Hayes.

'It happened in this wise,' he continued. 'A month or two before our arrival, Hayes had dropped anchor in Apia, and some ugly stories of recent irregularities in the labour trade had come to the ears of Mr Williams, the English Consul. Mr Williams, with the assistance of the natives, very cleverly seized his vessel in the night, and ran her ashore, and detained Mr Hayes pending the arrival of an English man-of-war to which he could be given in charge. But in those happy days there were no prisons in Samoa, so that his confinement was not irksome, and his only hard labour was picnics, of which he was the life and soul.

'All went pleasantly until Mr Pease — a degenerate sort of pirate who made his living by half bullying, half swindling lonely white men on small islands out of their coconut oil, and unarmed merchantmen out of their stores — came to Apia in an armed ship with a Malay crew. From that moment Hayes' life became less idyllic. Hayes and Pease conceived a most violent hatred of each other, and poor old Mr Williams was really worried into an attack of elephantiasis (which answers to the gout in those latitudes) by his continual efforts to prevent the two desperadoes from flying at each other's throat.

'Heartily glad was he when Pease — who was the sort of man that always observed *les convenances* when possible, and who fired a salute of twenty-one guns on the Queen's Birthday — came one afternoon to get his papers "all regular," and clear for sea. But lo! the next morning, when his vessel had disappeared, it was found that his enemy Captain Hayes had disappeared also, and the ladies of Samoa were left disconsolate at the departure of the most agreeable man they had ever known.'

This stirring yarn can be unravelled by comparing it with Consul Williams' diary. For a start, the *Albatross* arrived in Apia on 11 October 1870, six months after Hayes had absconded. 'The schooner *Albatross* arrived this morning bringing the Earl of Pembroke,' wrote Williams on that date. 'His lordship called on me in the afternoon, he is quite a young man and agreeable, affable.' His lordship's identification of the vessel that carried Hayes away was quite correct, though, as John Williams had noted the arrival of the *Pioneer* on 11 March. The master who had called at his office to register his arrival had been a very chatty man, with lots of interest to relate — 'that he had a fight with some of the Islanders on the Line for they had killed one of his traders, but the cause of them killing him was because the *Samoa* belonging to Mr Weber had forcibly taken away the Chief's daughter she was the greatest lady on the island & the king's only child & it was revenge why they killed his man & that they are threatening the German vessels.

'Capt Peas also states that a bark had taken away 400 people of the islands just about 4 months ago,' Williams' recounting went on, 'he also stated that he knew of an instance that the crew of a vessel 26 in number who went on shore & drove the people of the island into the boats & then took them off. Also people had been enticed into the Cabin & when below spirits had been given to the people & then put in irons by the crew & forced into the hold of the ship — this was done repeatedly & when the beachcombers on shore heard of it, prevented the natives going on board. He said that the African slave trade was nothing in comparison to this, there was some honour there, but here nothing of the kind.'

Though Pease was giving every appearance of being honest and honourable, and was inoffensive in appearance, being small and scrawny, it did not take long for John Williams to learn that he was a hard master, as prone to mad rages as Bully Hayes. Three days later, two of the crew of the *Pioneer* came in and asked for their discharge, pleading that their time was up. They were keen to get away, they said, because serving under Captain Pease was such a nerve-racking experience. Once, when their skipper was irritated by the way the rigging was being handled, he had produced a gun and fired a few shots into the air, wounding a fellow in the topgallant yard. 'Capt Peas is a tartar I think,' wrote Williams.

What Pease did not fire was a salute on Queen Victoria's birthday (24 May), despite the Earl of Pembroke's claim. That was impossible, because he, Hayes, and his vessel were long gone. The shipmaster from Massachusetts did, however, recognise the patron saint of Ireland — 'The *Pioneer* fired in honour of St Patrick,' wrote Williams on 17 March. The story that Pease and Hayes had been openly quarrelling may also have come from Williams himself, the consul writing in the course of his bitter description of Hayes' escape that 'Capt Pease has been speaking against Hayes & Hayes against Pease'. The real deception, though, was an argument about a dog. 'Capt Hayes has been the last three or four days making a great fuss about his dog, saying that it was stolen, taken up to Vailete by Tawai, by Mr McFarland's orders,' wrote Williams. Evidently Hayes had absconded while pretending to go to Vailete to fetch back the animal, because the consul added, 'this was a scheme of his to deceive me'.

Emily Hayes, summoned to the office, denied knowing anything at all about the plot. Then she contradicted herself by saying that she believed that Hayes, with Pease and the *Pioneer*, was headed for Niue, where a copra trader named McKenzie had stockpiled coconut oil for Mr Betham. Hearing this, Betham immediately boarded the *Adoph*, which was headed for Sydney via Niue, bearing a warrant signed by Williams — 'He has defrauded him so much, so I gave him the power to arrest him, also wrote to the chiefs telling them to assist Mr Betham.'

*

Then the consul returned to his work. Only four of the Pukapukans were still alive, which distressed him so greatly that he easily dismissed a report that the *Pioneer* was at Savaii, considering it so unlikely that it was not worth his attention. He should have paid more heed — as he wrote on 2 May, 'They have robbed J. Moss at Savaii — purchased 3000 yams from him promising to pay next morning and as a blind requested him to keep a fire burning all night so they should be off the place bright & early next morning for his pay, but when morning came there was no vessel she was gone.' Then the rogues had indeed sailed for Niue, getting there before

Betham and the *Adolph* arrived — 'They have not only defrauded Mr Betham, but robbed him by taking away the produce from Lupo at Savage Is., they having forged McFarland's name.'

By 27 September, when H.M.S. *Rosario*, the ship-of-war Williams had needed so much, finally hove to in the harbour, there were only Manihiki people to give evidence to the commander, all the Pukapuka men and women being dead. Then, having put their story on record, Moete and his charges were at last free to leave. Betham, who had returned from his fruitless hunt for Hayes, promised to give them work until he had a chance to return them to their island. For John Chauner Williams, the saga should have been over.

But there was one more disillusionment to come. George Boatswain, one of the two seamen who had taken his discharge from the *Pioneer*, turned up to give his own evidence to Captain Challis. 'Geo. Boatswain also appeared & made a statement against Capt Pease, how he took people off the islands & robbed them of their oil,' wrote Williams.

So the crimes that Captain Ben Pease had gossiped about were actually crimes that he had committed himself. Williams had been doubly fooled.

*

The old comrade Hayes had sailed off with was indeed a very tough customer. Though much smaller and skinnier than Bully Hayes, Ben Pease was notorious as a captain who personally flogged his crews. A tale told about him is that he punished a seaman by confining him in a hen-coop for a month. When accused of this, Pease retorted that it was a damned lie — it was a turkey-coop and it was only ten days. What he failed to add was that when he finally released the poor man, he then marooned him on a waterless atoll.

Born on Martha's Vineyard, Massachusetts, to a proud whaling family, he had cruised in the Orient with William Hayes and then moved to Ponape (now spelled Pohnpei), in the Caroline Islands, to set up a coconut plantation. Now, he robbed copra traders belonging to rival firms with no compunction, simply by force of arms. It was a brutal business, but it paid very well. In 1868, Pease had gone to Shanghai with enough money in his pocket to buy a fast ex-opium runner, a brig with two piratically raked masts called *Water Lily*. Taking her back to Ponape, he heavily armed and manned her, and renamed her *Pioneer*. Then he recommenced his foray about Micronesia, robbing lone traders of their stockpiled oil, or waiting until they were somewhere else, to take their stock unchallenged.

In December 1869, G.F. Hazard, a planter from New York, filed a complaint with the consul in Shanghai, accusing Pease of committing 'the most daring robberies, and even murders, with impunity'. While Hazard had been away from his trading store at Mili, in the Marshall Islands, Pease had arrived 'in the armed British brig *Pioneer*, belonging to Messrs. Glover & Co., Shanghai, and having landed with two boats full of men, armed to the teeth with breech-loading rifles, revolvers, & c., robbed my station of the whole of my property there'. This included pigs and poultry as well as trade goods, copra and oil, as Hazard made money out of supplying the whaling vessels. The *Pioneer* carried 'twenty old beach-combers' as a kind of marine squad, as well as a crew of well-armed Malays, he claimed.

It was a charge that set off an official hunt and was to change the history of not just Pease, but of Captain Hayes as well.

*

The copra and coconut oil trade owed much to whaling masters like Pease's more law-abiding relatives. Since about 1820, American whaling ships had prowled about the tropical islands and atolls of Micronesia in search of prey, but the general philosophy of the masters had been to keep to their business in deep waters and avoid sending boats onto the beaches. There was nothing much on shore that they considered of value, and the natives were regarded as untrustworthy — with good reason, as the average chief of an island in the Carolines, the Marshalls or the Gilberts (modern Kiribati) considered any foreign craft fair game, regardless of whether it was a canoe or a full-rigged ship. Reports of cuttings out and massacres were common.

But then the natives became addicted to tobacco, which made all the difference. American plug tobacco was plentiful and cheap, and the whaling captains carried lots of it, to sell to their crews as well as for trading purposes. The problem for the newly friendly chiefs and villagers was that they had nothing to exchange for the highly desirable stuff — apart from their good-looking girls. The shipmasters were still too wary to send boats on shore, so the natives paddled out in canoes, carrying the 'daughters' of the village (female slaves, in fact) to the ships. The scenes that resulted were sordid in the extreme, but it was the only way the villagers (and the whalemen) could satisfy their craving. Then, in 1849, the chiefs found that they had something else to sell — the oil that their villagers squeezed out of the inner meat of coconuts and used for cooking, as well as a cosmetic.

For the whole of history, the coconut palm had served Pacific Islanders in all kinds of ways. The trunks provided timber for framing houses, while the leaves could be used as thatch, and the shells were burned as fuel. The coir, or fibres in the husk, could be twisted into cords; it was this sennit that tied canoe planks together and was spun into rigging. The water inside the young nuts was not just thirst-quenching but healthy, too, providing an uncontaminated drink for atoll dwellers with little access to clean fresh water.

And the meat of older coconuts was scraped out and dried to make copra, which when packed into a mesh (made from the bases of coconut leaves) and pressed, produced a fine, clear oil. But while it had been used by the villagers for uncounted centuries, it was not the kind of oil that the whaling masters were hunting. In Europe in 1841, however, a process was invented for turning coconut oil into a mild soap with a luxuriously silky texture and none of the offensive smell associated with soap made from animal fat. And the whaling masters discovered another source of profit.

It was easy for them to take advantage of this. Not only did the ships carry stocks of barrel staves, but they had expert coopers to set them up into casks, so the oil was easily taken on board and stored for transport. The captains had already built up contacts among the island chiefs, who were easily bribed to order the villagers to extract a lot more oil from their nuts. There were even Englishmen and Americans on shore, miserable beachcombers who had run away from their ships, or had been castaway by shipwreck. Having survived months or years on the beach, with native women as partners and with a fluency in the language, they had the qualifications to be recruited as traders, easily set up with stores of tobacco and other trade goods, to buy and stockpile oil for the next time the ship called by.

The first whaling master to discover the benefit of this new trade was Captain Ichabod Handy of Fairhaven, Massachusetts. After years of sailing in the northwest Pacific, he could speak and understand the Gilbertese language, and had good relations with both the high chiefs and the missionaries who were starting to create a foothold in Micronesia. From 1849 to 1851, on the voyage of the whaling bark *Belle*, he collected 1850 barrels (just under 60,000 gallons) of coconut oil, which fetched $1 a gallon in Sydney — oil that he had bought for the equivalent of five cents a gallon in tobacco.

Unsurprisingly, other whaling masters were swift to follow his example, and not long after that opportunistic traders moved into the islands, getting to know the chiefs, clearing and planting coconut plantations, and establishing trading posts on shore. These copra traders, usually ex-seamen, were carried to the atolls by shipping captains, men who were commissioned by entrepreneurial merchants, like Robert Towns in Queensland, Godeffroy & Son in Samoa, and Charles Augustus Williams of Stonington, Connecticut. After landing a supply of casks, basic provisions and trade goods, the shipping captains then sailed away, returning months or years later to pick up the coconut oil that these men had collected.

It was not as easy as it may seem. While the people back home imagined life in a tropical paradise to be replete with lissom maidens, abundant food and an unvaryingly wonderful climate, it was in fact a precarious existence, demanding either remarkable courage or great desperation. The trader might fly his national flag over the thatched hut where he lived, but for protection he relied on the good nature of the island king. And, while keeping the high chief plied with gifts helped to ensure his safety from attack by the villagers, the resident copra trader was still vulnerable to the depredations of men like Bully Hayes and Ben Pease.

It was no wonder that so many became drunks.

*

It was one of these copra traders who provided the background to what happened next on the *Pioneer*. His name was Alfred Restieaux. A 38-year-old adventurer from England, he had been employed by Pease as a coconut oil trader on Ponape, and was there when Pease originally set out for Apia, headed for a surprise reacquaintance with Hayes.

According to Restieaux, Pease's reason for going to Samoa was that he wanted to negotiate a partnership with Theodore Weber, who was the manager of the German firm of Godeffroy & Son. It was a doomed ambition, Weber's philosophy being so different from Pease's rough and ready methods. When Theodore Weber interviewed a likely trader, he asked just three questions: 'Can you speak the language? Can you keep your mouth shut? Can you live among the natives without quarrelling with them?' And then, having received three affirmatives, he would advise the new recruit to steer clear of missionaries, and have his own woman, to avoid local jealousies.

After that, the recruit would be taken to a likely beach, where he and the woman would be set down with trade goods and the materials to build a house. The shipping captains, who dropped them there and returned at reasonably regular intervals to pick up their oil and dried coconut (copra), were paid a monthly stipend of $25, plus an incentive of three per cent of the profits, to keep them lively and hardworking. The system was working well, and it did not need interference from a man with very different methods. But when Weber informed Pease that Godeffroy did not need partners, Pease lingered in port, trying to smooth-talk his way into a better answer, and so he became reconnected with William Henry Hayes.

Restieaux also reveals what happened next, writing that Hayes talked Pease into spiriting him out of port by promising him half of the plunder they could pillage from the stations at Savaii and Niue, on the way to the northwest Pacific. Hayes reneged on the deal, claiming the lot once it had been stolen from the stations and was stowed in the holds of the *Pioneer* — 'Hayes said, No, it was all his, he had shifted it as freight,' wrote Restieaux. 'Pease called him a liar and said he was a trader, not a common carrier. Hayes called him a bloody pirate.' It looked for some moments as if the matter would be settled with pistols, but as Pease was by far the better shot, Hayes let the matter rest.

But then, they arrived at Ponape. It was August, 1870, and the American warship *Jamestown*, which had been hunting the Caroline Islands for Pease, had sailed for Hawaii just five or six weeks earlier. It would not be long before Commander Truxton came back, people said, as he was utterly determined to snare the pirate from Martha's Vineyard. 'Hayes worked on this and made Pease afraid to go to Shanghai,' remembered Restieaux. 'So he decided to send the brig to Shanghai in charge of Pitman the mate and stay at the islands until he saw how things went.'

Pease confirms that Pitman took over the *Pioneer* in an affidavit he wrote for the consul at Shanghai. After the vessel had arrived at his station in the Bonin Islands, he said, he found his wife, Susan Robinson Pease, in bad health, and so, 'I placed my brig under command of my chief officer, and dispatched her to Shanghai, expecting her back in a few months.' But five months passed by, with no sign of the *Pioneer*.

Growing impatient, Pease bought a schooner from a Frenchman, signed on a crew, and headed north of the Bonin Islands, to cruise all Micronesia in the hunt for Pitman, Hayes, and his vessel. Then he made the mistake of calling at Guam, where orders for his arrest were awaiting. No sooner was he reported in the harbour than a party of soldiers arrived on board, and he was forced off his craft and thrown into jail. Charged with piracy and murder, he was transferred to Manila, where he was confined in Bilibed prison to await the arrival of the first United States ship.

This turned out to be the mighty first-rate steamship-of-war U.S.S. *Colorado*, with Rear-Admiral John Rodgers, commander-in-chief of the Asiatic Fleet, on board. Carried in chains to Shanghai, Pease was put in prison there ... and managed to bribe his way out. After triumphantly returning to the islands, he bought another vessel, the schooner *Tom*, but never managed to catch up with Hayes. Instead, on 9 October 1874, he vanished. People whispered that he had been murdered by a black man named Spencer, but the full truth of his disappearance has never been known.

*

Ben Pease's biggest mistake had been to give Hayes the job of selling off the cargo that had accumulated in the holds of the brig. The moment the *Pioneer* arrived in Shanghai, Hayes sold all the goods that he and Pease had stolen — on his own account. 'So you see Pease got all the blame and Hayes the profit of that little transaction,' wrote Restieaux. Then Hayes took over command and sailed away. Once well offshore, he painted her a brilliant white and renamed her *Leonora*. And after that he sailed about Micronesia, setting up his own copra plantations and coconut oil trading stations, and robbing other traders, just as Pease had done, but keeping well out of Captain Pease's way.

CHAPTER 15

Neva

In Australia, the news of Hayes' sudden possession of Pease's brig came from Bangkok. 'By the arrival of the *Restless*,' revealed the *Brisbane Courier* on 17 August 1871, the editor had learned 'that Captain Hayes, who was reported to have been killed several times, is still alive and active. He is now in command of the brig *Leonora*, formerly the *Water Lily*.' The brig had arrived at Bangkok on 4 April 1871, in a leaky state, having run aground on the river Don–Nai while coming out of Saigon with a cargo of rice. As she was taking in over four inches an hour, she needed extensive repairs, so she was in port for two weeks.

'At 1.30 p.m. of April 27, Hayes again put to sea light,' the report went on, 'having had the *Leonora* repaired, caulked, and coppered, and leaving behind him his rice cargo as payment for the work, as well as other expenses incurred.' While the rice may have covered the total involved, as usual there was someone whom Hayes had cheated — 'It is reported that he chartered a small schooner from a Musselman at a monthly rate of charter to go to the Philippines, and thence to the South Sea Islands.' There, it was expected that the schooner would fall in with the *Leonora*, at which time 'the Musselman would for ever lose all vestige of his craft'.

Carrying on through the South China Sea to the Caroline Islands, Hayes arrived at Strong's Island (Kosrae) in October 1871, to discover a schooner named *Neva* lying at anchor. Intriguingly, though an American-built craft, she was flying French colours. Alfred Restieaux, who was now trading on behalf of Hayes (Pease having disappeared into prison), is the man who described what happened next. According to him, Hayes immediately introduced himself to the owner of the *Neva*, Captain Lechat, and invited him on board the *Leonora* for dinner and a gossip.

The two men got along well, as Lechat had an interesting history of trading in Japan. 'Hayes told him some of his adventures about the Islands,' Restieaux went on, adding, 'He could be very entertaining when he liked.' Then voices were lowered. Waxing confidential, Hayes told Lechat about a nearby lagoon that positively teemed with sea slugs, which fetched a good price in the Chinese and Japanese markets as the ingredient of a virility-restoring soup. Here, he said, the *bêche-de-mer* was so plentiful that in places it was almost knee-deep. No one had harvested it yet — 'I intend to work it when I get time but I am too busy,' he said.

'But someone else might find it,' the Frenchman protested, at which Hayes became very thoughtful. The problem, he confided, was finding a trustworthy manager, at which Lechat became meditative too. He took a while to mull it over, but the result was predictable — 'The Frenchman made a proposal to Hayes that they should work the *bêche de mer* together and share the profits.'

Captain Lechat's first mate was William Wawn, a Briton who had left the dusty desk of an architect's office for the romance of the sea and, like many young men of the age, had wandered the tropics in search of exotic adventure. 'At that time,' as he ruefully commented later, 'neither the Owner nor myself were acquainted with the true character of the notorious Bully Hayes.' When Lechat came to Wawn and the other two European seamen, Mac and Elsen, with the proposition that they should stay on shore with four of the Japanese seamen, to oversee them as they collected a cargo of *bêche-de-mer*, they were not at all averse 'to trying an island life for a change' — as Wawn put it — so agreed readily to the idea.

Then both the brig and the schooner prepared to sail, Hayes assuring Wawn that they were going to Samoa to get American papers for the schooner, but would be back in three months' time to pick them up, along with the *bêche-de-mer*. Then the two craft would sail with the cargo to Japan. It sounded perfectly plausible, so Wawn and the two others watched serenely as the two vessels set sail, and from then on they enjoyed a relaxed and pleasant time. Wawn lived amicably with a German trader named Hartmann, while Mac and Elsen lived with the island king on the other side of the island, close to the *bêche-de-mer* lagoon. They had plenty of trade goods and provisions, and the four Japanese who did most of the harvesting and processing were willing workers. Wawn, on his side of the isle, kept himself busy repairing a derelict cutter named *Coquette* that Hayes had left behind. He had been told that it had started life as the luxury yacht of a gentleman in Shanghai, but it could well have been the small schooner that Hayes had chartered from 'a Musselman' in Bangkok.

In January 1872, this peaceful existence was rudely disturbed when a trading ketch named *Lilian* arrived, carrying Lechat, who was in a towering rage. '*He son grand voleur; un sacré Corsair!*' he shouted when asked about Hayes, and dashed his hat on the sand. 'It appears from Lechat's story that instead of remaining on board the *Neva* & keeping her papers in his own possession, he had taken himself & his baggage onboard the *Leonora*,' Wawn recounted. Hayes' first mate, Ebenezer 'Aloe' Pitman (the same man who had been Ben Pease's chief officer), was then put in command of Lechat's schooner, with four seamen to take the places of the Japanese who had been left behind on Kosrae. This is confirmed by the logbook of the *Neva*. Aloe Pitman's first entry, dated 19 October 1871, runs, 'Came on board. Took charge of the schooner. Came on board from Brig *Leonora* the following persons — Charles Roberts, Maniller Peter, Wahoo John, Old Penna.' Charles Roberts was the first mate, while the others served as crew.

The two vessels then sailed in company to Mili, where part of a rice cargo was transferred to the schooner, along with a good portion of the trade goods the brig was carrying. Lechat should have become suspicious, because Hayes filled the gap this made in his manifest by robbing the station of James Lowther, an Englishman nicknamed 'Billy the Steward', who was a trader employed by Robert Towns. However, he remained tranquil, even though the fuss Lowther made about being plundered was answered with the threatening roar of cannon.

'Tuesday, Novr 7th, 1871. At 11 a.m. arrived the Brig *Leonora* — alias *Pioneer*, alias *Water-Lilly*,' Lowther wrote in the deposition he made at Sydney, a year later. According to his statement, Hayes sent a boat on shore with a polite invitation to come on board, which Lowther reluctantly accepted. Once on the deck of the brig, he learned that Hayes had come 'to settle up the affairs of Glover, Dow and Co., bankrupt'. After that came an offer to buy Lowther's oil for $20 per ton, along with Robert Towns' casks and tanks, which Hayes proposed to pay with 'a Bill on the French Government of New Caledonia'.

Lowther angrily refused, saying that it all belonged to Mr Towns, and he did not have the right to sell his employer's property, at which Hayes became menacing. Though he allowed the trader to go back to the beach, Lowther was deliberately led past four guns mounted on the deck, with more coming up from the hold, which made him very nervous. No sooner was Lowther on the beach than the island king paid a visit on board, and Hayes took the chance to demonstrate his mighty firepower by saluting the high chief's arrival with '3 broadside Guns to Starboard as the King went alongside over his head', while at the same time the American flag was smartly hoisted to the peak of the main mast.

Hayes gave the king a message for Lowther, which the island chief passed on as soon as he was back on shore — a warning that Hayes was prepared to seize the oil and casks by force. Still determined to safeguard Robert Towns' property, Lowther asked the king to store the casks of oil in his compound, which the chief agreed to do once Lowther had paid him $5 and one hundred heads of tobacco. However, no sooner were the barrels in transit to the king's house than Hayes came on shore with a gang and carried off the lot, handing Lowther a worthless receipt in exchange. Angry recriminations only made the situation worse — 'he jumped in a fearful rage, and told me if Jesus Christ and God Almighty stood at the door he would fight for it'. When Lowther protested that he would be answerable to Robert Towns for his actions, Hayes retorted, 'who was Towns, he was but a man'.

On 15 November, the *Leonora* sailed. It was not the last of the affair, however. A week later, to Lowther's horror, the brig reappeared, shrouded in smoke from another great firing of guns. This time the salute was to intimidate the king, as Captain Hayes proceeded to misappropriate a stock of oil that the island chief had been keeping on behalf of yet another firm, Capelle & Co. When the king objected, Hayes bought him off with cannon, powder and ball — and then he stole eight of Lowther's pigs. 'I remonstrated but he told me he would take all I had if I was not civil — became afraid for I did not know what extent he would go to.' And so, on 28 November, Lowther again stood helplessly on the beach as the *Leonora* stood to the south, 'Hayes taking my oil R. Towns and Co. Hogsheads and Tanks — my Pigs.'

On Friday, 5 January 1872, the *Leonora* hove into view again, 'with a cargo of copra bound for the Samoas'. For once it was a peaceful visit, everything worthwhile having been stolen already. Two days later the brig departed again, still with the tranquil Captain Lechat on board, on her way to Apia.

*

According to Restieaux, Hayes treated Lechat splendidly during the passage to Samoa, 'gave him one of his women and anything else he wanted and told him he was his partner until the Frenchman gave up the ship's papers'. But then they dropped anchor in Apia, and the moment the United States commercial agent, Jonas Coe, had stamped the new registry papers for the Frenchman's absent schooner — along with a change of name to *Emily* — Hayes showed his true colours. After deliberately getting into a political argument, as Alfred Restieaux related, Hayes called Lechat 'a damned son-of-a-bitch. What, said the Frenchman. You dare to call me a French gentleman that. By God sir.

If I had my revolver here, I will shoot you like the dog you are. My revolver is always ready, said Hayes and knocked him down with his fist. He then beat him and kicked him most unmercifully and almost killed the poor fellow and then put him on shore'.

The wonder is that Bully Hayes had had the nerve to put into Apia, let alone play such a blatant trick there. However, his arrival made so little stir that John Chauner Williams did not even note it in his diary. The British Consul, like all the European residents, was preoccupied with an outbreak of tribal war that threatened to devastate the village, and the man with the biggest grudge against Hayes, Montague Betham, was preoccupied with fighting with a Captain Dunlop, whose copra he had seized in lieu of repayment of a debt. Nor was the wretched Lechat given any mention in Williams' journal, though he did note that '1 French citizen' turned up at a meeting of Europeans to discuss the precarious peace in Apia. Then Lechat disappeared from the island, having chartered the ketch *Lilian* to take him back to Kosrae, where he arrived in January 1872, to tell Wawn the bad news.

William Wawn, once he had digested the full extent of Lechat's foolishness, was not at all sympathetic, particularly when Lechat tried to appropriate the little *Coquette*, which Wawn had finished repairing. 'As the partnership — Hayes & L. — appeared to be a thing of the past,' he wrote, 'it was now Every man for himself.' He and Mac formed their own partnership, and seized the *Coquette* and ship's boat that Hayes had left, in lieu of the wages they had never received. 'L- called us very hot names in consequence', but it made no difference to their determination to sail to Ponape on the *Coquette*, towing their goods behind them in the boat. Then the American missionary on the neighbouring island of Ebon, Benjamin

Galen Snow, wrote a letter to the king, in which he said that if the white men did not leave Kosrae, he would not visit the island any more, but send a man-of-war, instead. Accordingly, the island chief stalled the flow of food to Wawn and his companions, which speeded up the provisioning of the *Coquette* for the voyage.

Lechat was ordered to leave the island, too, the king helping him out by selling him the long boat of a wrecked whaler and the wood to half-deck it. And so the erstwhile complement of the schooner *Neva* made their way to Ponape. Wawn and Mac, with the woman Mac had taken as his wife, and a number of other natives who wished to leave, being 'heartily sick of the tyranny of the old king', sailed first, in the leaky *Coquette*. Two weeks later, Lechat, Elsen and the Japanese followed in the hastily prepared long boat.

And so the Reverend Benjamin Snow's wish was granted and Kosrae was free of the corrupting influence of the South Sea traders — for a while.

*

On 19 February 1872, the strange fact that Captain Hayes had had the nerve to come back to Samoa caught the attention of the inhabitants of Apia in the most dramatic fashion possible. Early in the morning, the rapidly approaching smoke of a steamer was spied, and shortly after that a ship-of-war appeared in the harbour, flying British colours and firing a salute of nine guns. Then, as Williams recorded, 'as soon as the Pilot boat was alongside them the British Colors were substituted by the American — the vessel soon came to Anchor when a boat with Marines was despatched to Capt. Hayes' vessel the *Leonora* & he was taken off as a prisoner to the *Narragansett*'.

That was excitement enough, but more was to come. When Williams returned to his office, after yet another meeting with the local chiefs about the worrying outbreak of tribal hostilities, it was to find a letter from Rev. Thomas Powell in Tutuila, with the news that Captain Meade of the *Narragansett* had annexed the port of Pago Pago, after negotiating a treaty with chief Mauga. This put the British Consul into a quandary. Naturally, he was a loyal and patriotic Briton, but there was always the chance that the sight of American naval power would discourage the chiefs from waging war with each other. Accordingly, his approach was cautious when he paid his official visit on board the steamship-of-war next day. 'Saw Capt. Hayes on deck, shook hands with him,' he wrote, and kept silent about the rest of the call.

There was much more to note after Captain Meade returned the visit the next day — 'told me he intended to tow the brig to Tutuila then ballast her & send off to California with Capt. Hayes in charge of an officer & six of his crew'. Meade's charge was that 'Capt. Hayes had violated the Navigation laws, for he flogged his Crew, knocked them down', and had marooned one of his chief mates on a lonely atoll. 'Moreover he was too heavily manned, 16 of a crew, has 6 Guns & a lot of small arms.' Captain Meade had found out how and where Hayes got his money, too, as he had heard that Hayes had misappropriated 2500 bags of rice, out of a cargo of 3000 bags that he was supposed to carry to a proper destination. All this, he said, had been taken from the evidence of one of the scoundrel's own crew.

Williams must have murmured something about Hayes' miraculous escape from his last imprisonment in Apia, because Meade went on to vow that this rogue, whom he described in his own papers as a 'swindler, a scoundrel and a dangerous man', would never get away from him. Betham had evidently been in touch, because the American commander then went on to observe that if he were Betham, he would send to California to claim the *Leonora* in lieu of all the money owed to him by Hayes. Meditated Williams after Meade had gone, 'By the Captain's conversation I think Hayes is a doomed man.'

All greater the shock, then, when a man raced into the consul's office the next day, exclaiming that Captain Hayes had been acquitted — '& quite free, for he had just heard it from Mr Coe. We replied he must surely be mistaken'. But no, it was true. 'This is indeed astonishing news,' Williams wrote in wonder, 'especially after what the captain had said to me.'

Newspaper editors, once they heard about it, were equally bemused. 'The *Narragansett* visited the island of Apia, on the 18th of February, and detained the brig *Leonora*, W.H. Hayes, master, on suspicion of cruising about in an unlawfully armed vessel, levying contributions on the native chiefs among the Islands,' revealed the *Press* of Christchurch, on 16 April, 'but there being no evidence to sustain the charge, Hayes was released.' The *Queenslander*, three days earlier, had published the same news, but with the extra titbit that Captain Hayes, once released, was 'brought back in triumph to his own ship, which immediately displayed a variety of bunting in honor of the event'.

The editor of the *Maitland Mercury*, knowing that there was a lot of local interest, waxed still more eloquent, musing on 4 April that Hayes had got away with his crimes yet again, 'being sharper than those with whom he had been dealing'. The captain of the *Susannah Booth*, just arrived from Apia, had reported that Hayes had been charged with piracy, on the basis that his brig was both over-manned and armed like a privateer, but, when a search of the *Leonora* was made, 'no arms were found, and his crew was proved to be short of the required number'.

Evidently, the crew had stowed the guns and cutlasses in some deep and secret place in the hold, or had sent all the arms on shore, and numbers were down because the five men sent to the *Neva* had not been replaced. Also, according to Restieaux, 'Frank Benson and the mate both perjured themselves and got him off', Frank Benson being one of Hayes' interpreters. Whatever the ploy, the notorious Captain Hayes had evaded the long arm of the law yet again.

Hayes returned in triumph to Mili, where the logkeeper of the *Neva* noted that the brig came into sight on 11 April 1872, and dropped anchor the next morning. 'Capt. Hayes and a passinger in the Brig came on board the schooner,' the entry ran on. The passenger was the American actor-turned-auctioneer, J.G. Alvord. According to James Lowther, who had watched the re-arrival of the *Leonora* with dismay, Hayes passed off Alvord 'as the Vice-Consul of the Samoas, and the man acknowledged the same'. Privately, though, Alvord told Restieaux that he was simply travelling for his health — which was plausible enough, as he was addicted to kava, the soporific drink of the Pacific.

Hayes also lied to Lowther that Robert Towns' shipping captain, John Daly, would not be back at Mili until August, meaning that Lowther, who was out of trade goods and provisions, needed to get to the station on Nonouti to apply for relief. Lacking any other transport, he was forced to buy passage on the *Leonora* for himself and his family, paying with the 589 gallons of coconut oil he had accumulated since the last time he was robbed.

On 27 April, the schooner was painted with her new name, *Emily*. Seven days later, Aloe Pitman went on board the *Leonora* to pilot the brig to Majuro Atoll, and a seaman named Powless, who had been hired in Samoa and had moved onto the *Emily* to act as first mate, took temporary command, while Charles Roberts was sent back to the *Leonora*. Once all that was accomplished, along with some shifting about of cargo, the *Leonora* sailed — only just in time, because two days later the British ironclad *Barossa* arrived. The commander, Lewis J. Moore, sent officers on board the *Emily*, ex-*Neva*, to inspect her papers, but everything was in order. And, of course, Powless had no idea of where Hayes might be. So, by 9 May, when the *Leonora* returned (still with Lowther on board) and Pitman took back the command of the schooner, the *Barossa* was well away.

Two days later, the *Leonora* weighed anchor and left the schooner behind again, this time headed off on a much longer voyage. Pitman was told to cruise about Mili, collecting what cargo he could while Hayes sailed away on a cruise 'to put men on different stations'. Then, once the *Leonora* had come back and resupplied the *Emily*, they would talk about where to go next.

At least, that was the plan.

*

The first call the *Leonora* made was at Providence Island (Ujelang) which, as Lowther noted in his continuing diary, they reached on 16 May. Four days later, 'Hayes and his ship's company went on shore and secured by force 5 natives and brought them on board: after detaining them about 5 hours dismissed them, giving them a few trinkets and telling them he was going to land his men.' Having suitably cowed the inhabitants, Hayes landed two traders, 'namely, Henry Gardiner, an American, and William Knight, British', with a gang of thirteen natives from other parts of the Pacific. Their job was to clear the ground for a coconut plantation and set up a trading post, which would be the hub of Captain Hayes' operations in the Pacific.

From there the brig cruised widely about the eastern Caroline Islands, Hayes landing traders and bringing others off, and demanding money as 'payment for Glover, Dow and Co. of Shanghai' from rival traders, just as he had with Lowther, who was a cynical witness to all this. On 25 May, the *Leonora* was at Pingelap, where Alfred Restieaux brought his wife, Letia, on board, along with all the oil and copra he had collected, so he is a witness to this voyage, too. Five days later, the *Leonora* was back at Kosrae, where the former crewmen of the *Neva* were long gone, having sailed to Ponape — 'Came to an anchor in the South Harbour and demanding payment for Glover, Dow and Co of Shanghai,' wrote Lowther, without naming the victim of Hayes' intimidating tactics this time.

On 9 June, the brig dropped anchor again at Providence, and there, returning to his old business of blackbirding, Hayes and his men 'hunted the bush for the natives'. They captured fifteen, who were thrust on board, and over the following days more were kidnapped, including three women who were distributed among the crew — '1 to the mate,' wrote Lowther, '1 to Allen, 1 to Bill, both the latter before the mast.' On that same day, 14 June 1872, the trader wrote, 'This night he committed a rape on the little girl he got from M'Caskill against her will.'

M'Caskill was Pingelap, so the girl must have been kidnapped the previous month, though neither Lowther nor Restieaux mentioned her being lured on board, or how she had been treated in the meantime. That same night, six of the captured Ujelang natives did their best to run away, but were recaptured within hours — 'Taken aboard, and got a punching about the head with Hayes' fist — got all their eyes blackened: they continued to cry. To punish them still further he committed a rape on the young girl of Providence.' The men pleaded with him to let 'their daughter' alone, so he tied their hands to the cable chain, and each had a belaying pin thrust across his open mouth and tied about the back of the head, to shut up his noise. Then Hayes sent the two girls he had violated to Lowther's native wife, 'to administer to their wants'.

And so Lowther's litany of brutality continued. Natives made more attempts to escape, only to be recaptured. Then they were robbed. Hayes sailed away from Ujelang with twenty tons of dried coconut and the masts and rigging of two canoes on board, leaving a warning that by the time he returned the inhabitants must have a cargo of arrowroot ready, or face the destruction of their village. At other islands he either purchased what he wanted with liquor or simply carried it away by force. A foremast hand who annoyed him had four teeth knocked out with a belaying pin. As Restieaux observed later, 'every crime was committed on that ship except murder', and if Hayes had killed the Malay seaman whose jaw he had broken, 'then murder would have been added to the list'.

For James Lowther, the terrible voyage was about to come to a sudden end. On 22 August 1872, when Hayes found the schooner *Ida* of Sydney at Tarawa, he ordered Lowther to take his family off his ship and buy passage for the rest of the way from the *Ida*'s Captain Eury. Naturally, the coconut oil Lowther had paid for passage to Nonouti was not refunded. But he had his revenge when he finally arrived in Sydney in March 1873, by copying the relevant part of his diary for Robert Towns, to be used in evidence against Hayes.

*

The reliability of Lowther's hostile testimony is a matter for debate. The Pingelap girl confirmed the rape six or seven years later, when she talked to another planter, George Westbrook, but her story differed in important details. The assault did not happen on board the brig, for a start. Captain Hayes, she said, took her for a walk on the beach, and when she came back she was bleeding. Hayes said she had simply fallen and staked herself on a stick, but she told Westbrook that she was so badly injured she could not be any man's wife. According to what she also told Westbrook, the rape occurred at Swain's Island — Olosega, in the Samoan group — and not at Ujelang. And it happened after Lowther had left the brig, not while he was there, so evidently he was reporting gossip as if he had actually been there.

James Lowther was aware that he might not be believed. He added a note to the transcription, saying that Hayes had put a trader by the name of 'James Gascon' (Jim Garstang, whom Restieaux called a murderer) on Drummond Island (Tabiteuea), and two more, Frank Benson and Henry Mulholland, on Matthew Island (Abaiang), who 'will confirm what I have stated in these writings, but I am sorry to say you will have to intimidate them, or charge them as an accomplice'.

*

While Hayes was robbing traders and intimidating natives in the Carolines, the schooner *Emily* (ex-*Neva*) was cruising the isles and atolls about Mili, dropping traders and collecting copra and coconut oil, just as Pitman had been instructed to do. And all the time their provisions were running out, as they waited with increasing desperation for the *Leonora* to come with much-needed supplies.

On 21 May 1872, the mate, John Powless, noted that they were taking passengers on board — '5 males, 4 females, 8 natives to work, cook, mate and master, making in all 20 souls'. The eight men who had come on board 'to work' were paying for their passage with labour, so helped weigh the anchor at the start of a miserable little voyage. The weather was rough, the mainsail split, and the eight native seamen did not understand a word of English. Captain Pitman 'and self are obliged to be everywhere and do everything all at once — the best part of our running rigging is rotten but the hull of the schr is staunch and tight'. The cook, an old whaleman, was seasick every time the *Emily* was in the open sea; still worse, if possible, he turned out to be a thief, and was cruel to the ship's monkey. 'Taken altogether,' the mate mused ironically on 10 June, 'Capt. Pitman and John N. Powless have had a gay time of it.'

By 10 August, they were back at Mili, having delivered all their passengers — including the native men who had worked their passage — to their various atolls. But still there was no sign of the *Leonora* with supplies. The ropes, like the men's tempers, were fraying, and the crew were desperate for 'civilised' food. Even local food was short, as the breadfruit season was over, so they were existing on a few provisions they had begged from a passing German vessel. As Powless wrote, it was imperative 'to go somewheres to get something to eat'.

Five days later, they set sail for Arno Atoll, to see if they could beg provisions from 'George the Trader', a man who worked for Hayes and might have been better supplied than they were. 'At noon got under weigh for Arno with all sail set,' the logbook ran. 'Our crew consists as follows: E.A. Pitman, Master, John N. Powless, mate, Peter of Guam, cook, Peter of Rotumah, seaman, Tony, a Japanese cooper, Johnny, a native of one of those islands (civilised), 2 large dogs and 3 cats.'

On the way out they were brought to by U.S.S. *Narragansett*, and were questioned severely and given a stern warning. Then, when they got to Arno, George the Trader informed them that Captain Hayes had ordered him not to give them anything. Furious, Pitman bought fifty barrels of coconut oil to top up their freight, for which he paid his own money, and then he marched back on board and told Powless that he had given up hope of ever seeing Hayes again and was heading for the next proper port. Everyone on the battered schooner was delighted with the idea, so they foraged coconuts from the beach, spent their last trade goods on preserved pandanus paste, and shaped a course for Honolulu.

It was a long, hungry passage. As Powless dryly observed, old coconuts and pandanus paste were 'not food calculated to produce a great amount of gaiety in a seaman's heart'. The cats and dogs survived on vermin, and escaped being eaten themselves only because they were so thin. But at long, long last, the schooner raised her destination, docking at Oahu on 23 October — and the crew immediately filed a suit for wages, which they won.

The schooner was sold at a marshal's auction on 15 November 1872, along with her tackle and cabin furniture, and so 'John N. Powless, Peter, Tony, Miho, and Peter of Guam' got their rightful pay, according to the legal notice. The freight had already been claimed and sold by Aloe Pitman. He donated $5 to the Bethel and $5 to the missionary paper, *The Friend*, pocketed the rest and headed back to the States on the steamer *Ajax*.

Then, once back in Massachusetts, he spent a respectable retirement in Marblehead, one of the few men in history to cheat Hayes and get away with it.

CHAPTER 16

Leonora

It was still August 1872 when the *Leonora* arrived back at Mili, so Hayes had only just missed the *Emily*, ex-*Neva*. His own provisions were running low, but he waited as long as he could before he decided that the schooner must have been wrecked, and prepared to make sail. As merciless and resourceful as ever, he steered back to Pingelap, where he held two chiefs hostage until the locals had provisioned the ship with coconuts, and after that he sailed to Kosrae, to make up the shortfall in copra and oil.

Once the anchor was dropped he sent everyone on shore, save Alvord and himself, and would not allow them back or give them any food until they had collected enough oil to make up for what Pitman was supposed to have delivered. Finally satisfied, he took the complement on board and set sail for Samoa — missing H.M.S. *Blanche* by just a handful of days. In October, the master of the naval supply bark *Tusso* told the shipping reporter of the *Sydney Morning*

Herald that H.M.S. *Blanche* had arrived at Kosrae in September, hot on the trail of Bully Hayes, only to learn that the *Leonora* had sailed for unknown parts just a few days earlier.

In December, the *Leonora* arrived back in Apia, where Hayes and Restieaux learned what had really happened to the *Emily*, ex-*Neva*. 'A ketch owned by Sam Dowsett of Honolulu came in. This was Christmas 1872,' Restieaux remembered. 'Captain English came and told Hayes and myself all about the schooner.' Not only did he reveal that Pitman had stolen the schooner, but also that the *Emily* 'was sold by auction and fetched just about enough to pay the men and other expenses'. William Wawn (who was now a shipping captain for Godeffroy & Son) heard that Pitman had sold the cargo for as much as $1000 — 'gave 50 to the Missionary society & then cleared out to San Francisco'.

Wawn, like Restieaux, was amused. Hayes, on the other hand, was 'like a madman', as Restieaux described. 'If ever I get hold of that son-of-a-bitch Pitman,' he raged, 'I will not quite kill him but I will leave him so that he wished he was dead.' It was impossible to hunt 'that bastard Pitman' down, however, as both Honolulu and San Francisco were 'altogether too dangerous' for him, as Hayes regretfully concluded.

'So,' Restieaux concluded with a smile, 'you see rogues do not always prosper.'

*

Alfred Restieaux had been mightily relieved to walk off the deck of the *Leonora*. The promissory note Hayes had given him for the oil and copra he had collected at Pingelap turned out to be worthless, but at least he had escaped. And, immediately after Captain English had related with relish the story of Pitman absconding with the schooner *Emily*, someone else in Apia got the better of Bully Hayes, which made Restieaux the narrator of one of the most popular stories ever about the so-called buccaneer.

Going home in a vile temper after learning how Pitman had cheated him, Hayes found Emily in an equally bad mood. A neighbouring publican, who was known familiarly as 'Black Tom', had been stealing her chickens, and she knew it for a fact, because she had found him stuffing feathers inside a pillow case. So Hayes stamped round to Black Tom's grogshop, which had a fine display of bottles behind the bar. Wreaking his wrath and frustration, Hayes smashed the lot with a few hearty swipes of his cane, raging at the secretly smiling owner meantime. And after that, Hayes went home. Feeling much better, he ate a hearty supper and went to bed.

In the morning, however, a bill arrived for damages. Black Tom had filed a complaint with the American Consul, along with a detailed inventory of the damage. And, rage again as he might, Hayes had to pay up in full before the consul would consent to clear the *Leonora* for her next voyage.

The joke was enjoyed by the entire village (except, perhaps, for Emily Hayes), as everyone knew that the smashed bottles had been filled with coloured water, and not the expensive liquor that Tom had claimed for, and that Hayes was forced to repay.

'Tom reopened in grand style,' Restieaux related, and this time, the contents of the bottles were real. A fiery spirit that had been known as 'Hamburg blue ruin' was rechristened 'the Bully brand', as Restieaux recounted, 'and became the most popular drink in Apia'.

*

It was imperative for Hayes to get out of Apia, no matter how expensive leaving port might be. In June 1872, a tough Imperial Statute known as the Kidnapping Act had been passed, empowering British Navy commanders to seize any vessels suspected of capturing their cargoes of natives. No less than nine British men-of-war were either hunting the Pacific, or in the process of being commissioned in Sydney, and one of these, an enormous 1790-ton screw-sloop heavily armed with six 64-pounder guns, H.M.S. *Dido*, was currently in Fiji. The Gilbert Islands, where Hayes knew the lagoons, seas and islets well, was a much safer option than lying exposed in Apia harbour, and so that is where he fled. By March 1873, he was in the Tuvalu Group — and because Restieaux was also in the area, having been shipped to Nukufetau to set up a trading post for Godeffroy & Son, he was a witness to much of what happened next.

Restieaux also knew the background, because he had been on board the *Leonora* when, late the previous year, Hayes had called at Abaiang, an islet to the north of the main island of Tuvalu.There, Hayes had found a trader by the name of George Phillimore Winchcombe, collecting copra and oil for one of Robert Towns' shipping captains, John Daly. Originally from Bristol, England, Winchcombe was a shiftless, devious fellow who told people he was qualified as a lawyer, but did not seem very intelligent. Hayes had summed him up as a pigeon ready for the plucking, and now, on this second visit, he reckoned it was time to take advantage of his naiveté.

According to the story Restieaux told later, Hayes walked into Winchcombe's trading post and said, 'Have you seen anything of Daly?'

'No,' said Winchcombe. It was strange, as he went on to muse aloud, that Captain Daly should be so late, as he was usually punctual.

'Well,' said Hayes. 'You are not likely to see Daly again. He is in gaol for killing his cook. If he does not get hung, he is sure of a long term of imprisonment.'

This, as it happens, was perfectly true. Captain John Daly, who operated the *Lady Alicia* on behalf of Robert Towns, had been arrested soon after dropping anchor in Sydney, on 22 January 1873, just two months earlier. His passengers, Rev. William Osborne and family, had reported that Daly's cook, Michael McCarthy, had committed suicide during the voyage. The cook was hopeless at his job, and after Captain Daly had given him a thorough scolding, McCarthy had jumped overboard, to meet his doom. So, when Hayes had last seen the papers, the notice from the Water Court reported that Daly was incarcerated, awaiting trial and sentencing. What he perhaps did not know — and Winchcombe certainly did not — was that though convicted, Captain Daly had been let off with a five-shilling fine, and was currently clearing out for the islands again.

George had heard enough of the scandal to believe Hayes, so immediately panicked about his future. Listening to this, Hayes said, 'the best thing you can do is to sell out to me and leave'. Winchcombe dithered, as it did not seem right to sell Daly's property, even if he were due for the hangman's noose, but then Hayes warned him that as long as he stayed on the island his life was in danger. This flustered George even more, so when Hayes promised to put him on 'a good missionary island, Nui, in the Ellice Group', where he would not only be safe but was bound to make a fortune, George was easily persuaded to take himself and all his goods on board the *Leonora*.

It was a three-month voyage to Nui, which must have been an interesting time for the innocent Englishman. The crew was the usual rough and polyglot lot, the first mate being a Dane by the name of Nahnsen, and the second mate a half-caste Fijian, Bill Hicks. The three seamen were German, English and Malay, while the carpenter, Ah-So, and the cook, Ah-Ho (who had two wives on board), were both Chinese. There was also a trader by the name of Henry Mulholland, but he was put on shore at Abaiang to take over Winchcombe's post, which should have made George Winchcombe suspicious, but apparently did not.

When they arrived at Nui, it was too rough to land. Winchcombe wanted to go on to Samoa, but Hayes put into neighbouring Nukufetau instead. 'I will land you here,' he told George; 'and if you do not like the place I will take you to Nui when I return.' There was the slight problem that he had very few trade goods to spare, but there was enough for Winchcombe to go on with in the meantime, and he expected to be back in two months, with plenty. 'So,' related Restieaux, 'he gave him a few pieces of cloth, a few shirts, no hardware, no tobacco — not a smoke for himself.'

'How about provisions?' said George.

'I have none for myself,' said Hayes, which puzzled Winchcombe, as all his provisions had been put on board at Abaiang. Then Hayes said, 'I suppose that damned Chinaman has used them.' The mate was laughing, somewhat to Winchcombe's puzzlement, but Hayes simply promised that when he came back with the trade goods, he would bring provisions too.

Winchcombe, who, like all the European traders, was convinced he would break out with huge black boils and die in agony if he lived on native food, cried, 'But what am I to eat in the meanwhile?'

'Eat?' echoed Hayes. 'Nukufetau is the Garden of the Pacific. Plenty of breadfruit, yams, taro, bananas. In fact, everything a man needs.' And then, when Winchcombe still protested, he gave him an order on Alfred Restieaux, who had his own Godeffroy-funded trading post on the island, and sailed away.

Restieaux was extremely surprised when the stranger turned up with a long list of what he needed. He was short of provisions himself, as the Godeffroy vessel was overdue, but he did give Winchcombe what tobacco he could spare, and from then on helped him keep body and soul together. This challenge included the new trader's love life. When Winchcombe noticed that Restieaux had a native wife, he asked him if she had come to Nukufetau with him. As it happened, though Restieaux and Letia had been together for some years, including a stint on Pingelap, she was originally from Nukufetau. So, after he had been assured that she was a local girl, George went a-courting — 'he used to put on clean clothes, oil his hair & parade before the school every morning whistling & singing to draw attention to himself when they came out. He would shake hands, touch them on the breast, then touch himself and say: Wifey you me?' — which the whole village found extremely funny.

But he was lucky enough, eventually, to find the amenable Jemima, and so he settled down.

*

After leaving Nukufetau, Bully Hayes cruised the islands and filled his holds with both legally and illegally acquired copra and oil. In August 1873, he turned back for Apia, where the shipping correspondent for New Zealand papers reported that the *Leonora* dropped anchor on the 13th with a full cargo. 'She is under the command of your old Auckland friend Captain Hayes,' the reporter dryly added.

While it was risky for Hayes to return to Apia, both H.M.S. *Conflict* and H.M.S. *Blanche* being in the area at the time, he had a compelling reason. When he had set sail from Apia so hastily, he had left Emily pregnant with another set of twins. This could not have made her very happy, as she had the seven-year-old girls, Leonora and Laurina, to look after. However, the new set were a boy and a girl, so Hayes at last had a son.

Having admired the additions to his family, he set sail again in October, running into the bark *Metaris* on the way out. As the *Fiji Times* noted on 27 October, the *Leonora* was making an involuntary sternboard at the time, surging backwards instead of sailing ahead. Many years later, Thomas Brownell, a deck officer on the *Metaris*, wrote a reminiscent account of the embarrassing accident, which the *Auckland Star* published on 13 December 1919. 'As soon as the anchor was off the ground the *Leonora* began to drift rapidly towards our vessel,' he remembered. As both captain and first mate were on shore, the writer was in charge, and when he saw what was happening he ordered the crew to pay out 'all the cable the barque possessed in order to get out of the way of the drifting brig, but to no purpose'.

With a shuddering crash, the *Leonora* collided with their jibboom, 'carrying it away, and also the fore-top-gallant mast, and then drifted clear of us, and again dropped anchor'. While the writer was supervising the clearing of the wreckage, Hayes came on board, 'and most courteously apologised for the damage done, and paid for it. He could be a gentleman when the occasion required,' the writer admitted. 'Next day,' he went on, 'the *Leonora* left Apia for the purpose of going to Levuka, but when we reached there some days later, there was no *Leonora*. But H.M.S. *Blanche* was there, a fact of which the acute Bully Hayes had evidently got wind, so he gave Levuka a wide berth.'

*

There was a veritable fleet of Royal Navy ships to keep clear of — H.M.S. *Dido*, which had been stationed in Fiji, was threading through the Gilbert Islands on her way to Sydney, preceded by H.M.S. *Clio*; H.M.S. *Basilisk* was hunting the waters north of New Zealand, her commander emboldened by his capture of the blackbirder *Krishna*; and H.M.S. *Rosario* was on her way to Levuka, where H.M.S. *Conflict* was also stationed. But, though Hayes did not know it, fate had granted him a temporary respite — by nothing less than another rumour of his own death. And, even more ironically, it came from the warship he so narrowly avoided in Levuka.

On 2 October, while the *Leonora* was still in Apia, the editor of the *Evening News* of Sydney reported that he had received a letter from Melbourne, written by one of the officers of H.M.S. *Blanche*, 'relating the end of the notorious Captain Hayes — freebooter, swindler, pirate and murderer, who has at length met with his just deserts in the shape of a long rope, a short shrift, and a swing from the yard arm of the *Blanche*.

'This ruffian has been for years known as the pest of the Pacific,' the letter ran on, 'and his last exploit was only in keeping with a lifetime of similar atrocities.' According to the story, Hayes had put into one of the Tokelauan Islands on a kidnapping mission, enticing large numbers of natives on board, trapping them below, and then destroying their canoes by dropping large weights on them. 'The *Blanche* chased him, caught him red-handed, and after a trial at Levuka, Captain Hayes was sent aloft to the fore yardarm by the agency of a rope, at the end of which a number of natives hauled with hearty good-will.'

If true, the editor remarked at the end, Captain Simpson of the *Blanche* had done mankind a service, but in the meantime he was treating it as just another rumour. 'Further information on the subject will be looked for with anxiety.'

*

Unaware of this, Hayes had wasted no time in getting away from Apia, so was not there to witness a personal tragedy. Amy Williams, the wife of the British Consul, John Chauner Williams, who was friendly with Emily Hayes, recorded on 3 November 1873 that the baby girl was ill with thrush; that she had had it for ten days and was 'very bad', and that 'they want me to give her medicines'. Next day, Amy wrote, 'I prescribed for the poor baby, but it was no use, she died yesterday afternoon.'

At the same time that Emily was mourning the loss of her third daughter, Hayes was paying a call on Winchcombe at Nukufetau. According to Restieaux, who heard the story from Winchcombe two days later, Hayes asked first how much copra Winchcombe had collected over the four months that had elapsed since he had dropped him here.

'Three bags,' said George.

'No more than that?'

'I had no suitable trade.'

'Well, where is the trade?'

'Gone.'

'Gone where?'

'Well, you gave me no provisions and I had to live.'

'Oh,' said Hayes, and then shrugged. 'Well, you had better pack up & come on board. I have brought back Tahiti Bob. His wife belongs here. Perhaps he will do better.'

'How about my wife?'

'Ah, bring her on board of course. I will take you to Nui as we agreed.'

So Tahiti Bob came from the brig to the beach, and the same boat that had brought him took George and Jemima on board. As Restieaux related, 'George said Hayes was very kind, invited him into the cabin, brought out a bottle of gin & said: "You know, I do not drink myself but that is no reason you should not help yourself." He then poured out a liberal nip which was disposed of. Presently, Hayes pretended to hear himself called. "Hello, I am coming," he said. "Excuse me, George. I must go on deck. But do not spare the bottle. There is plenty more where that come from."

'He then went on deck. Instead of going forward he touched Bill Hicks, a Fiji half caste who was now 2nd Mate, on the shoulder & they went and peeped down the skylight. George got up & walked around. Then he filled a tumbler with gin, drank it off, filled another good nip & sat down. Hayes laughed & went forward. In about half an hour he went below. There was George under the table, the bottle almost empty. He called a couple of men who carried George up & laid him on the main hatch. Hayes then took Jemima by the hand and led her below. She said afterwards as soon as they got in the cabin Hayes shut the door, downed her on the sofa & so forth.'

When Hayes came back on deck, he found that 'George, who wore no trousers, had kicked off his sulu & was exposed to public view. The mate, a German named Hansen or Nansen, had been doing something with a pot of coal tar & brush, came along & playfully put a little dab of tar on George's person. Hayes, who had finished amusing himself with Jemima said: "Damn it all, do it properly." So he took the brush & painted poor George, his belly, thighs, backside & all rubbing it well in. He then called Bill Hicks & said: "Take two men in the boat & put that fellow on shore. Chuck him on the beach. Anywhere. He is a disgrace to the ship."

'About 4 o'clock a boy came & told me George was lying on the beach dead. Hayes had killed him. I went & looked: but he was only dead drunk & in a nice mess. I told the natives to carry him to his house.' At that, Tahiti Bob objected, saying that the house belonged to him now. Restieaux protested that if Winchcombe was left in the sun, he would die, but Tahiti Bob was adamant, so Jemima's family was persuaded to take the hapless fellow into their home. He was as much a nuisance for his in-laws as he was for Restieaux, but Jemima never stopped claiming to anyone who would listen that 'George Phillimore Winchcombe was the Strongest & Handsomest man in the South Seas'. 'Perhaps he was,' Restieaux mused, 'but I am no Judge of Beauty.'

*

On 17 January 1874, having dealt with Winchcombe, Hayes was back at Mili, awaiting a delivery that he had negotiated during the short time he had been at Apia. This was with Williams and Macfarlane, the Williams being Samuel, the son of John Chauner Williams, who was in charge of the consulate in the absence of his father. The other partner was Mary Macfarlane, Samuel's sister, who had married a scion of the Auckland firm of Henderson and Macfarlane, general merchants and island traders. The delivery they had commissioned was of a worm-eaten ketch called *E.A. Williams*, which Hayes was to sell to an island chief. And the supercargo on board was an eighteen-year-old adventurer, George Lewis Becke, who called himself 'Louis Becke'.

Born 18 June 1855, in Port Macquarie, New South Wales, Becke was the son of a clerk of petty sessions. Undoubtedly, he was expected to follow in his father's path, and be tied to a dusty desk for the whole of his working life. Instead, like many young men of the time, he was seduced by the allure of the tropical Pacific. At the age of sixteen he stowed away on the bark *Rotumah* and was put ashore at Apia, where he got a job as a bookkeeper at Mrs Macfarlane's store. Obviously, he impressed his employer with his keenness to get to sea, as he was given the pleasant task of sailing with the old ketch to Mili, for an appointment with fate.

Becke's orders, dated 3 December 1873, were plain and formal enough. 'You will proceed from hence to Milli, Mulgrave's Island, for the purpose of selling the ketch *E.A. Williams*,' the instructions began. He would find Captain Hayes waiting there, 'so you will please consult with him, as he is acquainted with the people who wish to purchase the ketch'. Mary Macfarlane and Samuel Williams hoped that the near-wreck would go for the value of £500 in oil and copra, so Becke was to try for that, if possible, and then stow the produce on the *Leonora*, getting Hayes to sign the bills of lading. 'Do not sell the chronometer unless you get a good price for it. Sell the few things you take to the best advantage. None of the Samoans are to remain, but come back to Apia. Have the ketch painted up on your arrival at Mille.' And that was that, the letter ending with good wishes for 'a prosperous and speedy voyage'.

Though the instructions implied that Captain Hayes was a knowledgeable and experienced master, trustworthy enough to be consulted, Becke had heard many stories about him, so had some idea what to expect. 'When I joined the brig in Milli Lagoon, in the Marshall Group,' he wrote many years later, in 1913, 'I was not surprised to find over thirty native women on board. Some of them were half-castes; and fourteen out of the number were the especial *protégées* of Hayes.' All these women were young and good-looking, and destined for sale at the rate of £20 per head — but, he added, the goods had to be willing. One was sold to the captain of the *Acors Barnes* — 'a greyhaired man of 60' — but the woman was happy about it.

It is probably little wonder, then, that when Hayes offered Becke the berth of supercargo on the *Leonora*, the young man eagerly accepted. The ketch was sold to a local chief, and the produce taken on board, and when Hayes sailed to Ponape, instead of directly to Apia to deliver the proceeds of the sale, Becke made no objection. And still he kept silent the night that the *Leonora* anchored near the wreck of the brig *Kamehameha*, and Hayes and a few men dropped stealthily into a boat. Hayes sat in the stern sheets, holding a full bottle of gin, while the men took the oars and the boat disappeared into the darkness.

Shortly afterwards, voices rang over the water, one of them Hayes' distinctively jolly tones. The cooper of the *Kamehameha*, left to guard the wreck against pilferers, was not just being plied with alcohol, but distracted with famous yarns, as well. An hour or so later, the party clambered back onto the deck of the *Leonora*, bringing two casks and some ship gear with them. All of it had been foraged from the wreck. The salvage rights had been bought by another man, Captain Edward

Milne of the German schooner *Mantantu*, but Hayes cared nothing for that. Instead, he inspected his loot. One of the casks contained molasses, which was useful, so he sent it down to the hold. The other held whaleline and spare sails, which were taken out, also being handy. Once emptied, the cask was filled with rubbish and sent back to the wreck. The blocks and tackle that had also been brought on board were retained. Then the *Leonora* sailed away.

The next target was the palm-fringed beach of Pingelap atoll. The *Leonora* hove to off the reef, while Hayes crossed the sparkling lagoon to the shore in a boat. After an interval he came back with a guest — the island chief, who was ushered into the cabin for a well lubricated dinner. An hour or so went by, and then the second mate, Bill Hicks, was called down into the cabin, to guard the king while Hayes sent a native to shore with a ransom demand. Until the locals had supplied the brig with 5000 coconuts and two pretty girls, their king would be held hostage, he said. 'The natives brought off between 3,000 cocoanuts and one girl,' one of the crew testified later. 'The girl was crying and did not want to come. Hayes then let the chief on shore, and we sailed for Strong's Island.'

According to the account Becke wrote later, the brig arrived off Kosrae in the first week of March 1874, and dropped anchor in the northernmost harbour, Lelu (called Lêlé by Becke), to find the island 'in a very disturbed and excited state'. Two weeks previously, two American whaleships had dropped an unpleasant horde on the beach, consisting of five white beachcombers and a large number of natives, who were now terrorising the locals.

These intruders were refugees from a tribal war on Nauru. Evidently, they had taken to the sea in seven whaleboats, with the intention of sailing and rowing to Ponape, but when 300 miles out they had been sighted by the two whaleships, the *Europa* and the *St George*, both of New Bedford. The shipmasters, James Knowles and James McKenzie, had not liked the look of the people they were rescuing, so had simply towed the boats to Kosrae, where they left them. And now, as Becke went on to relate, the high chief, King Togusa, approached Hayes with a plea for relief.

Hayes settled the situation by threatening to wipe out the invaders' huts with a broadside of his guns, with such immediate effect that the highly relieved and grateful Togusa promised to pay him two tuns of oil. The five white beachcombers, led by an American, Harry Skillings, came on board, and arranged with Hayes to go with the brig to Providence Island (Ujelang), where Henry Gardiner and William Knight were still struggling to establish a trading post and plant a coconut plantation. There, as agreed, they would work for Gardiner on Hayes' behalf, collecting oil and copra, and paying a yearly tribute. And, as Skilling's team would need their own gang of workers, the Nauru rebels were herded into the hold of the *Leonora*.

The brig sailed to the other side of the island to collect fresh water, dropping anchor in an inlet called Molsron Utwe by the natives, but known to the Europeans as South Harbour. The two American whaleships were already in the lagoon, and Becke was just about to go on board of one of them for supper, when the wind abruptly dropped. Then the brig began to roll heavily on an incoming swell.

Hayes came on deck, looked around, and then sent a boat over to the nearest whaleship, to warn the two captains that a typhoon was on the way. His advice was for them to run out to sea, but they chose not to accept it, as the ships would have to be towed out through the gap in the reef, there being no breeze, and they thought this too risky. So Hayes returned to the *Leonora*, and had the royal and topgallant yards sent down. It was too late to tow the brig out, so everyone waited for the storm to rise, while the air grew hot and sultry, the mounting breakers crashed rhythmically on the reef, and dark descended.

Below, the natives were begging to be allowed out. Hayes gave permission, and ten men and six women dived over the rail into the black water, too terrified of the oncoming tempest to even think about sharks. Other women and children crawled into hiding places on deck, while men huddled in groups about the white beachcombers, many of them holding muskets and knives. Then the wind arrived in a mighty blast, showering the brig with branches, leaves and sheets of hail-like spray, while the brig spun about her anchor chain, lurching up and down.

Like thunder, a sea came out of the night to crash down on the bows of the brig, rushing inboard to wipe away the forward deckhouse. Killing four people in its wake, it poured into the cabin, where Becke, helped by some of the native women, was packing up arms and ammunition, the ship's chronometers, the navigation instruments and the charts, along with Hayes' accumulated loot — 'about six thousand silver dollars in bags, the ship's books and some silver plate'. Up into the open all this was hoisted, to be lowered into the beachcombers' whaleboats, while with a mighty smashing the starboard guns broke loose, carrying the port ones with them as they rumbled across the deck and over the side.

The brig was under water forward, but still she rolled dreadfully, while the stern banged up and down on the coral. Hayes bawled the order to abandon ship. However, there were still five on board, including himself, when 'a thumping sea came thundering down, and swept the lot of us over the stern'.

Dawn rose just as the storm subsided, to reveal the battered survivors clustered on the beach, the half-submerged wreck lying on her starboard side — and the two whaleships making a hasty departure through the gap in the reef. The captains were beating a diplomatic retreat, knowing perfectly well that Bully Hayes, backed by his crew, the beachcombers and the Nauru natives, was capable of seizing one of their ships to make up for his loss.

It was the morning of 15 March 1874.

CHAPTER 17

Rosario

'H.M.S. *Rosario*, three guns, Captain Dupuis, returned yesterday from the South Sea Islands,' reported the Sydney *Empire* on 2 November 1874. 'The ship left Sydney on the 22nd March, reached Fiji on the 13th April, and cruised at the various islands of that group till the 22nd July, thence proceeded to Rotumah, remained for a few days, then cruised through Marshall's, Ellis's and Gilbert Groups. The object of this visit was to get information regarding the notorious Captain Hayes. Afterwards went to Strong Island, where Hayes came on board, and piloted the *Rosario* into the place.'

The hunt had been triggered by Captain John Daly of the *Lady Alicia*, who had emerged from jail after paying the fine of five shillings imposed for the scolding that led to the suicide of his cook. After taking a hasty departure, he had sailed to Abaiang to pick up George Phillimore Winchcombe and all the oil and copra he had collected, only to find both George and produce gone. It had not taken him long to learn who was responsible, news that was confirmed when he called at Tuvalu. After getting back to Sydney in March, he first of all reported the loss to Robert Towns, and then, on 10 June 1874, he wrote a formal, itemised complaint to the Governor of New South Wales, Sir Hercules Robinson. Obviously, the Governor was impressed, because within three days the Commodore of the Australian Station, James Goodenough, had been given orders to collect comprehensive evidence of the crimes of 'the notorious Captain Hayes'.

The single-screw warship *Rosario*, on the Fiji Station, was immediately commissioned, with orders from Goodenough to look out for blackbirders in general, and in particular to 'collect evidence against and finally apprehend Mr Hayes, master of the *Leonora* and another vessel, he having committed depredations on property in various islands'. The first port of call was to be Rotuma, where Captain Daly of the *Lady Alicia* would be waiting with the details of Hayes' crimes. Then, after all the islands Daly had named were searched, the *Rosario* was to proceed to Providence Island, the place where 'Hayes has his home and central depot; and you may arrest him there and bring him to Sydney, should the evidence you have collected warrant it'.

For the commander of the *Rosario*, Arthur Edward Dupuis, this was a more ticklish task than it may have seemed to the angry Captain Daly. A 38-year-old career officer with high ambitions, Dupuis had been in command of the *Rosario* for only a few months, having taken over in January that year. He was also uncomfortably aware that previous captains had had bad experiences with apprehending blackbirders, because of flaws in the law. In 1869, in command of the same *Rosario*, Captain George Palmer had detained Ross Lewin's notorious *Daphne*, but the case had been thrown out of court, on the grounds that the British Trade Act did not apply in the South Pacific Ocean. Worse still,

Palmer had been accused of permitting 'his zeal somewhat to outrun his discretion', which was something no naval commander wanted on his record. So, since then, the commanders had satisfied themselves with forcing suspect captains to sign declarations of illegality. But Goodenough, prodded by the directive from Sir Hercules Robinson, wanted much more, something that taxed Dupuis greatly.

After being given the name of George Phillimore Winchcombe by Daly, who assured him that the trader would testify against Hayes, Dupuis sailed for Nukufetau. Once tracked down, however, Winchcombe stubbornly refused to admit that he had been robbed by Captain Hayes. Instead, the trader complained 'that Daly treated him very badly'. After he was dumped on shore at Abaiang, he said, 'he was much in dread of the natives; and on Hayes coming there at the beginning of 1873 he begged him to take him off the island, and offered to sell him all the trade he collected'.

That Winchcombe was so frustratingly uncooperative was confirmed by Restieaux, who was there when Dupuis was 'told a long story about the time he was on board of Dailey's vessel without pay; then he was left in Abaiang in danger of his life; how he had sold out to Hayes; & how Hayes had treated him. The Captain listened very patiently taking notes,' Restieaux remembered. 'When George had finished he said: "Well, from your own story it appears that you were hard up in Sydney & Mr Dailey very kindly took you on board & found you a place to trade & that you took the first chance you got to rob him & leave. Perhaps if I heard Mr Dailey's story it would look worst. I do not see that I can do anything for you," & so dismissed him.'

So it is little wonder, then, that Commander Dupuis noted in his report to Goodenough that he felt as if his 'case against Hayes was very weak, that I had gained no evidence worth mentioning against him, and that if I found him on Providence Island I could hardly arrest him'. The problem did not arise, as when the *Rosario* arrived at Providence on 19 September, Hayes was not there. Instead, the boat that was sent ashore found Henry Gardiner and William Knight, both looking ragged and thin. According to the log that was kept by Sub-Lieutenant George Wilson, they came on board to report that they had run out of supplies long since, having not seen a ship since the day they had been landed. Then they asked for passage away from the island, which Commander Dupuis granted.

Unlike Winchcombe, Henry Gardiner was keen to give evidence against Hayes, being very resentful that he had been left to starve. Indeed, it was hard to stop him talking. 'At Providence Island,' wrote Dupuis in his report to Commodore Goodenough, 'I heard the first direct evidence against him in a case of shocking brutal treatment of a young girl who he brought from the island of Pingelap. About July, 1872,' as Gardiner testified, when Hayes dropped anchor at Providence, he 'had a young Penjelap girl on board with him, and one day he brought her on shore and took her into the bush. About half an hour afterwards I saw the girl coming out of the bush. She was crying, and blood was running down her legs.' The girl, he said, was 'about ten years old'.

This gave Dupuis a problem. Even if he could find proof that the charge was true, arresting Hayes for rape was not part of his brief. As he wrote to Goodenough, 'I considered it would have been exceeding my instructions to apprehend an American subject on such charges.' Then, to complicate matters even further, when, on 25 September, the *Rosario* arrived at Kosrae, Hayes himself came out in a boat to help pilot the ship into harbour, as full of jovial talk and sunny humour as any man with a crystal-clear conscience.

And, when Hayes escorted him to the village he had established on shore, doubts of being able to establish a charge of rape were strengthened further. During the previous six months Hayes had turned South Harbour, Kosrae, into his private kingdom — complete with his own harem. As Dupuis wrote, he 'visited Mr Hayes' residence at South Harbour; he had made a regular settlement of it, and had collected a large quantity of oil. No less than five young women or girls were living in his house, who had all, with one exception, been living on board the *Leonora* with him'.

Idyllic indeed, but there were people who resented it. And at the head of the list was the American missionary in the Caroline Islands, the Reverend Benjamin Galen Snow, who marched across the beach to accost Commander Dupuis, soon after the commander's boat landed. While normally resident on Ebon, Snow had taken passage on the missionary ship *Morning Star* to get to Kosrae, after sending word to the authorities that the notorious Hayes was trapped on Kosrae, his brig a wreck. He had arrived on 19 September, and, unlike the Reverend James Chalmers seven years earlier, had not been at all charmed by Hayes.

'I have known said Hayes personally for a few years past, but have known much more of him by reports, which have almost invariably been great to his discredit,' Snow testified, 'or, as you Englishmen would say, he has the reputation of being "a very clever rogue."' What he had witnessed in the six days since he had arrived on Kosrae, 'only confirms, yes, even strengthens, previous evil reports I had heard of him, so that I am constrained to say, in all sincerity, and in the interest of our common humanity, that you will be doing a most praiseworthy act by taking him on board the *Rosario*, and taking him to Sydney, where he may be brought under the cognisance and jurisdiction of civil law'. He had, he admitted, tried to reform this difficult man, but with no success at all — 'I have hoped that a brighter phase might open up to his character from some source, but I have looked in vain.'

This was all very well, but Dupuis could hardly haul Hayes off to Sydney because a missionary happened to dislike what he had seen and heard, and had failed to turn this rogue into a Christian. When this was pointed out, Snow merely sniffed, 'I am fully aware of the difficulty and delicacy of your situation in this proceeding with a citizen of a foreign Power; but I think I can assure you, as a citizen of the United States, that our Government would gladly make common cause with our cousins across the water in arresting and bringing to justice such outlaws as this.'

Dupuis did his best to make a case. As Wilson noted in the log of the *Rosario* on 1 October 1874, 'Comr Dupuis investigated various complaints against Capt Hayes who was wrecked in the *Leonora* brig at the South Harb. of Island, six months previous.' Captain Milne, whose schooner *Mantantu* had dropped anchor here on 15 September, was willing to testify that Hayes had stolen 'a cask containing whale line and one lug sail' from the wreck of the *Kamehameha*, of which the salvage rights belonged to Milne himself. Milne, however, was sailing under German colours, so all Dupuis could do was refer the matter to the German Embassy after he got back to Sydney.

And then there was the matter of holding the chief of Pingelap hostage until the natives had supplied 7000 coconuts and two girls. This was corroborated by Nils Nahnsen, the first mate of the *Leonora*, plus a crew member, John Carstens, second mate Bill Hicks, and the Chinese cook, Ah-So. But this was not the evidence of robbing traders of oil and copra that Dupuis had been ordered to collect. And, as Dupuis was uncomfortably aware, holding chiefs hostage was a common device for getting the ship supplied at remote islands, a practice that dated back to the time of Captain James Cook.

The rape of the Pingelap girl was the most troubling charge. This, too, was confirmed by the four crew members, but then Bill Hicks added that the girl lived on board the brig for about ten weeks after the attack, apparently without making any trouble, and was returned safely to her home. Then a girl named Emma, a native of Ocean Island (Banaba), was produced, and through Captain Milne, who interpreted, she told an equally disturbing story. She had come to Kosrae 'about six months ago' in a whaleship — evidently either the *Europa* or the *St George* — as one of the refugees from Nauru. Two or three months after the wreck of the *Leonora*, Mr Hayes 'took her to his house and assaulted her; he used most brutal violence, and the girl bled very much'. The *Rosario*'s surgeon, Dr James Whitney, examined her, found that she still had trouble walking, and gave the opinion that 'she cannot be more than eight or nine years old'. A fellow islander from Pingelap 'actually saw the assault committed, and described it as being brutal in the extreme'.

This put Dupuis in a very difficult position. Naturally he was shocked and repelled, but his brief was to bring an infamous trickster and thief to justice, not to involve the Royal Navy in the sordid and sensational trial of a paedophile. On deep reflection, his only choice was to abandon the mission. Not only had Winchcombe failed to corroborate Captain Daly's charge of barefaced robbery, but Dupuis had no credible witnesses, as he was dealing with white riff-raff, incoherent natives, and a very biased missionary.

'There can be no doubt that Mr Hayes is a most unprincipled but shrewd man, one who has (I now have no doubt) committed many shocking acts of violence on the natives,' he concluded in his report to Goodenough, 'and to say the least of them, been guilty of many acts of dishonesty towards other persons; yet so clever is he in methods of proceeding, and so much has his name got to be feared by both natives and white residents on the islands, that though it was evident that at nearly all the islands I visited he was well known, yet it was impossible to find out much about him or his deeds. I was perfectly convinced that nearly the whole of the whites and natives were afraid to speak out.'

In short, Dupuis had not found enough evidence to make a reasonable case for arrest — which was ironic, as Hayes' nerve broke, and he ran. Sub-Lieutenant Wilson noted in his logbook, 'Captn Hayes finding the evidence too strong against him, deemed discretion the better part of valour, and with one white man and a native, made good his escape from the Island on the evening of Sunday 27th, in a small boat.'

*

The Reverend Mr Snow was not the only one who was glad to see Hayes go. Another was Togusa, whose kingdom had been usurped. 'My kind friend,' Togusa wrote to Dupuis three days after Hayes vanished. 'I am glad to see your ship to my island at this time. I think because you come Kaptin Hayes he go. I am very glad for this.'

The king would be equally delighted to see the back of Louis Becke, or so he confessed. 'That man no speak true,' he wrote. 'He tell Mr Snow, "I belong America," then when your ship come he tell you he belong England.' This low opinion was shared by Dupuis, who had been warned about Becke and the dubious affair of the ketch *E. A. Williams.* As Commodore Goodenough noted in his summary of Dupuis' report, he had been in Apia in H.M.S. *Pearl* in November 1873, and had seen a ketch under repair that turned out to be the *E.A. Williams*, 'belonging to the sons and daughter of Mr Williams, H.M. Consul for Samoa, one of whom, Mr Samuel Williams, is doing duty as Acting-Consul under a warrant from his father'.

As he went on to say, 'Mr S. Williams told me nothing of his intentions regarding his vessel, but gave me to understand that Mr Hayes was a great rascal, who had cleverly outwitted all inquiries.' Samuel Williams had even offered to obtain evidence against Hayes, evidence that had proved worthless, 'and yet on December 3, 1873, he actually enters into communication with this man against whom he had pretended to give me information'. The man needed firing from his job: 'I consider that he had been guilty of dishonest behaviour, rendering him unworthy to continue to occupy such a position.'

And Becke, if possible, was worse. 'This Mr Lewis Beck carried with him from Samoa orders from Mr Samuel Williams to put the *E.A. Williams* into Hayes' hands to be sold; and in course of business to have become so mixed up in Hayes' affairs, that the latter made him his agent.' As evidence of all this, Becke carried a number of papers. One of these, dated 3 December 1873, and from 'Messrs. McFarland and Williams to L.G. Beck', authorised him to sail to Mili, meet up with Hayes, and sell the *E.A. Williams*, while all the rest had been either written or dictated by Hayes.

Captain Hayes' appointment of Becke as his agent and representative was undersigned and witnessed by one of his seamen, Charles Roberts. 'Know all men by these presents,' the paper grandly commenced, 'that I, William Henry Hayes, master mariner, now residing on Strong's Island, in the North Pacific Ocean, have made, constituted, and appointed, and by these presents do make, constitute and appoint

Louis George Becke, of N.S. Wales, at present residing on this island of Kusaii or Strong's Island, my true and lawful attorney.' Not only did he bestow Becke with the right to take over his village and station on Kosrae, along with all the oil, casks, pigs, fowls and provisions, but he gave him an assistant, Harry Mulholland. 'Get all the cocoanuts you can, and keep making oil,' it concluded.

Evidently Hayes had made up his mind to leave the island before the *Rosario* had arrived, as this power of attorney was dated 19 August. A detailed memorandum of instructions was attached, accompanied by letters to Hayes' agents, all written on 26 September, the day before Hayes fled. Becke was to sell everything he could, pay Harry Skillings for the work he had done, and give away the rest. All the Samoans who had come with the ketch were to be taken home, unless they wished otherwise. 'My native boy Toby I want you to take to Samoa and look after him, as well as you can, and give him to my wife, also Kitty, as they have no father or mother, and both were given me by the king of Hope Island, or rather the head man, as there has been no king since the old one died.'

As for King Togusa, Becke was to make sure that he remembered 'that the king owes me ten barrels of oil for the two tripots, also there are two head of cattle that belong to me'. Furthermore, he should bear in mind 'that the king and chiefs owe me 12,100 (twelve thousand one hundred) cocoanuts, the balance of the item of 48,000 cocoanuts that they agree to pay to me for the loss of my property stolen by Strong Islanders at the time of the loss of the brig *Leonora*'.

Becke would have to deal with Hayes' agents as best he could, as the brig's trade book had been lost in the wreck — 'after you have settled up, you will please take the balance of money or property, and hand over the same to my wife, Mrs. Mary Emily Hayes'. Then, after concluding with a wish for 'every success and trusting you will arrive safely at Samoa', Hayes had penned notes to the agents at his seven stations in Micronesia: Garstang at Nukulili (Nukulaelae), Marshall at Oaitupu (Vaitupu), James Porter at Niue, George Brown at Aua, 'Rsin, Esq', at Maduru, Thompson at Funafati, and 'Jack, Agent to Captain Hayes, Mille or Mulgrave Island, Marshall Group'.

The letter to Jim Garstang, like the rest, was penned by Hayes himself. 'I am sorry to enform you of the loss of my vessell on this island, the 15th of last March, and I have never see a sail since that time till now. Mellon has come in with a small schooner, and since his arrival I have bin arrested by a English Ship of war, and they are goin to take me to Sydney on account of the things I took from Tarawa with Jim Porter. I don't now what they will do yet; I don't think they can do anything with me for it; if not, I will soon be with you again. Give my respect to Bookorow, not forgetting yourself.

'I have given Mr. Beck my power of attorney to settle with you, then you must do the best you can till you heer from me again. I remain, & c., W.H. Hayes.'

*

In view of the debts owed by Togusa to Hayes, it is little wonder that the king wanted Commander Dupuis to carry Louis Becke away. Dupuis agreed with him that the island was best rid of Becke, 'as a man likely to stir up much trouble on the island'. Five of the crew — John Carston, John McDonald, Ah-So, Ah-Ho and a Malay named Bob — were taken on board H.M.S. *Rosario* as well. 'The first mate I left on the island,' wrote Dupuis, 'recommending him to take charge of Hayes' property. The second mate ran away into the bush just before I sailed, and could not be found, or I should have taken him to Sydney with the others.' Then he concluded, 'Thinking the case over quietly afterwards, I cannot see how I could have arrested Hayes; it is, therefore, with great regret that I am obliged to report my failure to collect sufficient evidence against him to warrant my doing so ...

'A. E. Dupuis, Commander, to Commodore J. G. Goodenough, H. M. Ship *Pearl*.'

'Oct 2 Friday,' wrote Sub-Lieutenant George Wilson in his logbook. '3 PM Proceedd to Sea under steam (with six of the late *Leonora*'s crew as passengers to Sydney).'

CHAPTER 18

Lotus

Captain Hayes had not gone far at all. On 13 November 1874, when the missionary ship *Morning Star* returned to Kosrae to collect Mr Snow and take him home to Ebon, Captain Charles Gelett found Hayes back in residence. Undoubtedly, the Reverend Mr Snow had been as disgusted to see him return as Hayes himself had been to learn from Harry Mulholland that Becke had failed to follow any of his instructions. But, according to what Gelett told the missionary paper *The Friend* after the *Morning Star* got back to Honolulu on 3 February 1875, Hayes had done his best to placate the angry missionary — by claiming that he had come to be saved!

The editor of *The Friend*, highly intrigued, printed the news on 1 March 1875, under the simple headline, 'CAPTAIN HAYES —

'This person, who was for a number of years a notorious character among the islands of the Pacific, was recently "interviewed" by the Commander of H.B.M's S.S. *Rosario*, at Strong's Island,' the item ran.

Because he was American, Hayes was not arrested, 'but probably anticipating that he would, Hayes put to sea in a small boat with but one companion. After the *Rosario* had departed he returned to the island and presenting himself to the missionary declared that, repenting of past misdeeds, he intended to lead a correct life in the future'.

Despite Hayes' considerable acting skills, Snow had great trouble believing this — understandably so, considering that the missionary had testified to Commander Dupuis that he had already tried to reform the rogue, with no success at all. As the editor of *The Friend* meditated, 'It is not a matter for surprise that, until Hayes had given some real proofs of reformation the missionaries, to whom he had been such a strong opponent, were slow to believe in his conversion.' In the same issue, in the transcription of a speech by another missionary to Micronesia, the Reverend E.T. Doane, there was a claim that Hayes had forced the king of Pingelap to 'sign a treaty that no white man, no black man, no red man, no mulatto, should land for ten years, and to keep away all Missionaries'.

The *Hawaiian Gazette* printed its own story nine days later. 'The notorious Captain Hayes, after whom several war vessels have been dispatched, is reported to have reformed from his evil ways, and become a changed man,' it began. 'At present he is living on Kosrae, and endeavouring to lead a different life from what he has led in recent years.' But whether the editor — the same Henry Martyn Whitney who had published 'The History of a Consummate Scoundrel' in the *Pacific Commercial Advertiser*, back in the year 1859 — was any more credulous than the Reverend Snow is hard to tell from this, as for once he failed to add a commentary.

Captain Joshua Slocum, who was to become famous as the man to sail alone around the world in the *Spray*, was another witness to this apparent change of character. According to a story that he told to George Westbrook when he called at Apia, Samoa, in 1895, and which was eventually published in *Outing* magazine in March 1906 (after Century publishers had rejected his original manuscript), Slocum first met Bully Hayes when he arrived at 'the island of Outlan in the South Seas'. He gave the year as 1873, and told Westbrook that he was in command of the square-rigger *Northern Light* at the time, but both are impossible, as Slocum did not take over the *Northern Light* until 1881, and the encounter happened after the *Leonora* (ex-*Water Lily*, ex-*Pioneer*) was wrecked. Slocum's vessel, in fact, was the San Francisco sailing ship *Benjamin Aymer*, which had left Sydney, Australia, on 24 September 1874, on the way to the Orient with a cargo of coal.

Slocum related that when he backed his maintopsail, 'a six-oared yawl shot out' from the island, with none less than the 'most notorious scoundrel among the islands' at the steering oar. 'Bully himself came on board,' he told Westbrook, 'followed over the rail by Louis Becke.' And what did Hayes ask for, in exchange for the boatload of bananas that Captain Slocum wanted? A *Bible!*

Said he piously, 'My own copy of the Holy Scriptures has been worn out by much use, and my natives are sitting in darkness waiting for the reading of the Word.' Slocum's mate joked that Hayes certainly needed no coal, as he would find plenty of red-hot ones awaiting in hell, at which Hayes replied, 'My brother, we will all save fuel in the hereafter if we mend our ways in this life. Judge not that ye be not judged.'

Invited to breakfast on board Slocum's ship, Hayes said grace — 'a long blessing in a most serious manner with bowed head', Slocum told Westbrook. 'I have heard many clergymen do worse,' he declared in the printed piece. While they were eating, a note arrived from 'an old missionary, Rev. Mr. Snow, who has been in the islands for years and years, begging the old pirate to come to his village in a hurry and settle a row between a white beach-comber and his native wife. I saw the note,' Slocum went on. 'It said that the beggar had cut off one of his wife's ears', and she had retaliated with a few thrusts of a spear.

'Come quickly, dear brother,' Mr Snow had written, so Slocum (who had no idea that Snow was actually on Ebon) was completely understanding when the recipient left in a hurry. As he arrived back on deck, Hayes paused long enough to point out the wreck that had stranded him here. 'Yonder lie the bones of my ship, the *Leonora*,' said he, according to Slocum's printed story. 'She was once the *John Williams II.*'

'The mission ship?' asked Slocum.

'Exactly so,' Hayes replied. 'Lost in a gale of wind — total loss. But the crew was saved, thank the Lord.'

And, with that, he doffed his broad-brimmed hat in a courtly bow, jumped down into his boat, and was gone.

*

The next chapter in the saga was also published in Honolulu. It appeared in the *Pacific Commercial Advertiser* on 16 October 1875, and was reprinted in *The Friend* on 2 November. 'CAPT. HAYES AGAIN', the headline stated — 'When we last heard of this celebrated person, he was at Micronesia, claiming to have been converted from the error of his ways. Since then he went to Guam, on the whaleship *Arctic*, Captain Whitney.'

Though Captain Benjamin Whitney (no relation of the newspaperman) made no mention of this in the memorandum of his voyage that he gave once he arrived back in Honolulu, it is confirmed by a resident of Guam, Father Ibanez del Carmen. In the 1875 section of his 'Chronicle of the Mariana Islands', he noted that Hayes had arrived in Guam 'on the 28th of February this year aboard the barque *Arctic* under Captain Wilney [*sic*]'. Interestingly, Hayes had kept up his virtuous demeanour, the good father writing that such was his 'personal behavior' that many people thought 'he was something other than what he really is — which is still and all, a pirate'.

So that was how Hayes finally made his departure from Kosrae — by begging passage from the captain of a passing whaleship. While the log of the *Arctic* no longer exists, it must have been in January or even as late as the first week of February, 1875. Captain Bauldry of the whaleship *Arnolda* reported that when he had called at Kosrae in March 1875, a boat had come out with the news that the whaleship *Arctic* of Honolulu had been at the island some weeks earlier, 'clean' (meaning that they had taken no whales as yet), and this itinerary was confirmed by the otherwise taciturn Captain Benjamin Whitney, in his memorandum to the shipping list. Perhaps Hayes' display of piety convinced him to take him on board, or perhaps it was because Whitney was a fellow Mason. But Whitney did not mention Captain Hayes' name, let alone say why he had given him passage.

Something else that the captain of the *Arctic* failed to mention in his report was that before he left 'the Groups' (as the whalemen used to call the Gilbert, Marshall, Ellice and Caroline islands), he dropped anchor in Ponape. The logkeeper of another American whaler, *Triton*, described that when his ship arrived at Ponape on 13 February 1875, they found the *Arctic* 'lying in the Midle Harbour a-fitting of her spars reports all well and no oil'. Why Hayes did not leave the ship there is only a matter for conjecture. However, it probably had something to do with his thefts from the wreck of the *Kamehameha*. Or perhaps, not being aware that Ben Pease was dead, he wanted to avoid the man he had cheated of a vessel.

The whaleships *Arctic* and *Triton* were together again on 28 February, when the *Triton* called at Guam to get medical attention for the second mate — 'a Spanish steamer arived hear today and came to anchor at Aprar with 460 Spanish Prisoners on board for this Port allso the Bk *Arctic* Capt Whitney,' the *Triton* journal-keeper wrote. And that is where Hayes finally alighted, after a three- or four-week voyage from Kosrae.

Having solved the mystery of how Hayes got from Kosrae to Guam, the Honolulu papers revealed even more. 'There he repurchased a schooner that he formerly owned, and sailed away, having on board seven escaped convicts and a Spanish "commissary" absconding with government funds. On the side of the island opposite the capital, Hayes went on shore for water, and while taking a bath he was captured by soldiers looking for the runaways, and carried back to the city. Those on board the schooner, seeing this, made sail and escaped.

'Having got into the hands of the Spaniards, who are not given to be merciful,' the item concluded with palpable satisfaction, 'Hayes may be considered as near the end of his adventurous career.'

*

As happened so often, the editors in Honolulu had learned all this from shipmasters' gossip and foreign papers. This time, the story had originated from an item in the *Straits Times* of Singapore, which four months earlier, on 22 June 1875, had published a translation of an unsigned letter that had been sent to the Filipino paper, *Diario de Manila*. Written from Agana, Guam, this gossipy missive began: 'Mr Hayes, a citizen of the United States, and captain of the brigantine *Eleanora* which had been wrecked on one of the Caroline Islands, arrived at this island on the 28th of February last along with Captain Witney, a whaler, on board the American ship *Arctic*, with the object of buying a schooner which he said had formerly been consigned to him. After Mr Hayes had bought the schooner, he requested that the latter should be examined and cleared out. When these formalities had been duly gone through, he left the roadstead of this city at 9 a.m.'

While the letter writer forgot to give the date, Father Ibanez de Carmen's diary reveals that it was 4 April 1875. 'Notwithstanding that his craft was a swift sailer and that a smart breeze was blowing, he continued the whole day, sailing to and fro off this city,' the letter continued, 'two days afterwards, we became aware that he had carried off or kidnapped several natives. Captain Hayes anchored in Fasonan Cove on the northern peninsula, but as soon as our zealous Governor perceived this, he gave the necessary orders to Don Perez y Rivern, an adjutant, and twenty soldiers, who after posting themselves that night in the neighbourhood of the cove, seized the Captain when he was jumping ashore to bathe, and carried him off captive; as soon as those in the schooner saw that chase was being given to Captain Hayes, they weighed anchor and set off into the wide ocean without anything being heard of them since.

'After Captain Hayes had been conveyed to the chief town, he was put into prison and shut up,' the epistle concluded. 'From what I hear, the preliminary inquiries have been instituted for which reason I break off my narration, the matter being under the action of the law. Although historians are allowed to narrate public events, they are never permitted to prejudge cases pending in the courts.'

On the next page of the same issue of the Singapore *Straits Times*, the editor could not resist publishing his reaction to this sensational piece of news. 'The notorious Captain Hayes turns up most unexpectedly now and then,' he meditated. 'Only a few days ago, we heard of his leading a reformed life in one of the South Sea islands. Today, our readers will be surprised to learn, through our translations from the Manila papers, of his recent seizure and imprisonment in the Ladrone Islands. The name of his schooner, which is *Leonora*, not *Eleanora*, will doubtless be familiar to people in Saigon, who some time ago chartered her to carry a cargo of rice to Hong Kong; but instead of going to Hong Kong, the *Leonora*, through "stress of weather," made for Bangkok, and was next heard of at the South Sea Islands. If Captain Hayes is still in custody at the Philippines, doubtless many people in these parts will endeavour to get hold of him.'

Then it concluded, 'The reported loss of his schooner should, like all the other stories told by Capt. Hayes, be viewed with great suspicion.' And after that, there was silence, which as the editor of the *Straits Times* commented on 18 September, was both frustrating and strange. The translator of the Manila papers had fielded many inquiries, he went on, but all he could report was that he had had no luck at all in finding any further news of 'the renowned Captain Hayes, whom the Spanish authorities caught hold of at the Marianne Islands, and whose future progress would be rather interesting to traders and others in these parts'.

But then, on 11 December, a little light was cast by the arrival of the British trading schooner *Sea Bird*. Captain David Dean O'Keefe, the owner of the schooner (and later to become famous as 'His Majesty

O'Keefe', king of the island of Yap), reported an encounter with the same vessel that had made a brisk escape after Captain Hayes had been arrested. As the editor of the *Straits Times* wrote, 'The *Sea Bird* fell in with this very schooner, named the *Joaquin and Anna*, among the Pacific Islands. Her crew had put to sea, carrying with them the Secretary of the Government at Guam, who, we are told, was still in possession of the official seals. The offence charged against Captain Hayes was that he was carrying away from Guam people undergoing imprisonment, and no doubt the Secretary had boarded the vessel for the purpose of seizing her, when the cables were slipped and she put to sea with him.

'There was no one on board able to navigate the vessel, but after a time land was sighted, for which they made. The natives attacked and captured the schooner, but she was rescued from their hands by an American schooner that came in there for trade, the captain and crew of which now claim salvage on her. We understand that the unfortunate secretary was still alive and well at last advices, though with not much prospect of speedily getting back to his office.'

This is the first time that the schooner Hayes bought and fitted out was given a name. However, there is no record anywhere else of the *Joaquin and Anna*. Father Ibanez del Carmen, who wrote that Hayes had 'bought it in proper fashion' from Don Joaquin Portusach, seemed to think the name was *Rabbi*. This could have been a mis-hearing, as the *Sydney Morning Herald*, on 13 December 1875, published a report from Captain Edward Hernsheim of the German *bêche-de-mer* trader *Coeran*, who claimed that the schooner's name was *Arabia*.

As the Sydney *Herald* revealed, Hernsheim had told the shipping reporter that he 'was at Guam, towards the latter end of the month of April last, and Captain Hayes was there with the fore-and-aft schooner *Arabia*, 60 tons'. Also according to him, Hayes had charged the escapers $24 a head. When they saw their saviour being arrested and taken away from the beach, the fugitives had cut the cables and sailed away — which was when they realised that there was no one on board who could navigate. According to Father Ibanez del Carmen — who also said that Hayes had been betrayed by one of the *deportados*, Joe Fraile, who had been unlucky enough to be recaptured — there was a pilot on board, named Wilman, popularly known as 'Scar-face', but evidently he did not know his job.

There were passengers, too, including a German, August Martens, and a Chamorro woman, Bartola. The convicts who had escaped on the pilot-less schooner were 'Chamorros Don Mariano Aflague, Juan Camacho y Penglinan, Juan Chargualaf, Rose Mendiola with two small children, and Saturnino Duenas. There were also eight Spanish *deportados*.' So Hayes was not back to his old trick of kidnapping natives. Instead, the people who had paid to be smuggled away were political prisoners — aboriginal Chamorro people who were oppressed by the Spanish *conquistadors*, and Spanish activists known as *deportados*. In other circumstances, Hayes would have been commended for his action.

The *Arabia* drifted for the next nine days, or so Hernsheim described to the Sydney paper. Finally, she brought up in Palau, where those on board were rescued by Captain Holcomb, of the American schooner *Scotland*, who, 'seeing that there was no one on board the *Arabia* capable of navigating the vessel, took possession of her as an abandoned vessel'. This was doubly lucky for Holcomb. Not only did he get a second schooner — and only just in time, as the following year the *Scotland* was lost — but he gained a mistress.

Like Winchcombe on Nukufetau, he was searching for a wife, and the Chamorro passenger, Bartola, fell in love with him. And, like Winchcombe's Jemima, she was a staunch and loyal helpmate for many years after that.

*

In June 1875, at the same time the news of Hayes' arrest was published in Singapore, Captain Slocum was stranded in Manila. No sooner had he unloaded his cargo of coals than the *Benjamin Aymer* was sold from beneath his feet. Luckily, Slocum was also a shipwright, a trade that he was able to put to good use. A small boatyard was set up sixty miles from Manila, at the head of Subic Bay, close to an excellent stand of timber, and Slocum lived there for the next twelve months, after installing his family in a thatched house on stilts.

'One day in Manila,' he remembered in the 1906 *Outing* story, 'I received a note from U.S. Consul Griswold Herron,' saying that 'a countryman of ours, one Captain Hayes', had been brought to the port as a prisoner of the Spanish, the charge being that of 'stealing political prisoners'. Again, Slocum was either romancing or misremembering. Jonathan Russell was the United States Consul in Manila at the time; there was, in fact, no such person as 'Griswold Herron'. The probable reason for the old captain's confusion is that two of Russell's partners in his fibre-broking firm, Russell & Sturgis, were Frederick G. Heron and Charles Griswold. Heron became acting vice-consul after Russell died in September that year, but it was not until 1877 that he became the US Consul in Manila.

According to Slocum, 'Griswold Herron' revealed that 'Hayes insists that he knows you', and asked what he knew about the prisoner. Nothing damaging, Slocum admitted, and told him about the meeting at Kosrae, along with the details of saying grace at the table, and 'receiving messages from esteemed missionaries who called him "Dear Brother"'. In return, 'Griswold Herron' told him that Hayes 'had rigged the king's dug-out at Oulan as a schooner and with two of his old *Leonora* hands sailed for Ponape, where they took in provisions of cocoanuts and pigs *en route* for Guam'.

And there, while Hayes knew that there were Spanish prisoners in what was virtually a penal settlement, he 'did not dream' that any of them would sneak on board his schooner. But — or so he testified — that was what happened while he was taking an innocent 'surf bath'. Naturally, the 'account given by the guards was somewhat different'. Their story (or the one that was told to Slocum by the so-called consul) was that Hayes had 'stolen one batch of convicts and come ashore for more, when they pounced upon him from their ambush in the mango trees, and made him prisoner. When the convicts on board saw that Hayes was nabbed, they cut cable and made off before a fresh trade wind, carrying all sail. They managed to fetch up somewhere on the coast of Borneo, wrecked the schooner and made good their escape'.

The rest of Slocum's account is just as dubious. He called on Hayes at prison, he said, and found him chatting with the governor's family on the governor's veranda, at the same time reading the Bible Slocum had 'sold him at Oulan'. The officers of the gunboat that had carried him to Manila from Guam had written 'Christiano' by his name in the logbook, he said. Over the following months, 'Hayes became a chum of the governor of the prison, and also struck up a warm friendship with the priest, who baptized him in the Roman Catholic faith while he was locked up.' From there, he progressed to making 'an all-powerful friend', no less than the Bishop of Manila.

'The buccaneer was a penitent, and he made a most impressive and moving figure,' Slocum said. 'Fever had twisted and shrunken him until I recognized him only by his long beard and his unusual height and breadth. The light, free spring of his gait was gone, and he was the picture of the shuffling monk. To behold the old freebooter, penniless, reduced by sickness, tall, gaunt, with flowing white beard half a fathom long, marching barefooted, at the head of a religious procession, and carrying the tallest candle of them all softened the hearts of his enemies, if he had any in Manila.

'His accusers retracted their charges,' he claimed, 'and were covered with confusion. After his release, Hayes obtained passage from Manila on the ship *Whittier*, bound for San Francisco. The U.S. consul vouched for him as a destitute American seaman. He found himself in clover on the *Whittier*. Parcels containing comforts and knickknacks of various kinds were sent him from ships in the harbor, and the captain of the *Whittier*, being of a religious turn of mind, treated the reformed buccaneer like a brother.'

If indeed Hayes took passage on the *Whittier*, he did not leave Manila until late April 1876. The *Whittier* had arrived in San Francisco from New York on 4 January that year, and sailed onward to the Orient on 12 February, loaded with a cargo of flour. After arriving at Manila on 10 April, she had a remarkably swift turnaround, discharging her flour and loading with sugar, and getting back to sea by the end of the month. According to her commander, Captain W.H. Swap, he 'Sailed April 29th; had moderate weather in the China Sea; off Japan had two typhoons, lasting 12 hours each, wind SE to NW; thence to port moderate variable winds, with rain and much fog'. The anchor was dropped in San Francisco on 22 June, the same day that his report was published in the *Daily Alta California*. Like Captain Benjamin Whitney of the Honolulu whaler *Arctic*, Swap made no mention of his unusual passenger. Indeed, there was no passenger list at all.

*

Hayes arrived in San Francisco well before the end of June, as from the beginning of July onward his name appears in the social columns of the papers. On the Fourth of July, for instance, he was included in the list of invited guests on board the crack racing yacht *Lotus*, which was an observation boat at the Centennial Regatta of the San Francisco Yacht Club.

In the company of representatives from the local press and the Yacht Club secretary, H.G. Langley, Hayes cheered as the *Cousins*, sailed by Captain Frank Murphy, the San Francisco pilot, stormed into the winning place. The hospitality was lavish — 'a generous lunch was spread by "Harry," the steward, to which all were invited by Capt. Moody, and to which justice was done', wrote the reporter from the *Daily Alta California*. 'Our thanks and those of all on board the *Lotus* are due to Capt. Moody for the courtesy and kindness to his guests.' Altogether, as the item ran on, 'great credit is due to Commodore Ogden' and the rest of the club for the fine occasion.

It was just a step from being a welcome guest on board to the acquisition of the *Lotus* itself. According to the papers, her owner, Captain Edwin Moody, wanted to buy a larger and faster yacht for racing, but it seems that he was persuaded to go into a trading partnership instead. 'The yacht *Lotus* has been engaged to proceed to Apia, Navigators' Islands, and will start in a few days,' reported the *Daily Alta California* on 30 September. 'She has been coppered for the voyage, and it is quite likely that she will remain at the Islands trading.' A week later, the same paper noted that the schooner *Lotus* had cleared from port the previous day, commanded by Hayes, and headed for Samoa.

Her agent was Richard Livingston Ogden, the same man who, as the commodore of the San Francisco Yacht Club, had organised the highly successful Centennial Regatta. Though a soldier, not a sailor, Ogden was perhaps the most passionate yachtsman in the city, where he was affectionately known as 'Podgers'. In 1852, when he had arrived in San Francisco as a major in the US Army, there had been a sloop named *Restless* in struts on the ship's deck, and he sailed this as the first pleasure yacht to be seen in Californian waters. This was eventually sold for the very satisfactory price of $1000, and in 1868, according to his obituary in the *San Francisco Call* (7 October 1900), 'he built the large schooner-yacht *Peerless*, one of the handsomest yachts ever built here and one that took part in the first regular regatta ever sailed on this coast. She was sold by him to the King of Samoa and became the "Samoan Navy"'.

So there was a connection with Samoa already, which makes it seem likely that he was involved in the partnership too. Ogden was to be disillusioned, however. It was a bad year for him altogether, as his company, Kimball Carriage and Car Manufacturing, went broke, and on 15 November, the truth about the captain he had backed flashed into print, under the heading 'SKETCH OF THE NOTORIOUS CAPTAIN HAYES'.

*

The publication was the *Hawaiian Gazette*, and the editor who wrote the piece was none other than Henry Martyn Whitney, the same man who had made Hayes internationally notorious back on 24 September 1859. Early in the year 1870, Whitney had sold the *Commercial Daily Advertiser*, after a row with rich sugar planters who threatened to withdraw advertising, and in 1873 he had bought the *Hawaiian Gazette*, where he returned to publishing passionate commentary on political issues. And, as with the *Advertiser*, he specialised in breaking news and revealing unknown details about his chosen subjects — and again a favourite subject was that particular *bête noir*, Captain Hayes.

'This somewhat celebrated ocean rover is reported to have been last week at Kawaihae, in the yacht *Lotus*, of San Francisco, bound to the Navigator Islands,' this story began. Then, after noting that while they 'shall not probably have the pleasure of entertaining him in Honolulu', Whitney made the same excuse for publishing gossip that he had made in 1859 when he wrote 'History of a Consummate Scoundrel' — that 'it seemed a good idea to let the locals know something about this rogue's past and character.

'His last escapade at Manila and Guam surpasses all his former exploits,' Whitney went on. 'The last we heard of him, before he turned up at San Francisco, the Spaniards had him in prison, with evidence enough to have guaranteed the garrote of any ordinary man. But Captain Hayes was equal to the occasion, and suddenly and mysteriously appears on the other side of the stage, ready for another raid on his fellow men.'

Henry Whitney then shifted to Hayes' 'first appearance at these Islands' in 1858, on the *Orestes*, when he was 'accompanied by his wife, who is now living with his children at the Navigator Islands. In all his travels he is said to be accompanied by a female companion of some kind or other, whom he picks up and drops as the fancy takes him'. This was followed by another recounting of how Sheriff Treadway was tricked on board the brig, which set sail from Maui while he was being entertained. 'The sheriff was always fond of a good joke, but he was obliged to acknowledge that this was being *hazed* with a vengeance. But there was no alternative, and he had to leave, and witness his late prisoner triumphantly shaping his course for the setting sun.

'The next mail from the Coast brought the necessary papers to the United States Consul here, authorising him to arrest Captain Hayes and seize the brig. It appears that he had landed in San Francisco with a capital of fifty dollars, which he had borrowed when in Honolulu of the Rev. Dr. Damon. With this money for a basis of credit he bought the brig, fitted her for sea, stole somebody's wife, shipped a crew, and went to sea, paying for nothing but his water.' A sentence about the sinking of the *Ellenita* followed, along with an admission that Whitney did not know what happened next. 'He now disappears for some time, but finally is heard from at Batavia in a barque chartered for Europe with a load of coffee. The Dutch East India Company, however, becoming acquainted with some of his past history, was glad to pay him the charter money and get the coffee ashore again.

'His next voyage was from Hongkong to Melbourne, with a load of Chinese passengers. After being out some time he was informed by a ship which he spoke that he would have to pay fifty dollars per head on the Chinamen before he could land them. He kept on the even tenor of his way, however, until he arrived off Melbourne, when he choked both his pumps, started all his fresh water in the hold, and set his colour half-mast, union down, as if in sore distress. Two steamers soon came to his assistance and offered to tow him into port, but the captain's humanity overcame all selfish feelings, and he replied, "Save these people, and let the ship sink. If she is afloat when you return we will try and get her in." The Chinamen were landed, the steamers paying the head-money, but when they returned for Hayes, he was not to be found. His next cargo of Chinese were landed without trouble, as he had them all made British subjects previous to starting.'

*

There is absolutely no evidence that this ever happened. While there certainly was a poll tax of £10 per head for Chinese who landed in the state of Victoria, imposed by a law passed in June 1855, the tax could be evaded by landing the Chinese miners at Robe, in Guichen Bay, in South Australia, and this was exactly what Captains Goularte and Cambridge of the *Estrella do Norte* had been commissioned to do, back in 1857. When they ran out of money and tried to strand their passengers in Adelaide, they had been taken to court by the spirited Chinese — which was when Hayes entered the scene, organising bottomry on the vessel to get Goularte out of trouble. Then, though some of the unfortunate Chinese were taken on board the *C.W. Bradley* to be taken to Robe (but were dropped in Albany instead), the captain involved was Hayes' trading officer, Robert Parkinson.

So, while William Henry Hayes certainly had a reputation for carrying coolies in the Orient, he never carried coolies into Australia. As the editor of the *Timaru Herald* remarked as late as 6 May 1914, 'it is just a yarn, and no more'. Yet the Chinese coolie story has become part of the Bully Hayes legend, retold many times. So, where did the story come from?

It could have been influenced by personal prejudice. Henry Martyn Whitney had a history of opposing the importation of Chinese labour into Hawaii. Back in March 1857, he had lobbied for a curfew for Chinese, claiming that coolies were running about the streets at night and committing petty thefts, a campaign that had been successful, resulting in a statute imposing a 10 p.m. curfew being passed at the beginning of June. He also called out for stringent laws against any importation of Chinese indentured labour, claiming it was a form of slavery. It was this that had brought him into conflict with the sugar planters, who — like the cotton plantation owners in the South Pacific — needed cheap labour, and wanted the numbers imported increased. But whether some gossip he heard from other anti-coolie trade people was the origin of this unsupported story is impossible to tell.

Having related the Chinese coolie yarn, Whitney moved on to Hayes' arrest in Apia and his rescue by Pease, then his misappropriation of the *Leonora* while Pease was in prison in Shanghai; after that came the theft of the cargo of rice at Bangkok. 'We next hear of the U.S.S. *Narragansett*, Captain Meade, as being engaged in searching for him on account of his many alleged irregularities. He was found at Upolo, arrested, and taken on board the man-of-war, where he had no difficulty in winning the hearts of both men and officers in a very short time, and after three days' detention he was liberated, there being no evidence against him, and all were firmly convinced that he was a much injured and most worthy man. Insinuating to Captain Meade that he was in want of some sails, he was supplied with all he required, and the gentlemanly pirate departed with the best wishes of captain and officers.'

The theft of the *Neva* was then briefly described; as his readers were aware, the schooner was sold in Honolulu by 'Captain Pinkham', and was now familiar to many as 'the schooner *Giovani Apiani*, now in this harbour'. Finally, the article came to a close with Hayes' 'pious dodge' at Kosrae and then his conversion to the Roman Catholic religion, which 'bamboozled the clergy of Manila as effectually as he had the American missionaries'.

*

The acquisition of the San Francisco yacht *Lotus* was not mentioned by Whitney again, but the baton was taken up by the *Evening Post* in San Francisco. Two weeks later, on 28 November, the *Post* published a racy article devised to grab the attention of the reader, and which was guaranteed to send a chill up the spine of Richard Livingston Ogden — and Captain Edwin Moody, who was still in town, though he was supposed to be on the high seas.

'The ordinary landsman passing along the waterfront San Francisco a few weeks ago,' the story began, 'or, indeed, the ordinary mariner, engaged in plowing the sad waves, as he brushed by an elderly-looking, well-dressed man, whose beard descending swept his aged breast, would feel inclined to laugh in the face of the man who would tell him that he had just jostled a pirate.' But it was true — that elderly man was indeed a pirate, 'A pirate in the year of grace 1876!' And it was also true that 'hardly more than three weeks since the schooner *Lotus* left this port for Apia, as it is supposed, in command of a gentleman whose description we have already given, and whose piratical exploits would fill volumes — who has even given employment to the men–of–war of three different nations. The gentleman in question is Captain John Hayes, alias "Bully Hayes, the Pirate of the South Seas."

'At what time in the past John Hayes first imbibed his taste for a pirate's life — whether as a schoolboy from the dime novel, or when older grown from the weird yarns spun by ancient mariners in the middle watch, or when listening to the baritone voices of the rough tars as they celebrated in song the deeds of Captain Kidd, the "Blacksnake Privateer," or those who went

'Sailing on into Panama Bay,

'The mighty buccaneers —

'is unknown: but the old buccaneer spirits, wherever imbibed, obtained its full sway over him about 1868, when he was engaged to command a lumber bark.

'The bark was lying off Stewart-street wharf, ready to discharge, when one night, without troubling the Custom-house for his clearance papers,' Hayes sailed off to Mexico, where, as the writer claimed, the lumber found a market. 'The next thing heard of him was from Macao, where his bark was chartered to bring coolies to Sydney.' The story of tricking other men into paying for the coolies followed, though with a number of differences — the 'capitation tax' was $25 per head, and the two steamers were replaced by one tug. The result, however, was the same.

The theft of Lechat's craft — now described as 'a beautiful British schooner' — followed, though with a different setting, that being Bangkok. According to the editor of the *Post*, the rice cargo on the schooner was sold in Hong Kong, and then the craft was sailed to Strong's Island, where Hayes found the bark (presumably the lumber bark), in charge of the mate. This fellow, who 'by this time was sick of a life which sooner or later he saw might bring him to the yard arm or gallows', was given the job of sailing the schooner to Hong Kong, where 'he sold the schooner and her cargo for what he could get, and cleared out'.

Next came the story of that long-suffering commander of the *Narragansett*, Captain Meade, who, when he learned that Hayes was in Apia, steamed in under French colours, which he exchanged first for British colours and then for the American ensign, before sending an armed boat on board the bark to arrest the pirate. 'He was subsequently tried, but owing to the obstacles thrown in the way by the consular authorities, and the absolute terror all his sailors had of testifying against him, a conviction could not be obtained.'

No sooner was the pirate released by the Americans than 'Her Britannic Majesty's ship *The Pearl* received orders to cruise in search of him'. It took a long while, but at last 'Hayes was discovered at his favourite retreat, Strong's Island'. The harbour there had only one inlet, but Hayes 'took a boat, and going out to the war steamer, offered to pilot her in, informing the captain that that "pirate Hayes" had sunk his ship, and made his escape to another island. Before the Britisher discovered that he had been sold, Hayes succeeded in escaping in a whaleboat with his companions. The only one of the crew of the barque captured was a young English boy named Beck, who was found on the island. He was tried in Sydney about two years ago, and acquitted, as it was evident that the boy acted in terror of his life.

'Nothing further was heard of Hayes until about 18 months ago, at Manila, when it was reported by an American whaler, that he was round among the Philippine islands, and as the Spanish government confined political prisoners on some of the islands of the group, the authorities sent a man-of-war to look for him. The war vessel was too late, for when she touched at one of the smaller penal settlements, she found that 150 convicts had escaped in the schooner.' Hayes, however, was seized, and despite his plea that the convicts had run away with the schooner, he was thrown into prison to work out a nine-month sentence.

The experience almost killed him, so he was sent to San Francisco as a distressed seaman, on the advice of the American Consul, 'although when he landed on the bark *Whittier,* about April or May last, he had three chests of clothes, valuable instruments, and $10,000, which he had been paid by the friends of the political convicts. How he contrived to hold on to his treasure through all his sufferings is wrapt in mystery', meditated the editor, who was now on the verge of wrapping up the yarn with the story of the *Lotus,* 'well known to our yachting men, which he got from her owner, Captain Moody. He carried away with him $5,000 in cargo and money', so it would be no surprise, he reckoned, if many people in town were waiting in suspense to hear the next tidings from Samoa.

*

Remarkably, as the editor (Henry George) also meditated, 'Hayes, with all his faults, has friends who speak well of him. He has betrayed his trusts, he has stolen, and rumour says that he has committed murder. Indeed, it is evident that it could only be at the point of the pistol he or any man like him could keep his crew in order.'

And yet 'friends' were indeed speaking up, one of them to the extent of writing a letter to the *Evening Post*'s rival, the *Daily Alta California,* which was published on 1 December. 'In the *Post* of Tuesday last I observed an article on Captain William Hayes, reflecting severely upon that gentleman's character and accusing him of about all the crimes in the calendar,' this stern remonstrance began. 'I think I know the source whence the information came, and, if I am correct in my opinion, the whole story was prompted by malice and low spite.'

Captain Hayes had been in town for four months, the writer declared, and yet no one had spread such gossip at the time — 'No man in the place would have dared.' Instead, the source of the slander had waited until Hayes had gone, 'and then, in a cowardly manner, attacks him behind his back when he is not here to defend himself.

'As to the charges against him, they are gross exaggerations, with, in several points, not even the slightest grounds; in others there is just enough, probably, for a foundation to build on and let the imagination run riot', the writer claimed. Not only was it a load of 'bosh', but it would make good material for a 'dime novel of the blood and thunder order'. Granted, Captain Hayes had his faults — but who could claim to be fault-free? 'No better sailor or navigator ever sailed out of this port; with all the bravery, big heartedness and open-handedness of the true sailor, he is ever ready to divide his last dollar with a comrade; liberal to a fault. I have seen him give away his last two bits to a poor devil, and go without his own dinner. He did that while here, for in spite of the assertion that he landed with ten thousand dollars, I *know* that he did not have twenty-five.'

Whether he had run away with the *Lotus* remained to be seen, but the writer expected the 'croakers' to be disappointed by the sight of Hayes arriving back by the end of the year. 'It is to be hoped that now the bold buccaneer has sailed, little children and timid female will experience a sensation of relief, and the gentleman who furnished all the dreadful items of this fierce and dangerous customer can go out after dark with comparative safety,' he concluded with heavy sarcasm, and signed off with the pseudonym 'POSTED'.

*

Mr W. Lane Booker, the British Consul in San Francisco, was not nearly as trusting. He sent a circular to the marine boards of Pacific ports, 'respecting the movements of the notorious Captain Hayes'. In this, he stated that Hayes had sailed from San Francisco in the schooner *Lotus*, bound for Africa, but the craft was to be employed collecting *bêche-de-mer* in the Navigator Islands.

Naturally, shipmasters sailing in the region kept an eye out for both the yacht and the notorious owner, the first report coming from Captain Browne of the bark *Oriental*, which docked at Newcastle, Australia, in early April. 'The schooner *Lotus*, commanded by Captain Hayes, otherwise known as Bully Hayes, arrived at Manihiki in the Cook Islands on November 20, 1876,' he said. 'His crew consisted of himself, mate, and one American woman, three in all.'

Naturally, the intriguing news that an American woman was on board triggered even more intense interest, which was partially satisfied in June, when papers throughout Australasia noted receiving 'further particulars of the proceedings of the notorious pirate, Captain Hayes'. As the report revealed, 'It transpires that Hayes, after his release from prison in the Philippine Islands, made San Francisco, where he induced a speculator to purchase a schooner called the *Lotus*, and fill her up with trade for the islands, representing that he (Hayes) had a vessel in the South Seas, and the two vessels were to trade as a partnership.

'The *Lotus* was all ready for sea when Hayes' partner placed his wife on board, but had to return on shore, where he got mixed up in some row and was locked up. Hayes, failing to see the efficacy of waiting till next morning for his partner's return or troubling himself with Customs' delays, put to sea, taking with him his partner's wife, and only one man. The *Lotus* reached Samoa, where Hayes' wife and family were living, but the wife discarded him, and he sailed from thence for the Kingsmills, but before doing so made proposals to the crew of a schooner called the *Costa Sacramento* to run away with that vessel.'

*

Then even this choice piece of gossip was eclipsed, by astounding news that was first published by the *San Francisco Post*, and copied on 29 August by the *Sacramento Daily Union*.

'An American Captain Killed by One of His Men', ran the remarkably sedate headline: 'The schooner *Maggie Johnston*, just arrived from the South Sea Islands, brings news of the murder of Captain Hayes, of the schooner *Lotus*, of this port, by one of his men, while cruising among the Marshall group of islands.

'Hayes has been a notorious character in the South Seas; has been frequently credited with piratical acts, and was well known as a desperate character from Australia to Japan. He left here in the *Lotus* some months ago on a trading voyage to the Samoan group and neighboring islands. At Samoa he shipped a Dutchman as cook and seaman. An altercation ensued between the two as to the steering of the vessel, which resulted in the sailor's killing Hayes with the crutch of the main boom.'

The *Daily Alta California* had a few more details, which were reprinted with obvious relish by Henry Martyn Whitney in the *Hawaiian Gazette* on 17 October. 'If the following, which we copy from the *Alta*, is authentic, an individual quite well known in this part of the world has at last closed his earthly career, and in a manner quite appropriate' — he had 'been murdered in March last by the cook, a Dutchman, who shipped in Samoa as cook and seaman'.

According to information provided by the 'man acting as mate', the *Lotus* had left Jaluit, in the Marshall Islands, bound for Abaiang, when on the second day out 'the Captain spoke to the man at the wheel, who was the cook, about his steering. Some altercation followed, when the Captain went below. When he came up the companionway, sometime after, the man let go the tiller and struck Captain Hayes on the head with the crotch belonging to the main boom. He fell, and immediately expired. No firearms of any kind were found on him.'

The mate, named Elson, did not witness this, as he was below and asleep at the time. Coming on deck to find the captain breathing his last in the woman's arms, and the cook with blood on his hands, he took over and got rid of the evidence. 'The Captain was buried at sea,' the item continued. In short, the mate and the Dutchman heaved up the dead weight of William Henry Hayes and tossed his body overboard.

Then the schooner returned to Jaluit, to find the *Maggie Johnston* at anchor. After Elson had told Captain Bliven and his trading master, Captain Henry, what had happened, the two mariners inspected the ship's papers, and found that Elson had shipped informally, without signing ship's articles, so 'had no control over her at all'. Acting with the swift resourcefulness of adventurers all over the Pacific, they relieved him of command and seized the ship. Their excuse, according to the report, was that 'rumors about her going away to other islands in other hands' had got about, and so a rival copra company, Capelle & Co., had asked them 'as American citizens', to take over the vessel, 'until her owner in San Francisco could communicate instructions'.

Captain Moody, realising that he and Ogden could lose the yacht for the second time, responded in person. 'Captain Moody, the old Captain of the *Lotus*, left for the Marshall group of islands, in the South Pacific, on Friday,' noted the *Daily Alta California* on 22 September 1877. 'He has gone to settle up affairs connected with the death of Captain Hayes, and will bring the *Lotus* up to the Navigator Islands. He will be gone some six months or so.'

And it was almost exactly six months later, on 11 March 1878, that Moody arrived back in San Francisco, as a passenger on the *Maggie Johnston*, after a very rough passage. He had had to fight for the *Lotus*, other parties having claimed her as salvage, but with grit and determination he had hung onto his rights, and had sold her for $1400.

Undoubtedly, the moment he put a foot on shore, he was asked a raft of questions by the men from the press, and friends and fellow yachtsmen, too. However, he managed to keep his own counsel, undoubtedly helped by the fact that he was a total abstainer from alcohol, so his tongue could not be loosened. Accordingly, newspaper readers were kept in suspense until 7 February 1880, when the *Pacific Commercial Advertiser* published a letter from a traveller by the name of W.E. Wood, who had visited Jaluit in search of more detail 'regarding the death of the celebrated free-booter'.

After confirming that Hayes had sailed from San Francisco to Samoa, Mr Wood revealed the interesting detail that Hayes had picked up a passenger there — he 'got a Doctor to go with him to treat a King of one of the Islands to the westward, offering the disciple of Esculapius as a lure a fee of two thousand dollars, half to be paid shortly'. But once they had arrived at Jaliut, Hayes stranded the doctor on shore, saying that he was dissatisfied with the poor fellow, and that it was no use making a 'muss', as if he did, 'he might depend on having all his bones broken'.

'Meantime,' Wood went on, 'a Norwegian sailor on board the schooner, had deserted to the shore. Hayes, by offering a reward, got him on board again, had him tied up to the mainmast and unmercifully whipped. This affair cost Hayes his life.

'The schooner left Jaluit March 31st, 1877, April 8th she came back. The following facts I got from Dr Ingolis, the last victim of Hayes' tricks. The second night out from Jaluit, Hayes had an altercation with the Norwegian sailor and beat him savagely. The man still resisting, Hayes went into the cabin for a pistol, avowedly to shoot him. The sailor took the boom crutch in his hand (a heavy piece of iron) and when Hayes' head appeared above the companionway, the man struck him fairly and stove in the whole top of his skull. He fell back, and breathed his last in the arms of a white woman who is now in Honolulu.'

How she got to Honolulu was not explained; nor was her identity given. According to speculation then and since, she was Jenny Ford Moody, wife of Captain Edwin Moody. It is impossible to tell for sure, however, as there is no mention of a wife in his obituary. Another question is how Dr Ingolis knew all this in such detail, considering that he was on the beach at Jaluit at the time. But that was not explained, either.

CHAPTER 19

The Manufacture of a Modern Buccaneer

You can't talk long down in the Islands without the name
of Bully Hayes coming up — buccaneer, bad man, or
a nautical Robin Hood, whichever you like
to read into the beachcombers' tales.
— Spartacus Smith, *Sydney Mail*, 20 June 1928

Though the notorious Captain Hayes lay deep in his watery grave, public fascination refused to die. The saga that had been fostered by the newspapermen themselves, spearheaded by Henry Martyn Whitney in Honolulu, was still definitely alive, but now, while Hayes still pulled headlines, there was nothing new to write. Instead, the editors had to reshape old material.

As early as October 1877, the *Evening Post* of Wellington, New Zealand, published a racy recounting of the Bully Hayes story, complete with yet another version of the Chinese coolie yarn. The same happened in the 1 November 1885 issue of the *Daily Alta California*, under the descending titles, 'THE LAST OF THE PIRATES — An Account of the Bold Career of Skipper Hayes — THE MAN WHO DIED TWICE', which retold the Whitney article in a highly embellished account. Enthusiastically received, it was copied all about the Pacific, and reached as far as the Atlantic, being reprinted in the New York *Sun* on 3 January 1886, and the *Evening Star* of Washington, D.C., six days after that.

According to this version, Hayes was 'a quiet, sleek-faced rascal, who presented the appearance of a full-fledged Methodist parson of the old-fashioned type. He was never known to chew tobacco, to drink, or to give utterance to an oath'. After starting out as a well-liked officer on a Great Lakes schooner, he turned to a life of crime, beginning with the substitution of a wooden hobby-horse for a pedigree pony he had been supposed to deliver, but had sold instead. Escaping to the South Seas, Hayes then embarked on a blackbirding career, including a shipment of Chinese to Sydney, where he tricked the captain of a tugboat into taking his passengers, along with the due payment of the poll tax, by dropping a hose into the sea, connecting it to his pump, and pretending that the 'bright water' that came out of it was from a leak in his hold.

Turning up in San Francisco 'sick and penniless, as usual', he stole a yacht, hired a mate, shipped the mate's wife as his stewardess, and 'started off for the islands'. When they were well out to sea, however, the mate, offended by Hayes' approaches to his wife, expressed his views in some 'very forcible language'. Hayes, merely amused by this, announced that he was going below to fetch a pistol, at which the mate announced, 'Then I reckon I'd better kill you now,' and proceeded to do exactly that.

Just months later, on 9 August 1886, the New York *Sun* published yet another Bully Hayes story, with the subheading, 'Incidents in the Life of a Man who was the Terror of the Pacific'. Completely ignoring what they had printed in January, this version claimed that Hayes had started out as a pilot on the Mississippi River. 'He was a fine sailor, a reckless, dare-devil sort of a man, who, though he could hardly read, was a king among his fellows, owing to his great energy, force of character, and fertile brain.' He could have been just about anything he wanted to be, the writer claimed, but he chose to be a pirate. However, though nothing but a rogue, he 'struck everybody as uncommonly cute: so he had a sort of popularity, and at any rate was the most talked-of man in the Pacific'.

The editors of the New York *Sun* were rather cute themselves, because just three years later, on 29 December 1899, they published yet another version of the Hayes story. Headlined 'Bully Hayes, Pirate of the Pacific, the Thrilling Story of a Double Life', this so-called biography owed everything to fiction. The writer, Edward Wakefield, claimed that Hayes had been a respectable citizen of Nelson, New Zealand. Married to the daughter of a well-to-do farmer, he was highly regarded by all, though people did wonder where he got all his money, especially as he had a habit of paying in gold. Not much was said, as he was a stalwart of the church, with a 'magnificent tenor voice', but then, despite the gallant efforts of a half-caste Maori by the name of Peri, Hayes deliberately drowned his family.

Pictured next in the South Seas, where 'the name of Bully Hayes was a sound of terror', he hunted his prey (ships, as well as native people) on the notorious blackbirder *Black Diamond*. The British authorities retaliated by annexing the Fijian Islands, thus imposing their rule on the South Pacific, but Bully Hayes countered this attempt to trap him in his hideout in Levuka by marrying 'the buxom widow of a trader', and adopting the pose of a respectable sea captain on shore, while he continued his piratical depredations from the helm of the *Belle Étoile* of Tahiti. His adventures were brought to an abrupt end, however, when he was shot dead in a duel with the master of a smart China trader, Captain Magee — who, despite being gravely wounded, sailed to Fiji, and married the buxom lady, now the widow of Bully Hayes.

The New York *Tribune* also pandered to fiction, producing a startling new version of the wreck of the missionary vessel *John Williams*, which it published on 14 May 1899. 'PIRACY UNDER THE BETHEL FLAG', it headlined, the writer going on to claim, straight-faced, 'This is a true story.' After the *John Williams* came to grief at Niue, as the writer described, the wreck was bought by 'William G. Hayes, an American, who added a decided spice to South Sea life in the seventies, and who has not escaped fame under his common and well-earned designation of Bully Hayes the Pirate'.

After hauling the wreck off the reef and patching her bottom, Hayes changed her name to '*Lenore*', and sailed her to Apia. The Bethel flag — the blue flag with white palm leaves that proclaimed she was a missionary vessel — was still flying from the peak, and the Samoan missionaries, shocked to see 'flying at the fore their familiar flag', demanded it back. With a derisive laugh, Hayes nailed it to the mast, and proceeded to use 'one of the best known ensigns in the South Seas' to lure unsuspecting natives into his holds. The missionaries, naturally, were 'frantic at this desecration', but Hayes kept it flying until the wind mercifully tore it to shreds.

This imaginative approach to the Hayes story was also put to good use by Albert Dorrington, an Englishman who had drifted to Australia at the age of sixteen. After taking lodgings in Sydney, he wrote a few stories for the *Bulletin*, which found a good audience. In 1907, tired of Australia, he travelled through the Far East and India on a tortuous route back to England, where he settled down to make a living out of writing Bully Hayes fiction for *Pall Mall Magazine* and *Popular Magazine*. India was a favourite setting for these extremely popular blood-and-thunder tales, the reviewer for the *Queenslander* noting that the issue of *Pall Mall* for May 1908 carried another of Dorrington's 'briskly entertaining stories of the adventures of Captain Bully Hayes, the incident dealt with being an exciting experience with an Indian rajah's pet wrestler'.

Dorrington pictured Hayes as 'a fascinating sort of character', according to the reviewer, 'half pirate, half hero, whose creed may be summed up from one of his remarks to his mate — "We better take a walk ashore, Mr. Rowe. Maybe there's a few metal gods about that ain't screwed down. Many a poverty-whipped white man has come back from a walk through India with his pockets full of gold door-knockers"'. Australian newspaper readers loved this sort of stirring stuff, and Australian editors obliged by reprinting Dorrington stories whenever they could get hold of them. In December 1907, for instance, the *Australian Town and Country Journal* celebrated Christmas by publishing Dorrington's 'Mouth of the Moon-God', which pictured Hayes spinning yarns in an opium den in Darwin. 'I always had a notion that India was the place for me,' he informs his audience of pearl-fishers and layabouts. 'I always wanted to steal a peacock throne.'

*

Stirring as the fiction might be, some semblance of truth was generally preferred, so readers' personal recollections of Hayes were actively solicited. In August 1903, the *Press* of Christchurch called for reminiscences, the editor writing, 'The question has been raised whether Bully Hayes, of South Seas notoriety, ever entered the Hokitika river. We shall be glad if any of our readers can give us any trustworthy information on the subject, and also as to the visit he is said to have paid to Lyttelton in the early sixties' — and the replies poured in, to be published over the next few days.

Men were proud to boast that they had met him. 'I first had the pleasure of making Bully's acquaintance at Picton,' wrote William A. Moss. 'He landed there from a ten ton cutter with a crew of one boy and a French poodle.' W.H. Meikleham met him at Fairhurst's Hotel, Lyttelton, in the year 1865. 'I remember he gained some notoriety by sailing with two young girls belonging to the Port.' Wrote J.A. Morgan, 'I met Hayes first at Valparaiso in 1859. He was then engaged in trading to the Islands, I believe blackbirding for the Chilean mines at Sandy Point and shanghai-ing along the coast, and was a great smuggler, too.'

W.R. Turner remembered meeting Hayes at Day's Hotel, Sumner, Christchurch. 'I had several conversations with him. He was of a courteous and gentlemanly demeanour, a big man and well-proportioned.' Indeed, he could be likened to a locomotive, 'ready, compact, polished, and full of latent power for good or evil'. Mr Mosley, who had been the editor of the *Evening Mail* at the time, wrote that he regretted that he had been unable to accept an invitation to sail with Hayes — 'I found him a very well informed man, and to me he made himself very agreeable.' Alfred Gee was certain he would never forget meeting Hayes — 'a man of splendid physique, fully six feet in height, and proportionately well built'. And, while this Herculean figure had left Lyttelton with tradesmen 'bewailing' his departure, he came back to pay all his debts in full, 'partly in Spanish coin, which was afterwards changed at the local bank'. C.W. Chamberlain remembered him vividly, down to every detail of dress — 'I don't know whether he looked more like a reformed pirate, or a missionary who had done well in a native land.'

'An interesting discussion has been going on the columns of the Christchurch *Press* as to the visits of Bully Hayes, the notorious South Sea freebooter,' mused the editor of the *Newcastle Morning Herald*, on 29 August — 'there may be still old Newcastle residents who remember him. If so, it would be extremely interesting if they would give their recollections or experiences.' During his own wanderings in the Pacific, the editor had met many people who had known him — 'Hayes was truly a remarkable man, very handsome, and with an ingratiating manner.' Unfortunately, he received no mail. Though there were certainly living men in Newcastle and Maitland who remembered Hayes well, they were clinging to their secrets.

The quest for reminiscences was picked up again in March 1914, when the editor of the *Timaru Herald* observed, 'Already the aura of romance is round about Bully Hayes, the aptly named: but there are still in the flesh those who saw him and learned of his doings as current news of their day.' And even if 'their memories are at fault or their facts are second-hand', there were still people around to respond.

'Hayes said that he was born in Valparaiso in 1819,' declared a Sydney businessman to the *Daily Telegraph*, a wild claim that was published (and republished) without question. A man who signed himself 'Malaria' wrote to the *Register* of Adelaide in June 1928, reminiscing that a native captain in the islands of Papua–New Guinea had told him that Bully Hayes had once nailed his hand to the gunwale of his boat, and threatened not to release him until he gave up his pretty daughter.

Fijian memories of Hayes, contributed by Walter C. Hornaday, were published in the *Sunday Star* of Washington, D.C., on 8 November 1914. 'Many of the older residents of Levuka, remember well the buccaneer,' he wrote. 'He was about six feet tall, and his body strong and well proportioned. He always wore a long brown beard, that was kept well trimmed and combed. He exercised the greatest care and taste in his dress, his clothes being made by the most fashionable tailors in San Francisco, Shanghai, Manila, Melbourne or whatever port he happened to be in when he wanted a new supply of wearing apparel. Even when committing the bloodiest crime, or inwardly raging, what little could be seen of his face wore a bland smile.'

*

Inevitably, considering the extent of public interest, Hayes was featured in published books too. In the earliest, he was the subject of a chapter called 'The career of Bully Hayes', in a book with the title *Coral Lands*, by H. Stonehewer Cooper, which was published in 1880 by Richard Bentley. Though just a rewrite of Henry Martyn Whitney's 'Sketch of the Notorious Captain Hayes', it was widely read and received a great deal of publicity. Australian and New Zealand editors found the yarn about Bully Hayes and the Chinese coolies such a novel and newsworthy story that it was quoted almost in full in the various reviews, and so the myth lived on.

The first full-length book devoted to Hayes was called *A Modern Buccaneer*, written by a man who published under the name of Rolf Boldrewood, but who was actually an Australian government official by the name of Thomas Alexander Browne. Though he was not a professional writer, in his youth Browne had made some much-needed money by sending stories to the papers, which had such popular success that he had been encouraged to turn his hand to writing novels. By 1894, when *A Modern Buccaneer* came out, he was a prolific and well-regarded author of both fiction and non-fiction, his best-known book being *Robbery Under Arms*, which came out first as a serial in the *Sydney Mail* in 1882, was published in London in 1888, and is now considered an Australian classic. *A Modern Buccaneer* was his twelfth novel. It was largely based on a memoir by Hayes' one-time supercargo, Louis Becke, which Browne had paid Becke £10 to write, and because of this it is recognisable as a biography, though Hayes is renamed William Henry 'Bully' Hayston, and the book was sold as fiction.

Naturally, being based on Becke's experiences, Boldrewood's recounting commences in Apia, at the point when the narrator 'accepted the position of supercargo in a ketch which the junior partner of one of the principal firms in Samoa wished to send to the Marshalls to be sold'. Then, in the first sign of the oddly academic style that intrudes every now and then, the author goes on to quote Becke's letter of instructions word-for-word, though he changes the name of the ketch to *E.A. Wilson*. During the description of Becke's first encounter with Hayes, there is also a hint of the self-serving nature of Becke's account, because it stresses that the narrator accepted the job of supercargo only after extracting a promise that he would not be involved in anything illegal.

A cruise among the islands is then described, one that was much longer than Becke's reality, and which is punctuated with fictional action of the blood-stirring variety. At this stage some of Hayston's yarns are related, including a long account of his association with Pease (spelled Peese), who (according to the story) committed suicide by jumping overboard from the Spanish man-of-war where he was being kept captive. And another interesting detail is added — that when the *Leonora* and the two whaleships were trapped in the lagoon at Kosrae by the storm, the crew of the whaleship *Europa*, who were supposed to be steadying the *Leonora* by means of a hawser, deliberately sent her onto the rocks by paying out the cable.

Boldrewood then enlivens the description of life after the wreck with the intriguing detail that Hayston went mad — 'Some demon appeared to have taken possession of him.' Awful scenes of fighting and flogging follow, driving the narrator away from Hayston's village to live on the other side of the island, despite the captain's pleas for his supercargo to return. But then the missionary brig *Morning Star* arrives to deliver the Rev. Mr Morland — 'a portly, white bearded old gentleman' — and Hayston miraculously recovers his sanity. This, as in the real story, is closely followed by the arrival of H.M.S. *Rosario*, at which point Boldrewood reveals that Morland had sent for the man-of-war, having heard that Hayston had been stranded by the wreck.

Then, in another shift to the non-fiction form, Boldrewood quotes much of what was printed in the Queensland Government Gazette, though with some (but not all) of the personal names changed, and with the notable omission of the charges of raping young girls. The instructions to Commander Dupuis follow, along with much of the report he wrote to Commodore Goodenough; just as related by Becke and the newspapers, the narrator is arrested and taken on board the *Rosario*, while, meantime, Hayston escapes in a boat. And so, as the *Rosario* sails away, carrying the narrator to further adventures, Hayston is left behind, referred to only once again when memories flood the last pages of the book.

'He was not without resemblance to a yet more famous corsair,' Boldrewood concluded, 'immortalised by the poet —

'Who died and left a name to other times,

'Link'd with one virtue and a thousand crimes.'

Throughout the novel, it is obvious that the author (like Becke) was an admirer of his hero — Hayston is described as 'a thundering scoundrel' who was also 'one of the most fascinating companions possible', made distinctive by 'his great stature and vast strength, his reckless courage, his hair-breadth escapes, his wonderful brig'. It is little wonder that the book was so successful.

However, the author mainly responsible for turning Bully Hayes into a swaggering corsair was not Rolf Boldrewood but Louis Becke himself.

*

Back in September 1874, after being arrested by Commander Dupuis, Becke was carried from Kosrae to Brisbane, where he was acquitted of the charge of piracy. He then joined the Palmer River gold rush, worked at a cattle station, and served a few months in Townsville as a bank clerk. Eternally restless, he drifted back to the island existence, setting up a trading post on Nukefetau, and marrying a local girl. Just a few months after that he lost everything in a shipwreck, so he took up wandering again, first to New Britain, then to Majuro in the Marshall Islands, then back to Sydney, then back to Townsville, then Noumea, then Sydney again, where he stayed, immobilised by bad health.

Throughout this shiftless existence Louis Becke had never thought to scribble down his experiences, but Ernest Favenc, a man he met in a pub, was so fascinated with his yarns that he introduced Becke to the editor of the *Bulletin*. This man, Jules F. Archibald, taught him how to write for a general audience, and in 1892 his South Seas stories began to appear in print. Soon there were enough to make an anthology, which was bought by T. Fisher Unwin (the uncle of the man who bought out George Allen & Co., to create Allen & Unwin). An innovative publisher, Unwin had recently launched pocket books in a new, sumptuous design, tall and narrow in shape, with generous margins and much ornamental work. Becke's collection, trimmed down to 40,000 words, looked extremely well in that format.

Published in November 1894 under the title *By Reef and Palm* — and with a note in the front matter that most of the stories had already appeared in the *Sydney Bulletin* — the book was received so well that it went into three more editions by the end of that year. Bought by J.B. Lippincott, and published in New York in 1895, it had equal success in America. The reviewers, like the public, were impressed. Becke was favourably compared with Robert Louis Stevenson (being considered more authentic), and called 'the Rudyard Kipling of the Pacific'.

While there were no tales about Hayes in *By Reef and Palm*, the front matter exploited the connection. Becke had written to Herbert, Earl of Pembroke, sending him a copious autobiography (some of which was true), and soliciting an introduction for his forthcoming anthology. Evidently reading the manuscript brought back pleasant memories of the Earl's own jaunt about the Pacific, because the piece he wrote was generous indeed. Not only did it summarise Becke's romantic career, but it included the Earl's version of Hayes' escape with Benjamin Pease in the *Pioneer*, written from memory of what John Chauner Williams had told him when he had visited Samoa in 1870.

While reviewers, like the man who wrote for *The Academy*, lauded the 'charm and verisimilitude' of Becke's first book, it was this reference to the ever-popular Hayes that helped make *By Reef and Palm* a bestseller. And it also helped Becke to understand that he had a potential goldmine in his memories. The second collection — *The Ebbing of the Tide*, published by T. Fisher Unwin in 1895 — included two Bully Hayes stories ('A Tale of a Mask' and 'Lupton's Guest'), which worked so well that he and his publishers made sure that there was something about Hayes in every one of the many newspaper stories and thirty-plus books that Becke published after that. The culmination was a biography, *Bully Hayes, Buccaneer*, which was published in 1913, not long before Becke died.

The problem for Louis Becke was that his relationship with Bully Hayes, though filled with drama, had been very short. This meant he had to augment, embroider and exaggerate in order to eke out his material — which also meant, ironically, that Boldrewood's *A Modern Buccaneer*, which was published as a novel, was much closer to reality than Becke's memoirs. The eight weeks on the *Leonora* became inflated to four long voyages — 'it was my fortune to fill the distinguished position of supercargo to that eminent gentleman for two years', he wrote in 'The Wreck of the *Leonora*'. And, while Becke freely admitted quarrelling with Hayes and going to live on a different part of Kosrae after the wreck, he still felt able to depict him as a romantic, swashbuckling, charismatic figure.

*

Becke was not the first to lend an aura of authenticity to his stories by claiming that he had known Bully Hayes. Back in 1880, the writer of *Coral Lands*, H. Stonehewer Cooper, had made much of having personally met the famous rogue, remembering him as 'a handsome man of above the middle height, with a long brown beard always in perfect order. He had a charming manner, dressed always in perfection of taste, and could cut a confiding friend's throat or scuttle his ship with a grace which, at any rate in the Pacific, was unequalled', he wrote, judging his audience so effectively that others rushed to claim their own connection.

That association could be tenuous. Hugh Hastings Romilly, in his 1886 travelogue, *The Western Pacific and New Guinea*, devoted a whole chapter to Bully Hayes on the premise that not only had he met Hayes' wife, but he had a friend who was intimately acquainted with the 'last of the pirates'. This fellow, the Rev. James Chalmers ('Mr. C'), not only told Romilly 'that he never wishes to have a more amusing or better-informed companion', but also confided that though Hayes had landed Chalmers' own goods safely, the freight he had carried on behalf of the missionary society had mysteriously disappeared.

In 1887, London publisher Richard Bentley put out a book by another man who had never met Hayes himself, but had talked to people who knew him. This was William Churchward, who settled in Apia in 1881, and wrote an account of the next four years called *My Consulate in Samoa*, in which he devoted a complete chapter to Hayes. 'To write an account of any part of the Western Pacific without mention of its bold buccaneer and pet pirate "Bully Hayes" would be in the eyes of the old hands an unfriendly omission', Hayes being 'their most cherished hero', Churchward claimed, then launched himself into a series of yarns taken from the San Francisco *Evening Post*, complete with the Chinese coolie yarn and the hunting down by '*The Pearl*'. Yet, as he concluded, there was no one who would speak against him. Instead, he heard of many instances of 'humanity, daring and good-fellowship that in the eyes of the community completely overbalanced anything to his discredit'.

Frederick J. Moss, who published *Through Atolls and Islands of the Great South Seas* in London in 1889, commented with perfect accuracy that the ocean had been 'a region of romance' from the day that Balboa had named it; that since then the 'exploits of buccaneers, the work of explorers and missionaries, the strange customs and grace, kindliness and ferocity of the Islanders' had been hugely popular reading for a fascinated public. And the buccaneer of choice was Bully Hayes. As H. Stonehewer Cooper had observed earlier, no one could write about the romance of the Pacific without giving 'some account of this man's exploits'.

Though Moss was not able to boast about his own encounter with the so-called buccaneer, he was lucky enough to meet Restieaux, as well as other unnamed traders. Hayes was a 'magnetic' American, they told him, with a soft voice and persuasive ways. 'Mad as a hatter at times,' said one of those who had sailed with him. He was very fond of dogs, but shot one dead when the poor animal barked during a pig-hunt. Stricken with remorse, Hayes smashed up his cabin furniture, and spoke to no one for the next three days. Otherwise, Moss filled up his chapter with retold newspaper stories that were often garbled: he says, for instance, that Hayes discredited the evidence given to Dupuis of the *Rosario* by getting the testifiers drunk. Altogether, as he concluded, Hayes was a 'strange compound of unblushing roguery, rough humour, and strong sentiment dashed with insanity'. The Pacific would never see the like again.

In Edward Reeves' book, *Brown Men and Women*, published in London in 1898, Bully Hayes was the star of the very first chapter. And rightly so — or so Reeves reckoned, as he 'was one of the most remarkable of the pirate chiefs of this century — an able leader and persuader of men'. He had had a slight acquaintance with him, or so he claimed, and had been lucky enough to come away from the encounter unscathed. 'He enjoyed stealing a few pounds as much as seizing a merchant ship and making crew and passengers walk the plank.' He then fleshed out the chapter with farfetched yarns adapted from items in the New Zealand papers (including the story of the Chinese coolies). Most remarkable, however, is the conclusion, a highly coloured description of Hayes' death, where the '*beau ideal* gentleman-pirate' rushes up the companionway 'with a pistol in each hand and a knife in his mouth to murder a jealous rival'. Killed, the body is thrown overboard, 'still clutching in its death grasp the pistols and the knife'.

Another author who rewrote the stories told by the Reverend Mr Chalmers was his cousin, J. Inches Thomson, whose warmly reviewed book *Voyages and Wanderings* was published in 1913, well after the missionary's death (and consumption by his killers). If alive, Chalmers may very well have objected to the liberties Thomson had taken, such as crediting him for a story that Hayes deliberately ran his own ship onto a reef while the missionaries were on board, and that he then 'attempted to run down the missionary boat' at Rarotonga. 'Possessed of considerable culture, speaking German, French and Spanish fluently, his scandalous performances had made him an outlaw in almost every civilized port,' Thomson claimed, and proceeded to describe sundry exploits taken from the newspapers, including the ever-popular Chinese coolie yarn.

*

The romantics who painted Hayes as a charismatic ne'er-do-well went unchallenged for thirty years, but then about the year 1911, Alfred T. Saunders began to pay regular visits to his bedridden aunt. This was the seafaring Sarah Ann Allen, wife of Captain Thomas Allen, who had met Captain Hayes at least thrice, and had heard a great deal of gossip about him in ports from Singapore to Adelaide. Though eighty-two years old, her memory was sharp and her voice still eloquent, and when Saunders, intrigued by her yarns, checked some shipping lists, he found that her facts looked accurate. This led to a lifelong interest in Captain William Henry Hayes, and an obsessive crusade to get the facts right.

Saunders' intention was to write the definitive biography, debunking the romantic myths, a mission that became so compulsive that he went to great trouble and expense to contact archives in Singapore, Shanghai and Hong Kong. At home in Australia, he wrote a stream of newspaper articles, reporting on the progress of his researches. The first of these, 'Bully Hayes the Pirate, True History of the South Seas Buccaneer', was published in the Adelaide *Mail* on 30 August 1913. This reported what Aunt Allen had told him, so it had the appeal of coming from a firsthand source. More stories followed, as Saunders kept the public up to date with the progress of his researches, and reprinted the old news items that had been sent to him from afar.

The immediate and most irritating effect was to increase the sales of Louis Becke's books. Enraged, Saunders responded by writing a criticism of the author, written for the *Mail*, and published on 15 November 1913, nine months after Becke's death. Not only did Becke spend far less time with Hayes than he claimed, Saunders said, but when 'the romance which Becke and Boldrewood wrapped round Hayes is torn away, he is found to be a vile ruffian, who injured and defrauded everyone who trusted him'. Becke had deliberately misled his readers with romantic descriptions of happy girls and shipboard harems — Hayes drowned his wives, and his 'practice in the South Seas was to call at a remote island and compel the chief to send cocoanuts, girls and female children of tender years on board his vessel'. Furthermore, his violation of two young girls was proven.

This, too, was reprinted all about the Pacific, but with unanticipated consequences. Letters to editors were written in defence of Captain Hayes — Hayes had just as much intention of murdering the man at the helm of the *Lotus* as Mr Saunders would have had in similar circumstances himself, snapped a writer to the *Samoanische Zeitung* in January 1914, while another vowed in a missive to the same paper that Hayes 'was a man who never counted the cost when he could render assistance to a fellow sailor in distress'.

Saunders kept doggedly to his guns, real facts being his passion. He was famous for pointing out errors in other people's works, once writing to Joseph Conrad to tell him about his mistakes. Conrad, though surprised, was polite and gentlemanly about it, but other men tended to be much less tolerant. Saunders also had a habit of posting hostile reviews of biographies of Hayes, inserting the bracketed word 'rubbish' into quotations, which was not well received. When he wrote to the editor of the Sydney *Daily Telegraph*, informing him that the story about Hayes smuggling twenty tons of gunpowder into Hokitika was false, it was curtly pointed out that Saunders was not above repeating false stories himself. For instance, Mr A.T. Saunders gave credence to the Chinese coolie story, yet 'Hayes did not bring any cargoes of Chinamen to Australia'.

Saunders was certainly not immune to errors. Despite the San Francisco and Singapore shipping lists, he was convinced that Hayes had arrived in Singapore in July 1854 in the bark *Canton*, having usurped the command. He also insisted that Amelia Littleton Hayes had been murdered during the 1858 voyage to Hawaii, writing to the Adelaide *Mail* as late as 2 January 1932, 'The wife he married from South Australia went from Melbourne in the *Orestes* with Hayes, and was not again heard of. It is alleged that he threw her overboard.' And this despite his own reprinting of Whitney's 'History of a Consummate Scoundrel', which described Amelia — 'a lady of interesting demeanour' — as alive and well (and very angry with her husband) when she stepped on shore in Honolulu.

Despite acrimony and criticism, Saunders' stream of newspaper stories, book reviews and letters to the editor continued, culminating in a booklet that was printed in 1915 by the office of the *Sunday Times* in Perth, Western Australia. On 3 June, the *Register* of Adelaide, South Australia, noted that 'Mr. A.T. Saunders has issued for private circulation a pamphlet of 40 pages which, besides being a fine example of careful research and patient investigation, has a distinct historical value'. The title, as the editor commented, 'is significantly expressive of its contents — *Bully Hayes, Barrator, Bigamist, Buccaneer, and Pirate: An Authentic Life of William Henry Hayes, of Ohio or New York, U.S.A.; born 1829, killed 1877.*

'In a remarkably thorough and painstaking way the author traces the wild career of the great freebooter and scoundrel in general,' the item continued, the reviewer taking special note that Hayes' experiences in Port Adelaide held great local interest — and 'although Mr. Saunders indicates that certain romantic incidents which have frequently been connected with the name of the pirate are not well founded in fact', the pamphlet was a 'really substantial addition to Australasian history'.

*

But popular history had already claimed Hayes. This 'authentic' listing of the man's petty and major crimes, complete with newspaper exposés of him, completely failed to persuade the public that the man was bad. Instead, they wanted to read more about him than ever — and, as Dorrington had found in the first decade of the century, fiction featuring Bully Hayes was a money-maker. Back in 1898, Edward Reeves commented that when Robert Louis Stevenson mentioned Hayes so casually in *The Wrecker*, the great writer had failed to realise that in the life of this pirate 'there was a book of adventure second to none that ever was written' — and he was right, as Bully Hayes was readymade for fiction of the 'blood-and-thunder' genre.

A writer who took this up with relish was John G. Rowe, who, in his 1929 book for children, *Bully Hayes, Slave Trader*, depicted Hayes as meeting his death 'with a pistol in each hand and a knife between his teeth, his face looking perfectly devilish with desperate ferocity'. His end was noisy, too — 'Thud! The tiller, wielded with both hands by his ex-mate, descended with sickening force upon his head, smashing it in like an egg-shell.' This novel, ran the rave review in the Sydney *Sunday Times* on 20 October 1929, 'is exactly the kind of book needed by those stuffed in offices or schools while their adventurous hearts go roaming'. It was a book with it all — 'A tale holding truth, humor, adventure, and thrills, with a wreck in it, and some ripping incidents in the South Seas.' Rowe, with an audacity that Hayes would have admired, sold the same book in 1939, under the title *Bully Hayes, Blackbirder: A Story of Wild Adventure in the South Seas*, to the British-published Newnes Adventure Library, using the pseudonym Gregory Dunstan. It is still sold as two separate books, though the text in each one is identical.

Another novelist to capitalise on the Bully Hayes potential was Will Lawson, whose book, *The Laughing Buccaneer*, was published by Angus & Robertson in 1935. Warmly reviewed as a rousing tale of the South Seas, it depicts Hayes as an attractive character with twinkling eyes and a boisterous laugh, a man designed to appeal to the readers of the *Australian Women's Weekly*, which republished it as a supplement on 1 October 1938. Even more bizarre than Bully Hayes becoming a ladies' drawing room hero was the fate of the short biography researched by the Australian historian Thomas Dunbabin for a chapter in his 1935 book *Slavers of the South Seas*. This was reworked as a story, called 'Bully Hayes and Ben Pease', in a collection of 'true episodes of sorcery and the supernatural, as well as gory events on sea and atoll', titled *Horror in Paradise*, edited by A. Grove Day and Bacil F. Kirtley, and published in 1986.

*

Bestselling maritime author Basil Lubbock, who was as meticulous as Saunders in tracking down what he could find of the facts, produced

Bully Hayes, South Sea Pirate in 1931. Though he called it a biography and ended each chapter with lists of facts, he recounted the popular Bully Hayes yarns in a fictional manner, as conversations on board a yacht in the Pacific. He, too, got rave reviews, on both sides of the Atlantic — but not from A.T. Saunders, who in January 1932 wrote an infuriated letter to the editor of the Adelaide *Mail*, saying he had received 'the prospectus' of Basil Lubbock's *Bully Hayes*, and was most unhappy about what it said.

'I have corresponded for years with Basil Lubbock,' he declared, and went on to reveal that he had given him a lot of helpful material. 'I sent him my pamphlet on Bully Hayes, and Lubbock seems to have distorted it, and written a lot of nonsense.' Lubbock had let the man off too lightly altogether, he reckoned. Like the reviewer of *Bully Hayes* in the *Singapore Free Press* (7 July 1932), he thought that Lubbock made light of the subject's misdeeds, 'in order to extol his very few virtues'. By contrast, the reviewer for the New York *Times* supplement, *Saturday Review of Literature* (28 May 1932), reckoned that Mr Lubbock had been too hard on Hayes. 'I confess to a liking for the blackguard,' he wrote, and expressed the suspicion that Lubbock liked him too.

When the mega-selling writer James A. Michener co-authored a 1957 collection called *Rascals in Paradise* (with the same Hawaiian professor, A. Grove Day, who collaborated on *Horror in Paradise*), he devoted a complete chapter to Hayes. Unlike the more objective Lubbock, Michener demonised his subject, claiming that not only was the Clevelander 'charged with murder and piracy and bigamy and blackbirding, and the foul destruction of his entire family', but that his name was used to terrify little children into going to sleep, and that native chiefs 'prayed to ancient gods that they might be spared visits from this terrible man'.

A bestselling author of Australian popular history, Frank Clune, took quite a different view. In his 1970 publication, *Captain Bully Hayes, Blackbirder and Bigamist*, the writer did his utmost to exonerate Hayes, pointing out that he had never been convicted for major crimes, his two imprisonments being for debt and for smuggling political prisoners. Interestingly, his book also includes what he calls 'the only known photograph of Bully Hayes'. The man in the picture, an abject-looking fellow wearing a monocle, does not fit the popular image of Hayes at all. But, as is typical of so much of the Bully Hayes story, the photograph has been reprinted many times, without anyone expressing any doubts. It has merely added to his enduring appeal. Like Spartacus Smith, Clune thought that Hayes was a fascinating character who was probably not as black as he was painted — and millions of readers felt the same way.

The blurb-writer for Lubbock's book, keeping potential sales in mind, meditated, 'Yet there was something heroic in his spirit which atoned at least for a few of his faults.' Hayes had friends and admirers as well as bitter enemies, and while he might have been terrifying at times, he was disarmingly attractive at others. As one of the last of the copra traders reminisced, 'When he wished it, he could be most agreeable, could sing a good song, tell a good story, and was a most amusing companion. In short, he was saint or demon as the whim moved him or the circumstances dictated.' And it was probably this strange contradiction that accounts for the enduring public fascination with the man, just as it intrigued those he met — even those whom he cheated.

CHAPTER NOTES

I owe thanks to many people for keeping my interest alive over fifteen years of researching Bully Hayes, and particularly for their lively help in providing suggestions, ideas and material. Individual names are included in these notes, but there are librarians to be thanked as well — at the National Library of New Zealand, the Alexander Turnbull Library, and the Beaglehole Library at Victoria University, all in Wellington, and the Mitchell and Reference Libraries at the State Library of New South Wales in Sydney.

The metamorphosis of a common debt-dodger into a swashbuckling buccaneer was traced by searching newspapers, which are all cited in the text. Most were read online, and are best found through their website titles, URLs so often going out of date. Hawaiian newspapers were read on the 'Chronicling America' site run by the Library of Congress; Californian newspapers through the 'California Digital Newspaper Collection'; Australian newspapers on the 'Trove' website run by the National Library of Australia; New Zealand papers on the 'Papers Past' site managed by the National Library of New Zealand; the *Straits Times* on the 'NewspaperSG' site established by the Singapore Government; and Hong Kong newspapers on 'Multimedia Information System' run by the Hong Kong Public Libraries.

*

Details of the *Otranto* and *Canton* were found in a paper, 'Ship Registers of New Bedford', produced as a Federal Project in 1940. I thank Judith Lund, curator alumnus of the New Bedford Whaling Museum, for this. Also see Barnard L. Colby, *For Oil and Buggy Whips* (Mystic, Ct.: Mystic Seaport Museum, 1990).

A.T. Saunders claimed that Hayes was on board the *Canton* when she first arrived in Singapore, on 11 July 1854, and that somehow, over the *Canton*'s passage from Sydney, Australia, he had taken over both the ownership papers and the command. Evidently he heard much of this from his aunt, Sarah Ann Allen, the source of much gossip about Hayes, though he also claimed that Bradley's consular report includes a note of the sale of the *Canton* to Harvey on 19 July 1854, with Hayes the seller or agent. However, it was impossible for Hayes to be in the Orient in July 1854, as he was recorded by the Californian newspapers freighting timber on the California coast for Davenport & Co., as the new owner of the *Otranto*. Either the consular report was misdated or the information given to Saunders was wrong.

The story about Hayes' background in the Chinese Navy was related by Captain Cocks, Harbourmaster at Levuka, and is described in a letter from Arthur Moore of St Clair, Hunters Hill, NSW, to Alexander Turnbull, dated 30 April 1914 (MS-1658, Alexander Turnbull Library). A copy of a bond between 'William Henry Hayes, master and part-owner of the American barque "Otranto", to Captain Robert McMurdo of Amoy for $1,259.50 ... dated Amoy, 30 November 1854', reference MS JM/F5/24, is held in the Jardine Matheson Archive, Cambridge University Library. That Hayes was a Mason is recorded in the diary kept by John Chauner Williams, British Consul in Samoa (micro-ms-coll-08-0037, Alexander

Turnbull Library). Names connected with Hayes in the Orient, the Bradleys in particular, were traced through the *Hong Kong Directory with list of Foreign Residents in China*, published in Hong Kong in 1859. Also very useful was a paper presented by Ferry de Goey at a 2010 conference at the Centre for Business History, University of Glasgow, called 'The business of consuls'. There is an excellent article on the Borneo Trading Company and John Harvey in the online Singapore Infopedia.

Much of the Eli Boggs story can be read in *China and Lower Bengal, being 'The Times' correspondence from China in the Years 1857-58*, by George Wingrove Cooke (London: Routledge, 1861). Pages 68–69 cover his trial. Also see A.G. Course, *Pirates of the Eastern Seas* (London: Muller, 1966), pages 173–178 of which were the major source for the Boggs capture story, with additional details from Grace Estelle Fox, *British Admirals and Chinese Pirates, 1832-1869* (London: Taylor & Francis, 1940, 1st ed, repub. Westport: Hyperion, 1973), and A.D. Blue, *Piracy on the China Coast* (Journal of the Hong Kong branch of the Royal Asiatic Society, 5, 1965).

Saunders and those who followed him claimed that the *C.W. Bradley junior* was named after the son of the United States Consul in Singapore, as a gesture of gratitude for registering the vessel. Charles William Bradley was indeed the consul from March 1854 to 19 April 1856, when he handed over the office to William Charles Siffken, who lasted until 31 October, when he was succeeded by his vice-consul, Thomas Biddle jr. (History of the Fiftieth Anniversary of the American Association of Singapore, printed 1967). However, while Bradley had a residence in Singapore, his main job was US Consul in Ningpo and Amoy, so it is unclear which of these men dealt with the registration of the bark, and it is more likely that the name was chosen because Charles William Bradley junior was a personal friend.

Captain Thomas Allen's biography is printed in *Notable South Australians* by George P. Loyau, published in Adelaide in 1885, pages 182–183. A stirring account of how Hayes bolted from Adelaide, written by 'An Ancient Mariner', was published in the Adelaide *Observer* on 6 May 1871. Helen O'Dea, genealogist, kindly provided background to Daniel Asaro Osborne. An excellent study of the Honolulu press at the time was found in *Press Time in Paradise: the Life and Times of the Honolulu Advertiser* (University of Hawaii Press, 1998) by George Chaplin. The notices of Amelia Littleton Hayes' applications for divorce are in the *Daily Alta California* for 10 October 1863 and the San Francisco *Bulletin*, 27 February 1864. The depositions of the raft survivors after the wreck of the *Ellenita* are in a collection of Pacific Islands Papers (qMS-1616) at the Alexander Turnbull Library. They differ little from the newspaper reports.

Hayes' theatrical career was fascinating to follow, as were the stories of the Buckingham Family. Again, I thank Helen O'Dea for a detailed genealogy. There is a biography of George Buckingham by Peter Downes on the 'Te Ara Encyclopaedia of New Zealand' website. For background to the Otago gold rush, see Roberta McIntyre, *Whose High Country?* (Auckland: Penguin, 2008: 62–83). Robert Gilkison repeats much of the Bully Hayes legend, including the cut ear, in *Early Days in Central Otago, Being Tales of Times Gone By* (Dunedin: Otago Daily Times & Witness Newspapers Co., Ltd., 1930: 75–85). There is also a retelling on the Arrowtown website. John Dunmore (*Wild Cards, Eccentric Characters from New Zealand's Past*, published in Auckland by New Holland in 2006) concluded in his chapter 'The Theatrical Pirate' that the burlesque on the cut-ear story was simply a marketing ploy. This seems very likely, considering that Hayes still managed the troupe after they all left Arrowtown.

An article called 'Black Diamond', by J.N.W. Newport, appeared in the *Nelson Historical Society Journal* vol. 3, issue 3, 1977. Memories of Bully Hayes at Akaroa were published in the *Akaroa Mail*, 14 March 1919. I am grateful to Ian Church for sending me a copy of his article 'Bully Hayes at Wanganui', which was published in the *New Zealand Marine News* (vol. 29, no. 2, 1978: 53–55). I also thank him for sending me a copy of Doug Edwards' article, 'Henry Boyden Roberts, 1810-1873', which was published in the *Historical Review, Journal of the Whanganui Historical Society* (vol. 18, no. 1, May 1987: 1–8). The story about the storekeeper on Rarotonga who tricked Hayes over the lime juice shipment came from an unpublished paper by Don Percival, called 'Dramas that Made Cook Islands History: Bully Hayes in the Cook Islands'. I thank Tony Monteith for sending this to me.

The history of blackbirding in the South Seas is a grim and engrossing one, about which much has been written. Useful were: a paper read by E.V. Stevens to the Historical Society of Queensland, 23 March 1950, called 'Blackbirding, A Brief History of the South Sea Islands Labour Traffic, and the Vessels Engaged in it', and Doug Hunt, 'Hunting the Blackbirder: Ross Lewin and the Royal Navy', in *Journal of Pacific History*, vol. 42, no. 1, June 2007, 37–53. The letter from Consul Miller at Tahiti to Lord Stanley, 16 December 1868, was quoted in Lubbock, 147–148. A biography of Robert Towns can be read in the online Australian Dictionary of Biography. For Rev. James Chalmers' account of his voyage with Hayes, see his *Autobiography and Letters*, edited by Richard Lovett (London: Religious Tract Society, 1912).

The journal kept by John Chauner Williams, British Consul in Apia, Samoa, was studied at the Alexander Turnbull Library, National Library of New Zealand, as part of the Pacific Manuscripts Bureau series (micro-ms-coll-08-0037). The complete collection of handwritten testimonials is held at the New Zealand National Archives, Wellington (as item R19684924, also available as micro S3623). I am very grateful to the librarians who made this material so accessible. The despatches presented to both Houses of Parliament regarding accusations of kidnapping and slave-trading against Captain W.H. Hayes of the *Atlantic* were published in the Queensland Government Gazette, 28 August 1875. While the case of Hayes is not mentioned, a very good background discussion is given by Reid Mortensen, as 'Slaving in Australian Courts: Blackbirding Cases, 1869-1871', *Journal of South Pacific Law*, article 7, volume 4, 2000. His examples of common law offences also illustrate the difficulty faced by Commander Dupuis (or any Royal Navy officer on a mission to apprehend blackbirders) in bringing charges for rape to the courts.

Benjamin Pease's past record, including his purchase and conversion of the *Water Lily*, the evidence collected by Commander Truxton of USS *Jamestown*, the charges of piracy brought by Admiral Rodgers, the informal inquiry held by the US Consul in Shanghai, George F. Seward, and the release of Pease from his prison on 5 June 1871, were all aired in an investigation of Expenditures in the State Department that was initiated by John Myers, Consul-General, Shanghai, 29 March 1877. This can now be read online as part of the Congressional Series of the United States.

For the history of Micronesia, a major resource is any work by Francis X. Hezel, either online (see the Micronesian Seminar) or in printed books. *The First Taint of Civilization: A History of the Caroline and Marshall Islands* (Honolulu: University of Hawaii Press, 1983) was consulted in detail, as was his *Foreign Ships in Micronesia: A Compendium of Ship Contacts with the Caroline and Marshall Islands* (Saipan, Mariana Isl.: Trust Territory Historic Preservation Office and the U.S. Heritage Conservation and Recreation Service, 1979), and his 'Beachcombers, Traders, and Castaways in Micronesia', and 'The Role of the Beachcomber', both on the Micronesian Seminar website. Also see, Dirk H.R. Spennemann, 'Ships visiting the March Mili Atoll', in the same Micronesian Seminar online series.

For the story of 'Aloe' Pitman and his dealings with Benjamin Pease and Captain Hayes, see Lawrence W. Jenkins, 'A Marbleheader Meets the Last of the South Sea Pirates' (Proceedings, Massachusetts Historical Society, October 1936–May 1941). For the birth (and death of the girl) of the Hayes twins, see 'Housekeeping in Samoa a Hundred Years Ago', in the Newsletter of the Pacific Manuscripts Bureau, January 1969.

The background to the coconut oil and copra trade is comprehensively covered in H.E. Maude, with Ida Leeson, 'The Coconut Oil Trade of the Gilbert Islands', in *Of Islands and Men, Studies in Pacific History* (Melbourne: Oxford University Press, 1968: 233–283). The log of the bark *Belle*, Captain Ichabod Handy, is catalogued by the Sag Harbor Whaling Museum, New York, and a microfilm copy is held at the Alexander Turnbull Library as part of the Pacific Manuscripts Series, PMB 680.

For a thorough discussion of Louis Becke and his strange relationship with Hayes, see Dirk H.R. Spennemann's study of Becke in his 1998

Collection of Essays on the Marshallese Past, on the Micronesian Seminar website. The Westbrook papers are essential reading for Hayes and the coconut oil trade in Micronesia. See: Westbrook, George Egerton Leigh, MS Papers 0061-072; further papers, MS Papers 5737, folders 72, 85, 87; papers concerning Pease, MS Papers 0061-079A. All are held at the Alexander Turnbull Library, as are the William Wawn memoirs ('Amongst the Pacific Islands', MS microfilm copy 0326), and the Asia Lowther diary (Depositions re oil stolen by Hayes, November 7, 1871-August 22, 1872. qMS-1164). I am grateful to Doug Munro for his active interest and help in this area of research.

An unpublished paper by Joseph C. Meredith, called 'Recollections of a South Sea trader; based on the reminiscences of Alfred Restieaux', is held at the Alexander Turnbull Library as MS Papers 7022, 7022-2, 7022-3. Jane Resture's website includes a page called 'In Memory of Alfred Restieaux', which reprints Westbrook's reminiscences of Restieaux. These originally appeared in a book edited by Julian Dana, *Gods Who Die* (New York: Macmillan, 1935). She also has pages devoted to extracts from the Restieaux reminiscences that were told to Westbrook and collected in the Westbrook and Meredith papers, as cited above. For details of the wreck, I relied on Louis Becke's story, which was published as 'The Wreck of the "*Leonora*," A Memory of Bully Hayes', in a collection of stories called *Ridan the Devil* (London: T. Fisher Unwin, 1899).

Sub.-Lt. George Wilson, in his Journal and remark book on H.M.S. *Rosario* (Alexander Turnbull Library, MS-2506) gave an unusual view of events on Kosrae. Commander Dupuis' instructions, collected evidence, and reports, plus letters from Hayes, were all published in the Queensland Government Gazette on Saturday, 28 August 1875.

The logs of the whalers *Triton* and *Arnolda* were read at the Alexander Turnbull Library as Pacific Manuscript Bureau microfilms 368 (*Triton*) and 721 (*Arnolda*). Walter Teller's biography, *Joshua Slocum*, was published by Rutgers University Press in 1956. Slocum's memory of Hayes, 'Bully Hayes, the Last Buccaneer, written from data supplied by Captain Joshua Slocum', was published in *Outing* in March 1906. His story that the *Leonora* was the rebuilt missionary vessel *John Williams* was widely believed, and published in the *Pacific Commercial Advertiser* on 28 June 1899. Ibanez del Carmen's *Chronicle of the Marianas*, translated by Marjorie Driver, was published by the University of Guam in 1970. Also see Francis X. Hezel's fascinating biographies of two men involved with the rescue of the schooner *Arabia*, 'A Yankee Trader in Yap: Philo Holcomb', and 'The Man Who Was Reputed to be King: David Dean O'Keefe', both online at the Micronesian Seminar. The puzzle of the identity of 'Griswold Herron' was solved by consulting *Elephants for Mr Lincoln: American Civil War-era Diplomacy in South-East Asia*, by William F. Strobridge and Anita Hibler (Rowman & Littlefield, 2006).

Commodore Ogden's obituary was published in the San Francisco *Call*, 7 October 1900, while Captain Edwin Moody's was published in the same paper, 8 September 1896. According to the *American Yacht List*, Moody was the owner of the *Lotus* in 1875. There is no record of a change of ownership, and after that year the vessel disappears from the record.

The Alexander Turnbull Library holds manuscripts written by Becke, none of them reliable: 'The True Story of the Real Bully Hayes' (MS 0156; micro copy on MS 0011), 'Fifty years ago, Old Sydney Harbour' (qMS-0150) and 'The Call of the South' (MS-papers-11946-042). At the same repository, there are collections that proved variously useful: Cliffe, Robert McKenzie ('Old Wire-whiskers'), typed MS marked 'not to be broadcast' and called, 'Pearls, pirates and blackbirders, tales of the tropical seas' (MS-0509A); Cox, Charles Percy, Letter to John Acland concerning career and character of Hayes (MS Papers 3288); McNab, Robert, Correspondence with Alfred T. Saunders, 1914-1916 (MS Papers 0859); Saville, Alfred Thomas, Misc. papers re Society Islands (Microfilm MS 1024); Scott, Very Rev. Donald David, Scrapbook, including Hayesiana (MS 0605).

An article about A.T. Saunders was published in the Adelaide *Mail* on 12 September 1925. Also see his biography in the online *Australian Dictionary of Biography*. Michael Hayes, in his doctoral thesis for the University of Wollongong (1997), 'Discursive Production of the Pacific in Australian Colonial Discourse', discusses the 'Bully Hayes Adventure Narratives' in chapter two (91-143). The copra trader who meditated about Hayes' contradictory moods was George Westbrook: the quotation comes from Julian Dana's *Gods Who Die* (New York: Macmillan, 1935), page 111.

Finally, I wish to thank all those at HarperCollins Publishers who have worked so hard to bring this book into existence, with special acknowledgement to publisher Finlay Macdonald.

INDEX

Abaiang, Gilbert Islands (Kiribati), 213, 220, 222, 235, 237, 273

Academy, The, 288

Aches, Edmund S., 142-43

Acors Barnes, whaleship, 230

Adelaide Mail, 292, 293, 294, 297, 304

Adelaide Observer, 37, 301

Adelaide, South Australia, 26*ff*, 52, 53, 56, 71, 72, 87, 152, 283, 292, 294, 295, 297, 301

Admella, steamer, 42

Adolph, schooner, 189, 190

Ah Ho (ship's cook), 222, 245

Ah So (ship's carpenter), 222, 245

Aitutaki, Cook Islands, 150, 151

Ajax, steamer, 216

Akaroa Mail, 23, 122, 302

Akaroa, New Zealand, 9, 121-23, 125, 128, 153, 165, 302

Akersten, Capt. William, 115-18

Alarm, brig, 30

Albany, Western Australia, 29, 264

Albatross, yacht, 186, 187

Algerine, brig, 89

Allen, Capt. Thomas, 25, 26, 30, 42, 64, 76, 77, 109, 292, 301

Allen, Sarah Ann, 25, 26, 30, 34, 42, 64, 76, 77, 109, 292, 300; meets Capt. Hayes, 25, 26, 76, 77; talks to nephew A.T. Saunders, 25, 34, 77, 109, 292, 300

Alvord, J.G., 158, 181, 209, 217

Amelia Francis, schooner, 137-38

Amoy, China, 16-17, 22, 300-01

Anderson, James Wright, 143

Antonio, brig, 64, 75

Apia, Samoa, 5, 7, 74, 149, 158-59, 160, 165, 172, 173, 177, 178, 180, 181, 186-87, 195, 204, 205-09, 218-19, 224, 226, 228, 229, 243, 265, 266, 268, 279, 284, 289, 302

Arabia, schooner, 255-56, 304

Archibald, Jules F., 287

Arctic, whaleship, 250, 251-53, 260

Argus, The (Melbourne), 40, 41, 42, 166

Armstrong, Mrs Catherine, 56, 62, 73

Arno Atoll, Marshall Islands, 215

Arnolda, whaleship, 251, 304

Arrowtown, Otago, 99, 100-102, 302

Askew, William, 112-13, 124

Aspasia, merchant ship, 54

Atiu, Cook Islands, 140-41

Atlantic, schooner, 160-61, 164*ff*, 176-180

Auckland Star, 142, 224

Auckland, New Zealand, 87-88, 89, 110, 144-46

Australian Town and Country Journal, 280

Australian Women's Weekly, 296

Baker, B. T., 27, 72

Ballarat, Victoria, 28, 39

Banham, William "Billy" (aka Pablo Fanque), 78-80, 86, 124

Barossa, H.M.S., 210

Basilisk, H.M.S., 225

Bauldry, Capt. George F., 251

Bêche de mer trade, 161, 162, 200, 201

Becke, Louis, 186, 229-34, 242, 243-44, 245, 284, 285, 286-89, 303, 304

Bell's Life in Sydney, 90

Belle, whaling bark, 194

Bendell, Captain, 106-07

Bendigo, Victoria, 28

Benjamin Aymer, ship, 249, 257

Bennett, Samuel, 69

Benson, Frank, 209, 213

Bentley (Lyttelton merchant), 137